Practice*Planners*

Arthur E. Jongsma, Jr., Series Editor

Helping therapists help their clients . . .

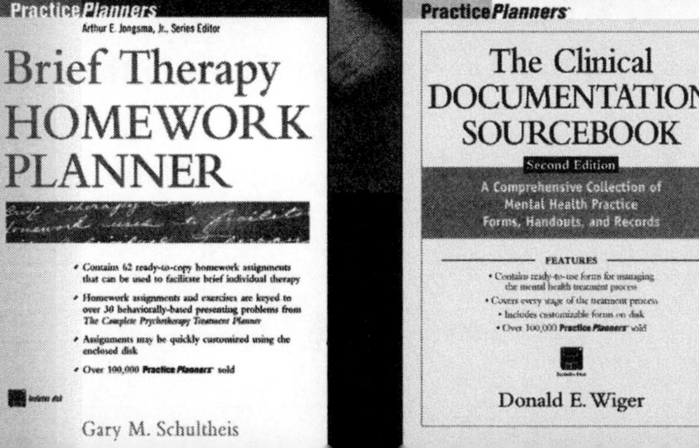

Practice*Planners*® Order Form

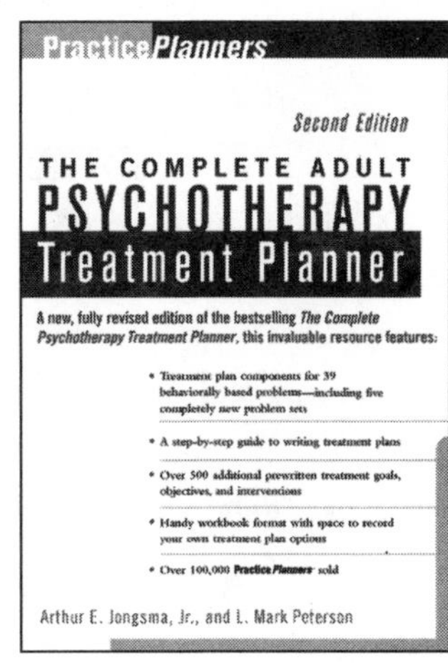

Treatment Planners cover all the necessary elements for developing formal treatment plans, including detailed problem definitions, long-term goals, short-term objectives, therapeutic interventions, and DSM-IV™ diagnoses.

- ❑ **The Complete Adult Psychotherapy Treatment Planner,** Second Edition
  0-471-31924-4 / $49.95
- ❑ **The Child Psychotherapy Treatment Planner,** Second Edition
  0-471-34764-7 / $49.95
- ❑ **The Adolescent Psychotherapy Treatment Planner,** Second Edition
  0-471-34766-3 / $49.95
- ❑ **The Addiction Treatment Planner,** Second Edition
  0-471-41814-5 / $49.95
- ❑ **The Couples Psychotherapy Treatment Planner**
  0-471-24711-1 / $49.95
- ❑ **The Group Therapy Treatment Planner**
  0-471-37449-0 / $49.95
- ❑ **The Family Therapy Treatment Planner**
  0-471-34768-X / $49.95
- ❑ **The Older Adult Psychotherapy Treatment Planner**
  0-471-29574-4 / $49.95
- ❑ **The Employee Assistance (EAP) Treatment Planner**
  0-471-24709-X / $49.95
- ❑ **The Gay and Lesbian Psychotherapy Treatment Planner**
  0-471-35080-X / $49.95
- ❑ **The Crisis Counseling and Traumatic Events Treatment Planner**
  0-471-39587-0 / $49.95
- ❑ **The Social Work and Human Services Treatment Planner**
  0-471-37741-4 / $49.95
- ❑ **The Continuum of Care Treatment Planner**
  0-471-19568-5 / $49.95
- ❑ **The Behavioral Medicine Treatment Planner**
  0-471-31923-6 / $49.95
- ❑ **The Mental Retardation and Developmental Disability Treatment Planner**
  0-471-38253-1 / $49.95
- ❑ **The Special Education Treatment Planner**
  0-471-38872-6 / $49.95
- ❑ **The Severe and Persistent Mental Illness Treatment Planner**
  0-471-35945-9 / $49.95
- ❑ **The Personality Disorders Treatment Planner**
  0-471-39403-3 / $49.95
- ❑ **The Rehabilitation Psychology Treatment Planner**
  0-471-35178-4 / $49.95
- ❑ **The Pastoral Counseling Treatment Planner**
  0-471-25416-9 / $49.95
- ❑ **The Juvenile Justice and Residential Care Treatment Planner**
  0-471-43320-9 / $49.95
- ❑ **The Probation and Parole Treatment Planner**
  0-471-20244-4 / $49.95
- ❑ **The School Counseling and School Social Work Treatment Planner**
  0-471-08496-4 / $49.95
- ❑ **The Sexual Abuse Victim/Offender Treatment Planner**
  0-471-21979-7 / $49.95

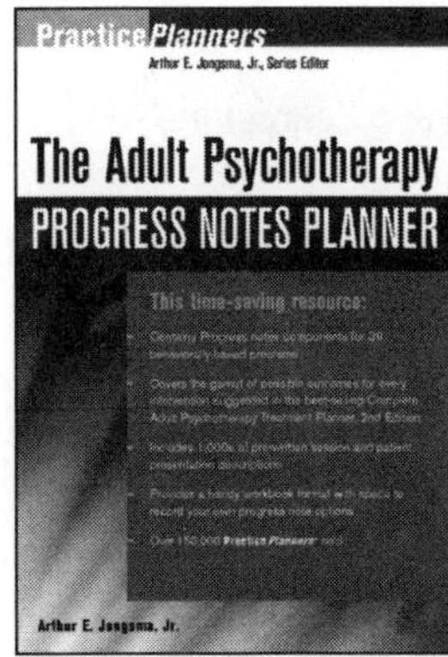

Progress Notes Planners contain complete prewritten progress notes for each presenting problem in the companion Treatment Planners.

- ❑ **The Adult Psychotherapy Progress Notes Planner**
  0-471-34763-9 / $49.95
- ❑ **The Adolescent Psychotherapy Progress Notes Planner**
  0-471-38104-7 / $49.95
- ❑ **The Child Psychotherapy Progress Notes Planner**
  0-471-38102-0 / $49.95
- ❑ **The Addiction Progress Notes Planner**
  0-471-10330-6 / $49.95
- ❑ **The Severe and Persistent Mental Illness Progress Notes Planner**
  0-471-21986-X / $49.95

Name____________________

Affiliation____________________

Address____________________

City/State/Zip____________________

Phone/Fax____________________

E-mail____________________

On the web: practiceplanners.wiley.com

To order, call 1-800-225-5945
(Please refer to promo #1-4019 when ordering.)

Or send this page with payment* to:
John Wiley & Sons, Inc., Attn: J. Knott
111 River Street, Hoboken, NJ 07030

❑ Check enclosed ❑ Visa ❑ MasterCard ❑ American Express

Card #____________________

Expiration Date____________________

Signature____________________

*Please add your local sales tax to all orders.

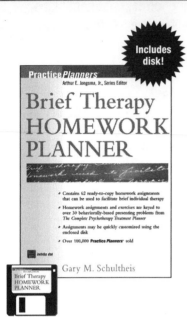

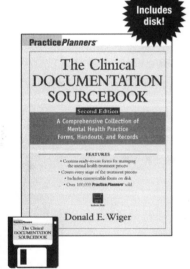

The Couples Psychotherapy Progress Notes Planner

PRACTICE*PLANNERS*® SERIES

Treatment Planners

The Complete Adult Psychotherapy Treatment Planner, 3e
The Child Psychotherapy Treatment Planner, 3e
The Adolescent Psychotherapy Treatment Planner, 3e
The Continuum of Care Treatment Planner
The Couples Psychotherapy Treatment Planner
The Employee Assistance Treatment Planner
The Pastoral Counseling Treatment Planner
The Older Adult Psychotherapy Treatment Planner
The Behavioral Medicine Treatment Planner
The Group Therapy Treatment Planner
The Gay and Lesbian Psychotherapy Treatment Planner
The Family Therapy Treatment Planner
The Severe and Persistent Mental Illness Treatment Planner
The Mental Retardation and Developmental Disability Treatment Planner
The Social Work and Human Services Treatment Planner
The Crisis Counseling and Traumatic Events Treatment Planner
The Personality Disorders Treatment Planner
The Rehabilitation Psychology Treatment Planner
The Addiction Treatment Planner, 2e
The Special Education Treatment Planner
The Juvenile Justice and Residential Care Treatment Planner
The School Counseling and School Social Work Treatment Planner
The Sexual Abuse Victim and Sexual Offender Treatment Planner
The Probation and Parole Treatment Planner
The Psychopharmacology Treatment Planner

Progress Note Planners

The Child Psychotherapy Progress Notes Planner, 2e
The Adolescent Psychotherapy Progress Notes Planner, 2e
The Adult Psychotherapy Progress Notes Planner, 2e
The Addiction Progress Notes Planner
The Severe and Persistent Mental Illness Progress Notes Planner
The Couples Psychotherapy Progress Notes Planner

Homework Planners

Brief Therapy Homework Planner
Brief Couples Therapy Homework Planner
Brief Child Therapy Homework Planner
Brief Adolescent Therapy Homework Planner
Brief Employee Assistance Homework Planner
Brief Family Therapy Homework Planner
Grief Counseling Homework Planner
Group Therapy Homework Planner
Divorce Counseling Homework Planner
School Counseling and School Social Work Homework Planner
Child Therapy Activity and Homework Planner
Addiction Treatment Homework Planner, Second Edition
Adolescent Psychotherapy Homework Planner II

Client Education Handout Planners

Adult Client Education Handout Planner
Child and Adolescent Client Education Handout Planner
Couples and Family Client Education Handout Planner

Documentation Sourcebooks

The Clinical Documentation Sourcebook
The Forensic Documentation Sourcebook
The Psychotherapy Documentation Primer
The Chemical Dependence Treatment Documentation Sourcebook
The Clinical Child Documentation Sourcebook
The Couple and Family Clinical Documentation Sourcebook
The Clinical Documentation Sourcebook, 2e
The Continuum of Care Clinical Documentation Sourcebook

Practice*Planners*®

Arthur E. Jongsma, Jr., Series Editor

The Couples Psychotherapy Progress Notes Planner

David J. Berghuis

Arthur E. Jongsma, Jr.

JOHN WILEY & SONS, INC.

This book is printed on acid-free paper. ♾

Published by John Wiley & Sons, Inc., Hoboken, New Jersey.
Published simultaneously in Canada.

For general information on our other products and services please contact our Customer Care Department within the United States at (800) 762-2974, outside the United States at (317) 572-3993 or fax (317) 572-4002.

Wiley also publishes its books in a variety of electronic formats. Some content that appears in print may not be available in electronic books. For more information about Wiley products, visit our Web site at www.wiley.com.

Library of Congress Cataloging-in-Publication Data:

Berghuis, David J.
The couples psychotherapy progress notes planner / David J. Berghuis, Arthur E. Jongsma, Jr.
p. cm. — (Practice planners series)
ISBN 0-471-27460-7
1. Marital psychotherapy—Handbooks, manuals, etc. 2. Psychiatric records—Handbooks, manuals, etc. I. Jongsma, Arthur E., 1943– II. Title. III. Practice planners.
RC488.5 .B478 2003
616.89'156—dc21

2002154098

Printed in the United States of America.

10 9 8 7 6 5 4 3 2 1

To my brothers, Timothy L. Berghuis and Michael S. Berghuis, with love and respect.

—David J. Berghuis

To the memory of my friend, Dr. Darrell Elders.

—Arthur E. Jongsma, Jr.

CONTENTS

Series Preface xiii
Acknowledgments xv
Introduction 1

Alcohol Abuse 4
Anger 14
Anxiety 26
Blame 37
Blended-Family Problems 44
Communication 51
Dependency 60
Depression Due to Relationship Problems 69
Depression Independent of Relationship Problems 79
Disillusionment with Relationship 87
Eating Disorder 97
Financial Conflict 104
Infidelity 112
Intolerance 121
Jealousy 129
Job Stress 137
Life-Changing Events 146
Loss of Love/Affection 154
Midlife Crisis 163
One Partner Unwilling to Attend Therapy 173
Parenting Conflicts—Adolescents 183
Parenting Conflicts—Children 194
Personality Differences 205
Physical Abuse 211
Psychological Abuse 220
Recreational Activities Dispute 230
Religion/Spirituality Differences 236
Separation and Divorce 244
Sexual Abuse 253
Sexual Dysfunction 263
Work/Home Role Strain 273

PRACTICE*PLANNERS*® SERIES PREFACE

The Couples Psychotherapy Progress Notes Planner is the next step in the evolution of the Practice*Planners*® series from John Wiley & Sons. This book is written as a companion to *The Couples Psychotherapy Treatment Planner* and provides a menu of sentences that can be selected for constructing a progress note based on the Behavioral Definitions and Therapeutic Interventions from the Treatment Planner. The content in this book is available in electronic form that can be imported into the treatment planning and record keeping software, Thera*Scribe*® 4.0. Using the simple point-and-click action, progress notes statements can be selected from the database to fit your client's session description.

This progress note format has evolved through several stages before it arrived at its final form for publication. Our hope and desire is that both students and seasoned clinicians will find this resource helpful in writing progress notes that are thoroughly unified with the client's treatment plan. We have provided a range of content covered by the progress note sentences that can document how a client presented and what interventions were used in the session.

The Practice*Planners* series has continued to expand, especially in the area of Treatment Planners. There are now 24 Treatment Planners published with several others in the development stage. The original flagship books of this series, *The Complete Psychotherapy Treatment Planner*, *The Child and Adolescent Psychotherapy Treatment Planner,* and *The Chemical Dependence Treatment Planner* have all been completely revised into new editions entitled *The Complete Adult Psychotherapy Treatment Planner, 3rd Edition; The Adolescent Psychotherapy Treatment Planner, 3rd Edition; The Child Psychotherapy Treatment Planner, 3rd Edition;* and *The Addiction Treatment Planner, 2nd Edition.* Books for specialized client populations continue to evolve such as *The Probation and Parole Treatment Planner* and *The Sexual Abuse Victim and Sexual Offender Treatment Planner*. All of these Treatment Planners are available in an optional electronic version that can be easily imported into the software, Thera*Scribe 4.0*, *The Treatment Planning and Clinical Record Management System for Mental Health Professionals*. The Practice*Planners* series also includes several psychotherapy Homework Planners that are coordinated with the Treatment Planners or can be used independently. Several Documentation Sourcebooks containing useful examples of clinical record-keeping forms, lecture outlines, and handouts round out the Practice*Planner* series.

ARTHUR E. JONGSMA, JR.
Grand Rapids, Michigan

ACKNOWLEDGMENTS

We want to thank many people who helped make this book a reality. The professional community has found these books helpful, hence, the series has continued to expand. This is the latest installment in making the Practice*Planners* a complete treatment package. We thank the clinicians who find our books helpful. This book is a companion book to *The Couples Psychotherapy Treatment Planner* by K. Daniel O'Leary, Richard E. Heyman, and Arthur E. Jongsma, Jr. We thank the authors for their work. Special thanks goes to the colleagues we have worked with over several years of practice. We are also indebted to the clients who have taught us so much about how to work with couples' problems, and we thank them as well.

As with each of the books in this series, the final product is a collaborative effort. Barb Berghuis did a great deal to complete the manuscript with her typing, revising, and unfailing support. Katy Berghuis worked hard to make each chapter fit into the format, as did Mike Berghuis. Jen Byrne compiled hundreds of pages of text into a manuscript that could be submitted for publication. Peggy Alexander and Cristina Wojdylo of John Wiley & Sons, Inc. have coached us through the publishing process. As always, Judy Jongsma understood how to grease the wheel when the process became tedious.

David J. Berghuis
Arthur E. Jongsma, Jr.

INTRODUCTION

INTENT AND FOCUS

The Couples Psychotherapy Progress Notes Planner is another step in the evolution of the Practice*Planners* series. This book is written as a close companion to *The Couples Psychotherapy Treatment Planner* by O'Leary, Heyman, and Jongsma (John Wiley & Sons). It provides a menu of sentences from which a clinician may select those appropriate for constructing a progress note based on the Behavioral Definitions and Therapeutic Interventions from *The Couples Psychotherapy Treatment Planner*.

Our hope is that both students and seasoned clinicians find this resource helpful in writing progress notes that are thoroughly unified with the couples' treatment plan. In our progress note sentences, we have provided a range of content documenting how a couple presented and what interventions were used in the session.

INTERFACE WITH *TREATMENT PLANNER*

Progress notes are not only the primary source for documenting the therapeutic process, but also one of the main factors in determining the client's eligibility for reimbursable treatment. Although the books can be used independently, *The Couples Psychotherapy Progress Notes Planner* provides prewritten sentences that are directly coordinated with the symptom descriptions in the Behavioral Definitions section and with the clinical activity description in the Therapeutic Interventions section of *The Couples Psychotherapy Treatment Planner*. Used together, you'll find these books save time while providing a guidepost to complete, integrated clinical record-keeping.

ORGANIZATION OF *PROGRESS NOTES PLANNER*

Each chapter title represents a couple's potential presenting problem, reflecting the chapter titles from *The Couples Psychotherapy Treatment Planner*. The first section of the chapter, Client Presentation, provides a detailed menu of statements that describe how that presenting problem manifested itself in the couple's behavioral signs and symptoms. The numbers in parentheses within the Client Presentation section correspond to the number of the Behavioral Definition from *The Couples Psychotherapy Treatment Planner*. For example, consider the following two items from the Communication chapter of this Progress Note Planner:

1. Frequent Arguments (1)

A. The client reported frequent or continual arguing with his/her partner.
B. The frequency of conflict between the partners has diminished.
C. The partners report decreased arguments due to the implementation of conflict resolution skills.
D. The client reported that his/her relationship with his/her partner has significantly improved and arguing has become very infrequent.

2. Poor Problem-Resolution Skills (2)

A. The client and his/her partner often have continuing arguments because they have poor problem-resolution skills.

B. The partners described unresolved conflicts that have led to sustained periods of distrust and alienation from each other.

C. As the partners have progressed in therapy, problem-resolution skills and communication have increased.

In this example, the numerals (1) and (2) refer to the first and second Behavioral Definition from the Communication chapter in *The Couples Psychotherapy Treatment Planner*. Within the Client Presentation section of each chapter, the statements are arranged to reflect a progression toward resolution of the problem. The latter statements are included to be used in later stages of therapy as the couple moves forward toward discharge.

The second section of each chapter, Interventions Implemented, provides a menu of statements related to the action that was taken within the session to assist the couple in making progress. The numbering of the items in the Interventions Implemented section follows exactly the numbering of Therapeutic Intervention items in the corresponding *Couples Psychotherapy Treatment Planner*. For example, consider the following two items from the Communication chapter in this Progress Note Planner:

6. Rephrase Mind-Reading (6)

A. One of the partners was identified as mind-reading the other partner.

B. When a partner was identified as mind-reading the other partner, the mind-reading partner was requested to rephrase statements in a manner that speaks only for one's self and expressing one's own perceptions.

C. The partners were provided with positive feedback as they decreased the tendency to mind-read.

D. The partners continued to focus on the internal thoughts of the other partner and were provided with additional feedback and direction in this area.

7. Teach Paraphrasing (7)

A. While one partner was serving as the speaker, the other partner was directed to paraphrase, rephrasing the speaker's major point.

B. The speaking partner was asked to acknowledge whether the paraphrasing partner had accurately described the intended message.

C. The partners were provided with positive feedback as they appropriately paraphrased each other's comments.

In these samples, the items numbered (6) and (7) correspond directly to the same numbered items in the Therapeutic Interventions section from the Communication chapter of *The Couples Psychotherapy Treatment Planner*.

Finally, all item lists begin with a few keywords. These words are meant to convey the theme or content of the sentences that are contained in that listing. The clinician may peruse the list of keywords to find content that matches the couple's presentation and the clinician's intervention.

USING THE *COUPLES PSYCHOTHERAPY PROGRESS NOTES PLANNER*

If you have not used *The Couples Psychotherapy Treatment Planner* to initiate treatment, then relevant progress notes can be found by finding the chapter title that reflects the couple's presenting problem, scanning the keywords to find the theme that fits the session, and then selecting the sentences that describe first how the couple presented for that session and then what interventions were used to assist the couple in reaching his/her therapeutic goals and objectives. It is expected that the clinician will modify the prewritten statements contained in this book to fit the exact circumstances of the couple's presentation and treatment. Individualization of treatment must be reflected in progress notes that are tailored to each couple's unique presentation, strengths, and weaknesses.

To maintain complete client records, in addition to progress note statements that may be selected and individualized from this book, the date, time and length of a session, those present in the session, the provider, provider's credentials, and a provider signature must be entered in the couple's record.

All progress notes must be tied to the treatment plan—session notes should elaborate on the problems, symptoms, and interventions contained in the plan. If a session focuses on a topic outside those covered in the treatment plan, providers must update the treatment plan accordingly.

As of April 2003, new federal regulations under the Health Insurance Portability and Accountability Act (HIPAA) govern the privacy or confidentiality of a client's "psychotherapy notes" (or process notes or progress notes) as well as other protected health information (PHI). If you keep detailed notes for each session that reveal personal information about the client, you may separate these psychotherapy notes from the rest of the client's file that contains PHI. PHI and psychotherapy notes must be kept secure in a locked file and access to it must be limited and protected by office policy and procedures. Psychotherapy notes require additional protection in that the client must sign a specific authorization to release this confidential information to anyone beyond the client's therapist or treatment team. For most of us, this regulation does not impose a new standard of practice since we have been protecting psychotherapy notes as confidential and requiring a release before sharing them. A new wrinkle that does result from HIPAA is that a client's psychotherapy notes are not available to insurance carriers or managed care organizations. Decisions about coverage for mental health services may not hinge on psychotherapy note information and the client may not be denied coverage based on the lack of access to this confidential information.

Does the information contained in this book, when entered into a client's record as a progress note, qualify as a "psychotherapy note" and therefore merit confidential protection under HIPAA regulations? The answer to that question is, "It depends." If the progress note that is created by selecting sentences from the database contained in this book is kept in a location separate from the client's PHI data, then the note could qualify as psychotherapy note data that is more protected than general PHI. However, because the sentences contained in this book convey generic information regarding the client's progress, the clinician may decide to keep the notes mixed in with the client's PHI, and not consider it psychotherapy note data. In short, how you treat the information (separate from or integrated with PHI) can determine if this progress note planner data is psychotherapy note information. If you modify or edit these generic sentences to reflect more personal information about the client or you add sentences that contain confidential information, the argument for keeping these notes separate from PHI and treating them as psychotherapy notes becomes stronger. For some therapists, our sentences alone reflect enough personal information to qualify as psychotherapy notes and they will keep these notes separate from the client's PHI and require specific authorization from the client to share them with a clearly identified recipient for a clearly identified purpose.

ALCOHOL ABUSE

CLIENT PRESENTATION

1. Frequent Use of Alcohol (1)*

A. The client frequently abuses alcohol.

B. The client's partner frequently abuses alcohol.

C. The client's use of alcohol has been so severe as to meet a diagnosis of alcohol abuse or alcohol dependence (e.g., interference in major role obligations; recurrent use in spite of danger to self or health, legal, vocational, and/or social problems).

D. The client's partner's use of alcohol has been so severe as to meet a diagnosis of alcohol abuse or alcohol dependence (e.g., interference in major role obligations; recurrent use in spite of danger to self or health, legal, vocational, and/or social problems).

E. As treatment has progressed, the partner's alcohol use has decreased or been eliminated.

2. Arguments about Drinking (2)

A. The partners report persistent arguments over the issue of the alcohol abuser's pattern of drinking.

B. The partners have frequently been at odds with each other over issues related to drinking.

C. As the alcohol abuser's pattern of drinking has been eliminated and he/she has gained sobriety, the arguments between partners have decreased.

3. Broken Promises (3)

A. The partner with alcohol abuse problems has consistently failed to keep his/her promises to quit or significantly reduce the frequency and quantity of drinking.

B. The alcohol abusing partner's failure to keep his/her promises about his/her drinking has led to friction within the relationship.

C. As the alcohol-abusing partner has developed his/her sobriety, the couple reports less friction within the relationship and an increase in trust.

4. Threats/Violence (4)

A. The client described periodic episodes of violence or threats of physical harm, especially when his/her partner has been intoxicated.

B. The client's partner described periodic episodes of violence or threats of physical harm, especially when the client has been intoxicated.

C. The abused partner has taken steps to leave the abusive relationship.

D. The physical violence and threats of physical harm have been terminated.

*The numbers in parentheses on Client Presentation pages correlate to the number of the Behavioral Definition statement in the companion chapter with the same title in *The Couples Psychotherapy Treatment Planner* (Jongsma, O'Leary, and Heyman) by John Wiley & Sons, 1998. The numbers in parentheses on the Interventions Implemented page correspond to the number of the Therapeutic Intervention statement in the companion chapter in the same book.

5. Relationship Deterioration (5)

A. The couple described a previous pattern of relationship deterioration, including little or no communication, shared recreation, mutually satisfying sexual intercourse, or attempts to meet each other's emotional needs.

B. The client and his/her partner continue a pattern of emotional distance characterized by poor communication, arguing, and infrequent sexual enjoyment.

C. The client and his/her partner have taken steps to spend quality time together to increase the degree of intimacy between them.

D. The couple reported that their relationship has been significantly reestablished, with better communication, shared recreation, mutually satisfying sexual intercourse, and attempts to meet each other's emotional needs.

6. Enabling (6)

A. The partner without alcohol abuse problems consistently enables the partner with alcohol abuse problems by making excuses for the other's drinking, doing anything to please the drinking partner, and denying the seriousness of the problem

B. The enabling partner has been disparaged or abused repeatedly without offering assertive, constructive resistance.

C. The partner without alcohol abuse problems has acknowledged being an enabler and is beginning to take steps to change this pattern.

D. As the partner without alcohol abuse problems has terminated the pattern of enabling, the dynamics within the relationship have changed.

7. Financial Pressures (7)

A. The couple described severe indebtedness and overdue bills that exceed their ability to meet the monthly payments due to the pattern of alcohol abuse, squandering money, loss of jobs, and/or low wage employment.

B. The couple has developed a plan to reduce financial pressures through increasing income and making systematic payment, as well as the discontinuation of substance abuse.

C. The partners have begun to reduce the pressure of indebtedness and financial pressures and are making systematic payments.

D. The couple has significantly reduced their financial pressures.

8. Social Isolation (8)

A. The partner with alcohol abuse problems is away drinking too frequently and/or spending time with fellow alcohol abusers.

B. The partner with the alcohol abuse problems has been emotionally unavailable to the sober partner.

C. The nondrinking partner has become passively withdrawn.

D. As treatment has progressed, the partner with alcohol abuse problems has decreased relationships with fellow alcohol users, and increased contact with the sober partner.

E. The partner with alcohol abuse problems continues to spend time only with alcohol abusers, but the other partner has become more socially involved with others.

INTERVENTIONS IMPLEMENTED

1. Hold Individual Session to Describe Negative Effects of Alcohol Abuse (1)

A. An individual session was held with each partner prior to any conjoint session to explore the negative effects of alcohol abuse on the relationship and the family.

B. The effects of intimidation and mutually supported denial were decreased by exploring the negative effects of alcohol abuse on the relationship and the family.

C. Each partner was provided with feedback about the description of the negative effects of alcohol abuse on the relationship and the family.

D. The client tended to minimize the effects of alcohol abuse on the relationship and the family and was urged to focus on this in a more realistic manner.

E. The client's partner tended to minimize the effects of alcohol abuse on the relationship and the family and was urged to focus on this in a more realistic manner.

F. Both partners were realistic about the effects of alcohol abuse on the relationship and the family and were supported for their honesty.

2. Controlled Drinking Contract (2)

A. The partner with alcohol abuse problems was directed to sign a controlled drinking contract that stipulates the frequency of drinking allowed per week (e.g., twice) and the maximum number of drinks per instance (e.g., three in two or more hours).

B. Positive feedback was provided to the partner with alcohol abuse problems for signing the controlled drinking contract.

C. The partner with alcohol abuse problems has followed the controlled-drinking contract, and the positive effects of this pattern were reviewed with both partners.

D. The client with alcohol abuse problems has broken the controlled-drinking contract and was directed to sign a nondrinking contract.

E. The partner with alcohol abuse problems has signed the nondrinking contract, and the implications of this were processed.

3. Assign Controlled Drinking Information (3)

A. The partner with alcohol abuse problems was assigned to read information on controlled drinking.

B. The partner with alcohol abuse problems was assigned to read NIAAA pamphlets *How to Cut Down on Your Drinking* and/or *How to Control Your Drinking* (Miller and Munoz).

C. The partner with alcohol abuse problems has read the information on controlled drinking, and key points were processed.

D. The partner with alcohol abuse problems has not read the information on controlled drinking, and was redirected to do so.

4. Require Alcohol-Free Sessions (4)

A. Both partners were informed that they must attend the sessions alcohol-free.

B. Both partners have agreed not to consume alcohol before a counseling session.

C. When it became apparent that alcohol had been recently consumed by one of the partners, the alcohol-free session rule was enforced firmly and consistently and the session was terminated.

5. Use Nonviolence Contract (5)

A. Both partners were directed to sign a nonviolence contract that prohibits the use of physically assaultive contact, weapons, or threats of violence.

B. The partners were provided with positive feedback as they signed a nonviolence contract.

6. Develop Safety Plan While Treating Anger (6)

A. The alcohol abusing partner was provided with individual treatment for anger issues prior to conjoint treatment.

B. Supportive counseling was provided to the sober partner to address anxiety and self-blame related to the violence.

C. A safety plan was developed to provide a means of escape from the partner's violence.

7. Discuss Couple versus Individual Treatment (7)

A. The appropriateness of providing individual treatment or couple's treatment was discussed.

B. Because the level of violence is severe and has caused injury and/or significant fear, individual treatment was recommended.

C. Because severe violence and fear were not occurring, couple's treatment was recommended.

8. Probe Benefits Sought through Alcohol Abuse (8)

A. The partner with alcohol abuse problems was probed regarding the benefits being sought in becoming intoxicated (e.g., reduced social anxiety, altered mood, lessened family demands).

B. The benefits that the partner with alcohol abuse problems is seeking in becoming intoxicated were identified and reviewed.

C. The partner with alcohol abuse problems was assisted in identifying healthier ways to get satisfaction of needs.

D. The partner with alcohol abuse problems failed to identify the reasons for abusing substances, has not been able to replace the substance abuse with healthier alternatives, and was provided with tentative interpretations in this area.

9. Emphasize Constructive Alternatives (9)

A. The partner with alcohol abuse problems was taught about how to produce the results sought in becoming intoxicated without using mood-altering substances.

B. The partner with substance abuse problems verbalized increased understanding of how to get good things out of life without using mood-altering substances.

C. The partner with the substance abuse problems rejected the concept of using constructive behavioral alternatives to produce the results sought in becoming intoxicated and was redirected in this area.

10. Teach Anxiety and Stress Reduction Techniques (10)

A. The partner with alcohol abuse problems was taught the use of stress-reduction techniques (e.g., deep muscle relaxation, aerobic exercise, verbalization of concerns, positive guided imagery, recreational diversions, hot bath).

B. The partner with alcohol abuse problems was assigned to relax twice a day for 10 to 20 minutes.

C. The partner with alcohol abuse problems reported regular use of relaxation techniques, which has led to decreased anxiety and decreased urges to abuse substances.

D. The alcohol abusing partner has not implemented relaxation techniques and continues to feel quite stressed in anxiety-producing situations.

11. Teach Anger-Management Techniques (11)

A. The partner with alcohol abuse problems was taught anger-management techniques (e.g. time-out, thought stopping, positive thought substitution, counting down serial sevens from 100).

B. The alcohol abusing partner reported regular use of anger-management techniques, which has led to decreased anger and decreased urges to abuse substances.

C. The partner with alcohol abuse problems has not implemented the anger management techniques, continues to feel quite stressed in anxiety-producing situations, and was redirected to use these techniques.

12. Teach Assertiveness (12)

A. The partners were referred to an assertiveness training group that will educate and facilitate assertiveness skills.

B. Role-playing, modeling, and behavioral rehearsal were used to train the partners in assertiveness skills.

C. The couple was reinforced for demonstrating a clearer understanding of the difference between assertiveness, passivity, and aggression.

D. The partners were referred to appropriate reading material (e.g., *Your Perfect Right* [Alberti and Emmons]) to learn about assertiveness.

13. Educate about Alcoholism Contributors (13)

A. The partners were educated regarding the social and biological factors that contribute to alcoholism.

B. The partners were assigned reading material on the subject of alcoholism, including *Alcoholism: Getting the Facts* (NIAAA) and *I'll Quit Tomorrow* (Johnson).

C. Positive feedback was provided when the partners displayed increased understanding of the social and biological factors that contribute to alcoholism.

D. Additional information was provided when the partners failed to gain a clear understanding of the social and biological factors that contribute to alcoholism.

14. Require Nondrinking Contract (14)

A. The partner with alcohol abuse problems was requested to sign a nondrinking contract that stipulates complete abstinence, cooperation with counseling, and attendance at AA meetings at least twice per week.

B. The partner with alcohol abuse problems was supported for signing a nondrinking contract that stipulates complete abstinence, cooperation with counseling, and attendance at AA meetings at least twice per week.

C. The partner with alcohol abuse problems declined to sign the nondrinking contract, and was strongly urged to reconsider this.

D. Because the partner with alcohol abuse problems declined to sign a nondrinking contract, conjoint counseling was terminated.

15. Respond to Contract Violation (15)

A. The partner with alcohol abuse problems was reminded that violating the nondrinking contract would cause conjoint treatment to be suspended.

B. The partner with alcohol abuse problems has violated the nondrinking contract, and conjoint treatment has been suspended.

C. Conjoint treatment has been reinitiated as the partner with alcohol abuse problems has identified explicit steps that will be taken in the next week to reestablish abstinence (e.g., daily AA meetings, detoxification treatment, inpatient or intensive outpatient treatment).

16. Refer for Antabuse or More Intense Alcoholism Treatment (16)

A. Because drinking has continued despite psychological interventions, the partner with alcohol abuse problems was referred to a physician for Antabuse treatment.

B. The partner with alcohol abuse problems was referred for more intense alcoholism treatment (e.g., residential, inpatient, or intensive outpatient treatment).

C. The partner with alcohol abuse problems has followed up on referrals for additional treatment, and the benefits of this treatment were reviewed.

D. The partner with alcohol abuse problems has not followed up on additional treatment and was redirected to do so.

17. Assign Favors (17)

A. Each partner was assigned to do small favors that would be appreciated by the other partner (e.g., help with or do a chore, run an errand, purchase a small present).

B. The client has completed small favors for his/her partner, and the benefits of this were reviewed.

C. The client's partner has completed small favors for the client, and the benefits of this were reviewed.

D. The partners have not completed small favors for each other and were redirected to do so.

E. Reasons for the partners not completing small favors for each other were identified and problem-solved.

18. Encourage Shared Recreational Activity (18)

A. The partners were encouraged to engage in shared recreational activities (e.g., a family outing, visiting friends together).

B. The partners were requested to stipulate who is responsible for what steps in implementing the activity.

C. The couple has increased their involvement in shared recreational activities, and the benefits of this were reviewed within the session.

D. The partners have not increased involvement in shared recreational activities and were redirected to do so.

19. Identify Communication-Interfering Behavior (19)

A. The partners were requested to describe the ways that each interferes with the communication process in the relationship (e.g., raises voice, walks away, refuses to respond, changes subject, calls partner names, uses profanity, becomes threatening).

B. The client was encouraged to describe the ways that he/she interferes with the communication process in the relationship.

C. The client's partner's interference in the relationship communication process was focused on, identified, and reviewed.

D. The partners were provided with positive feedback for their insight into the ways that each interferes with the communication process in the relationship.

E. The partners tended to minimize the ways in which each interferes with the communication process and were provided with feedback about this defensive reaction.

20. Explore Etiology of Communication Styles (20)

A. The partners were assisted in self-exploration about their own communication style and discussed how they have learned such styles from their family-of-origin experiences.

B. The partners were provided with positive feedback as they displayed insight into how they may have learned their communication styles from their family-of-origin experiences.

C. The partners displayed a poor understanding of how they may have learned their communication styles from their family-of-origin and were provided with additional feedback.

21. Review Conflict Discussion (21)

A. The partners were requested to choose a relationship conflict topic and discuss it in the session.

B. The couple was provided with feedback about their listening and communication styles to improve healthy, accurate, effective communication.

C. The partners were given positive feedback as they displayed a healthy pattern of conflict discussion.

D. A variety of communication suggestions were made to help the couple discuss conflict topics.

22. Reinforce Positive Communication (22)

A. Positive communication experiences between the partners that occurred since the last session were reviewed.

B. Positive feedback was provided for healthy communication experiences between the partners that occurred since the last session.

C. The partners were unable to identify positive communication experiences, and additional effective communication skills were reviewed.

23. Encourage Healthy Problem Description (23)

A. The partners were encouraged to describe a problem between them in a nonblaming, nonhostile manner.

B. Modeling and role-playing were used to provide problem-description guidance to the partners.

C. The partners received primarily positive feedback regarding their ability to describe a problem in a nonblaming, nonhostile manner.

D. The partners were provided with significant feedback and guidance on how to describe a problem in a nonblaming, nonhostile manner.

24. Teach Problem Solving (24)

A. Problem-solving techniques were taught, including using the following steps: (a) define the problem; (b) generate many solutions, encouraging creativity; (c) evaluate the proposed solutions; and (d) implement the solutions.

B. Modeling and role-playing were used to help the couple practice problem-solving techniques.

C. Feedback was provided about the partners' use of the problem-solving techniques.

25. Review Problem-Solving Techniques (25)

A. The partners were asked to use the problem-solving techniques in real-life situations between the sessions.

B. A review and critique was provided regarding the partners' reported instances of implementing problem-solving techniques at home since the last session.

C. Positive feedback was provided for the effective use of problem-solving techniques at home.

D. The partners have failed to consistently use the problem-solving techniques and were redirected to do so.

26. Encourage Making Amends (26)

A. The partner with alcohol abuse problems was encouraged to make amends by apologizing to each family member for specific behaviors that have caused distress.

B. The partner with alcohol abuse problems has made amends and this was processed with that partner.

C. The partner without the alcohol abuse problems was requested to provide feedback about the manner in which the alcohol abusing partner has made amends.

D. The partner with alcohol abuse problems has not yet made amends to family members, and was redirected to do so.

27. Identify Relapse Triggers (27)

A. The partners were assisted in identifying situations that trigger relapses of drinking episodes.

B. The couple identified a variety of triggers for drinking relapses, and these were processed.

C. The partners failed to identify many situations that trigger relapses of drinking episodes and were provided with tentative examples in this area.

28. Develop Alternatives to Triggers (28)

A. The partner with alcohol abuse problems was assisted in developing positive alternative coping behaviors as reactions to trigger situations.

B. The partner with alcohol abuse problems was reinforced in identifying specific alternative coping behaviors (e.g., calling a sponsor, attending an AA meeting, practicing stress reduction skills, turning problems over to a higher power).

C. The partner with alcohol abuse problems was provided with feedback about the use of alternative coping behaviors.

D. The partner with alcohol abuse problems has not regularly used alternative coping behaviors for trigger situations, and was redirected to do so.

29. Confront Enabling (29)

A. The partner without alcohol abuse problems was confronted regarding behaviors that support the continuation of abusive drinking by the other partner (e.g., wanting to cover up for the drinker's irresponsibility; minimizing the seriousness of the drinking problem; taking on most of the family responsibilities; or tolerating the verbal, emotional, and/or physical abuse).

B. The partner without alcohol abuse problems was provided with positive feedback regarding identifying the pattern of enabling.

C. The partner without alcohol abuse problems failed to identify the pattern of enabling and was provided with additional feedback in this area.

30. Practice Refusing to Enable (30)

A. Modeling and role-playing were used to help the couple practice examples of how the partner without alcohol abuse problems can refuse to accept responsibility for the behavior and/or feelings of the other.

B. Encouragement was provided as the partner without alcohol abuse problems displayed an understanding of how to refuse to accept responsibility for the behavior and/or feelings of the other partner.

C. The partner without alcohol abuse problems was reinforced for regularly refusing to accept responsibility for the behavior and/or feelings of the other partner within the home setting.

D. The partner without alcohol abuse problems has continued to enable the other partner and was provided with redirection in this area.

31. Encourage Confrontation of Disrespect or Abuse (31)

A. The partner without alcohol abuse problems was encouraged to confront the partner with alcohol abuse for disrespect or blatant abuse.

B. The partner without alcohol abuse problems was reinforced for confronting the partner with alcohol abuse for disrespect or blatant abuse.
C. The partner without alcohol abuse problems has failed to confront the partner with alcohol abuse for disrespect or blatant abuse and was provided with additional support and redirection.

32. Assign Budget Discussion (32)

A. The couple was assigned to discuss finances and prepare a mutually agreed on budget that begins to deal with the financial stress caused by the drinking problem.
B. The partners were supported for developing a mutually agreed on budget to deal with the financial stress caused by the drinking problem.
C. The partners gave positive feedback for their ability to develop solutions to financial stress problems.
D. The partners have not developed a mutually agreed upon budget to deal with the financial stress caused by the drinking problem and were redirected to do so.

33. Encourage Nonalcohol Social Activity (33)

A. The partners were encouraged to plan social activities with other couples in which alcohol will not be consumed.
B. Church, hobby, recreational groups, or work associates were identified as possible opportunities for social outreach.
C. The partners were provided with positive feedback for participating in social activities where alcohol was not consumed.
D. The partners have not developed social contacts where alcohol is not consumed and were redirected to do so.

ANGER

CLIENT PRESENTATION

1. Uncontrolled Anger (1)*

A. The client described a history of loss of temper that is perceived by the other partner as hurtful or threatening.

B. The client's partner has displayed a history of loss of temper that the client has perceived as hurtful or threatening.

C. The client and his/her partner have reported increased control over temper outbursts and a significant reduction in the incidence of poor anger management.

D. The client and his/her partner have reported no recent incidents of explosive outbursts that have resulted in the destruction of any property or intimidating verbal assaults.

2. Continued Threat (2)

A. The client continues to feel threatened even when his/her partner believes that expressions of anger have modulated.

B. The client's partner continues to feel threatened even when the client believes that expressions of anger have modulated.

C. The partners have begun to have a more realistic understanding of the level of threat imposed by expressions of anger.

D. As expressions of anger have become more normalized, the perceived threat has been decreased as well.

3. Coercion (3)

A. The client described that his/her partner often attempts to coerce him/her in order to enforce that partner's wishes.

B. The client's partner described that the client often uses coercive means to enforce his/her wishes.

C. The partners have become alienated from each other because of the dominating and controlling manner of coercion.

D. The partner's pattern of coercion has mellowed into consideration of the other's opinion and feeling.

E. The client's coercion has mellowed into consideration of the other's opinions and feelings.

F. The partners described that they are able to yield control to each other, which has decreased the need to maintain power and control.

4. Yelling/Cursing (4)

A. The client has engaged in verbal threats of aggression toward others, name calling, and other verbally abusive speech.

*The numbers in parentheses on Client Presentation pages correlate to the number of the Behavioral Definition statement in the companion chapter with the same title in *The Couples Psychotherapy Treatment Planner* (Jongsma, O'Leary, and Heyman) by John Wiley & Sons, 1998. The numbers in parentheses on the Interventions Implemented page correspond to the number of the Therapeutic Intervention statement in the companion chapter in the same book.

B. The client's partner has engaged in verbal threats of aggression toward others, name calling, and other verbally abusive speech.
C. Little or no remorse has been observed regarding the intimidation of others.
D. The blame for verbal outbursts tends to be projected from the intimidator onto others.
E. The client has shown progress in controlling his/her verbally aggressive patterns and seems to be trying to interact with more assertiveness than aggression.
F. The client's partner has shown progress in controlling verbally aggressive patterns and seems to be trying to interact with more assertiveness than aggression.

5. Throwing/Breaking Objects (4)

A. The client described several incidents of suppressing angry feelings, then exploding in a violent rage.
B. The client's partner described several incidents of suppressing angry feelings, then exploding in a violent rage.
C. The partner with anger control problems reported gaining greater control over aggressive impulses.
D. The partner with anger control problems reports successful control over aggressive impulses, with no recent incidents noted.
E. The partner with anger control problems identified situations in which assertively expressing feelings has helped to gain successful control over aggressive impulses.

INTERVENTIONS IMPLEMENTED

1. Teach Anger as a Natural Signal (1)

A. The partners were educated that the purpose of anger control is not to eliminate anger, because anger is an important, natural signal that something important is at stake.
B. Examples were provided to help the partners to understand the use of anger as a natural signal.
C. The partners were reinforced for displaying an increased understanding of the appropriate place for anger.
D. Additional information was provided as the partners failed to grasp the appropriate place for anger as a natural signal.

2. Teach about Anger as a Motivator (2)

A. The partners were taught about the concept that anger motivates the body's general response to fight a perceived threat.
B. The partners were taught about how the angry response to the perceived threat can either help or hurt one's self and the relationship.
C. The partners were reinforced as they displayed a clear understanding of how anger motivates the body's general response to fight a perceived threat, and how the response can either help or hurt the relationship.
D. Additional feedback was provided as the partners failed to grasp the motivating aspects of anger.

3. Educate about Goals of Anger Control (3)

A. The partners were educated about the importance of recognizing a provocative situation.

B. The partners were educated about the use of anger control to manage provocative situations in ways that strengthen rather than weaken the relationship.

C. The partners were provided with positive feedback as they displayed a clear understanding of the use of anger control to identify and manage provocative situations.

D. Remedial information was provided to the partners to assist in developing a greater understanding of how anger control can help to strengthen rather than weaken the relationship.

4. List Short-Term Negative Anger Impact (4)

A. Each partner was asked to describe the ways in which anger has been destructive to self or relationship in the short term.

B. The partners identified many immediate negative consequences that have resulted from poor anger management.

C. The couple's denial about the negative impact of anger has decreased, and each partner has verbalized an increased awareness of the negative impact of angry behavior.

D. Additional feedback was provided as the client failed to identify ways in which anger is destructive to himself/herself or the relationship in the short term.

E. Additional information was provided as the client's partner failed to describe ways in which anger is destructive to self or the relationship in the short term.

5. List Long-Term Negative Anger Impact (5)

A. Each partner was asked to describe the ways in which anger has been destructive to self or the relationship in the long term.

B. The partners identified many long-term negative consequences that have resulted from poor anger management.

C. The couple's denial about the negative impact of anger has decreased, and the partners have verbalized an increased awareness of the negative impact of angry behavior.

D. Additional feedback was provided as the client failed to identify ways in which his/her anger is destructive to himself/herself or the relationship in the long term.

E. Additional information was provided as the client's partner failed to describe ways in which anger is destructive to self or the relationship in the long term.

6. List Short-Term Gains (6)

A. Each partner was assisted in identifying the short-term reinforcers for anger (i.e., getting one's own way, being left alone).

B. The partners identified many immediate reinforcers that have resulted from anger outbursts.

C. Additional feedback was provided as the client failed to identify ways in which his/her anger is reinforcing in the short term.

D. Additional information was provided as the client's partner failed to describe ways in which anger is reinforcing in the short term.

7. List Long-Term Gains (7)

A. Each partner was assisted in identifying the long-term reinforcers for anger (i.e., intimidation, obedience).

B. The partners identified many enduring reinforcers that have resulted from anger outbursts, and these were processed within the session.

C. Additional feedback was provided as the client failed to identify ways in which his/her anger is reinforcing in the long term.

D. Additional information was provided as the client's partner failed to describe ways in which anger is reinforcing in the long term.

8. Review Anger Management Success (8)

A. Each partner was asked about ways in which anger has been managed or de-escalated appropriately in the past.

B. The client was encouraged to implement the technique of managing or deescalating his/her anger in the past.

C. The client's partner was encouraged to implement the previously successful techniques of managing or deescalating his/her anger.

9. Review Counterproductive Anger Experiences (9)

A. Each partner was asked about counterproductive ways in which anger has been managed in the past.

B. The client described his/her negative experiences regarding managing his/her anger in the past, and these were processed.

C. The client's partner identified past counterproductive attempts to manage or deescalate anger, and these were processed.

10. Identify Different Perceptions Regarding Anger Control (10)

A. The partners were helped to identify ways in which one partner's de-escalating strategies have been perceived as a provocation to the other partner (e.g., partner's withdrawal is perceived as a provocative rejection by the partner).

B. The partners were provided with positive feedback as they identified how one partner's de-escalation strategies were perceived as a provocation to the other partner.

C. Additional examples have been provided as the partners failed to identify how de-escalation strategies have been perceived as a provocation by the other partner.

11. Contract Regarding Anger Responsibility (11)

A. Both partners were focused on the need to accept responsibility for managing one's own anger, instead of managing the partner's anger.

B. Both partners were asked to verbally contract to accept responsibility for managing their own anger instead of managing the other's anger.

C. A written contract was used to focus the partners on taking responsibility for their own anger rather than the partner's anger.

D. Positive feedback was provided as both partners accepted the responsibility for managing their own anger rather than the partner's anger.

E. The partners were confronted as they tended to focus on managing the other partner's behavior rather than their own anger.

12. Contract Regarding Therapy Sessions (12)

A. Both partners were focused on the need to use therapy sessions for constructive purposes.
B. Both partners were asked to verbally contract to focus on constructive areas during the therapy session and to abide by the therapist's directions if the process becomes destructive.
C. A written contract was used to focus the partners on the constructive use of therapy sessions.
D. Positive feedback was provided as both partners accepted the responsibility for managing their own anger during the sessions and using the sessions for constructive problem solving.
E. The partners were confronted as they became verbally destructive with their anger during the sessions and ignored the therapist's directions.

13. Teach "Measured Truthfulness" (13)

A. The partners were taught the speaker skill of "measured truthfulness" (i.e., the speaker balances the need to comment about the other against a concern for the other's feelings).
B. The partners practiced the skill of "measured truthfulness" within the session, regarding areas of conflict.
C. Positive feedback was provided regarding the couple's use of "measured truthfulness."
D. The partners were provided with more specific feedback regarding situations in which they can use "measured truthfulness."

14. Contract for "Measured Truthfulness" (14)

A. Both partners were verbally contracted to use "measured truthfulness" at home and in the session when discussing anger-eliciting topics.
B. A written contract was used to assist both partners to use "measured truthfulness" at home and in session.
C. Both partners have regularly used "measured truthfulness" at home and in session and identified an increased level of emotional safety.
D. The client has failed to use "measured truthfulness," and this failure was problem-solved.
E. The client's partner has failed to use "measured truthfulness," and this failure was problem-solved.

15. Identify Low-Level Anger Cues (15)

A. The partners were assisted in identifying the behavioral, cognitive, and affective cues of being at low levels of anger (0–30 on a 0–100 scale).
B. The partners were provided with positive feedback as they identified a variety of behavioral, cognitive, and affective cues of low levels of anger.
C. The partners were provided with additional feedback regarding the common behavioral, cognitive, and affective cues of being at low levels of anger.

16. Identify Moderate-Level Anger Cues (16)

A. The partners were assisted in identifying the behavioral, cognitive, and affective cues of being at moderate levels of anger (31–50 on a 0–100 scale).

B. The partners were provided with positive feedback as they identified a variety of behavioral, cognitive, and affective cues of moderate levels of anger.

C. The partners were provided with additional feedback regarding the common behavioral, cognitive, and affective cues of being at moderate levels of anger.

17. Identify the Danger Zone of Anger Cues (17)

A. The partners were assisted in identifying the behavioral, cognitive, and affective cues of being at the danger zone of anger (51–70 on a 0–100 scale).

B. The partners were provided with positive feedback as they identified a variety of behavioral, cognitive, and affective cues of the danger zone of anger.

C. The partners were provided with additional feedback regarding the common behavioral, cognitive, and affective cues of being at the danger zone of anger.

18. Identify the Extreme Zone of Anger Cues (18)

A. The partners were assisted in identifying the behavioral, cognitive, and affective cues of being at the extreme zone of anger (71–100 on a 0–100 scale).

B. The client was assisted in identifying the behavioral, cognitive, and affective cues that are indicating emotional and/or physical abusiveness as a more likely response.

C. The partners were provided with positive feedback as they identified a variety of behavioral, cognitive, and affective cues of the extreme zone of anger.

D. The partners were provided with additional feedback regarding the common behavioral, cognitive, and affective cues of being at the extreme zone of anger.

19. Inquire about Constructive and Destructive Anger Levels (19)

A. The partners were asked about what levels of anger have been constructive in the past.

B. The partners were asked about what levels of anger have been destructive in the past.

C. Positive feedback was provided as the partners displayed significant insight regarding the constructive and destructive levels of anger in the past.

D. The partners failed to identify the constructive and destructive levels of anger in their past experience and were provided with additional feedback in this area.

20. Inquire about Erosion of Anger Control (20)

A. The partners were asked about the level of anger at which effective control over behavior has begun to erode.

B. Positive feedback was provided as the partners displayed significant insight regarding the pattern of anger control eroding.

C. The partners failed to identify the level at which effective anger control breaks down and were provided with additional feedback in this area.

21. Inquire about When to Use Anger Management Skills (21)

A. The partners were asked about what level of anger necessitates the use of anger management skills.

B. The partners were asked about when they have needed to use anger management skills in the past.

C. Positive feedback was provided as the partners displayed significant insight regarding the level of anger at which management skills must be implemented.

D. The partners failed to identify when anger management skills must be introduced and were provided with additional feedback in this area.

22. Teach Time-Out Techniques (22)

A. The partners were taught about the six components of time-out techniques (i.e., *self-monitoring* for escalating feelings of anger and hurt, *signaling* to the partner that verbal engagement should end, *acknowledging* the need of the partner to disengage, *separating* to disengage, *cooling down* to regain control of anger, and *returning* to controlled verbal engagement).

B. Positive feedback was provided as the partners displayed mastery of the time-out techniques.

C. The partners were advised about the potential for misuse and manipulation of the time-out techniques if used to avoid arguments or manipulate the other partner.

D. The partners have misused the time-out techniques and were provided with additional feedback in this area.

23. Practice Time-Outs (23)

A. The couple was coached in the session regarding their practice attempts to use time-out techniques.

B. Positive feedback was provided to the couple as they appropriately used time-out techniques in session practice attempts.

C. The couple was provided with additional feedback about how to use the time-out techniques.

D. The partners were assigned to practice the time-out techniques at home.

24. Teach Reasons for Anger (24)

A. The partners were taught about the three main reasons for anger: (a) to get something, (b) to assert independence, and (c) to protect self.

B. The partners were provided with examples of the three main reasons for anger.

25. Identify Anger to Get Something (25)

A. The partners were asked to identify episodes in which their anger was used to get something (i.e., anger that results in getting one's way or anger that results from frustration over not getting one's way).

B. Feedback was provided as the partners identified episodes in which their anger was used to get something.

C. The partners were provided with additional examples of the use of anger to get something.

D. The partners were assisted in discussing their use of anger to get something.

26. Identify Anger to Assert Independence (26)

A. The partners were asked to identify episodes in which their anger was used to assert independence (i.e., anger that results from perceptions that the partner is trying to exert control over one's life or actions).

B. Feedback was provided as the partners identified episodes in which their anger was used to assert independence.

C. The partners were provided with additional examples of the use of anger to assert independence.
D. The partners were assisted in discussing their use of anger to assert independence.

27. Identify Anger to Protect (27)

A. The partners were asked to identify episodes in which their anger was used for self-protection (i.e., anger that results from the perception that one has been hurt or is vulnerable).
B. Feedback was provided as the partners identified episodes in which their anger was used for protection.
C. The partners were provided with additional examples of the use of anger for protection.
D. The partners were assisted in discussing their use of anger for protection.

28. Assign Anger-Tracking Homework (28)

A. The partners were assigned to track anger experiences, listing the situations that trigger anger, which of the three goals of anger apply, and to recount the thoughts and behaviors that occur during such anger-eliciting situations.
B. The partners have completed the anger-tracking homework and were provided with feedback.
C. The partners have not completed the anger-tracking homework and were redirected to do so.

29. Review Anger-Tracking Homework (29)

A. The partners were asked to review their anger-tracking homework and to identify situations where they were trying to get something.
B. The partners were asked to review their anger-tracking homework and to identify situations where they were asserting independence.
C. The partners were asked to review their anger-tracking homework and to identify situations where they felt the need to protect themselves.
D. The partners were provided with feedback as they identified the different uses of their anger.
E. The partners have failed to identify the uses of their anger and were provided with additional information and feedback in this area.

30. Analyze Anger Situations (30)

A. The partners were shown how to organize a situational analysis.
B. From the homework assignments, each partner chose specific anger-eliciting situations and told the interpretations/cognitions, behavior, and the actual outcome; feedback was provided about this analysis.
C. An individual session was used to have the client identify anger-eliciting situations, his/her interpretations/cognition, behavior, and actual outcomes of the situation.
D. An individual session was used to have the client's partner identify anger-eliciting situations, interpretations/cognition, behavior, and actual outcomes of the situation.

31. Identify Desired Outcomes (31)

A. The partners were asked to describe a desired outcome from a specific anger situation.
B. In an individual session, the client was requested to describe what his/her desired outcome was for a specified situation.
C. The client's partner was requested to identify the desired outcome for a specific situation.

32. Review Verbalized Thoughts (32)

A. The partner was assisted in determining whether identified thoughts about the situation were helpful in getting the desired outcome.
B. The partner was assisted in determining whether identified thoughts about the situation were anchored to the specific situation described (i.e., situationally specific instead of global).
C. The partner was assisted in determining whether each thought was accurate (i.e., overt evidence could be marshaled to support it).
D. The partner was reinforced for the accurate, insightful views regarding cognitions in angry situations.
E. Additional feedback was provided to the partner regarding interpretive thoughts about anger situations.

33. Direct Rewording of Inaccurate Thoughts (33)

A. A portion of the partner's interpretive statements were identified as unproductive, not anchored in reality and/or not accurate.
B. The partner was assisted in rewording the thoughts so that they meet criteria (e.g., "She's always on my back about spending time with the kids" can become "She's exhausted and is looking for a break").
C. The partner was provided with positive feedback as interpretive thoughts were modified.
D. The partner was provided with specific examples of how to reword interpretive thoughts.

34. Develop Achievable Outcome (34)

A. The partner was assisted in determining whether the desired outcome was achievable (i.e., under personal control).
B. The partner was encouraged to reword unachievable outcomes in a manner so that the outcome becomes achievable (e.g., " I want him to listen to me when I'm upset" can become " I want to ask him to schedule a time for us to talk about problems that we're having").
C. The partner was provided with positive feedback as changed unachievable outcomes were changed into achievable outcomes.
D. The partner did not appear to understand the concept of achievable versus unachievable outcomes and was provided with remedial information about this concept.

35. Summarize Situational Analysis (35)

A. The partner was asked to summarize the lessons that have been learned from the situational analysis.
B. The partner was provided with positive feedback about the summarization of the situational analysis.

C. Additional feedback was provided to the partner to help summarize the situational analysis.

36. Request Talking about Angry Feelings (36)

A. The partners were requested to agree to label and talk about angry feelings, rather than acting them out.

B. Both partners committed to talking about angry feelings rather than acting them out.

37. Distinguish Unassertive, Assertive, and Aggressive Patterns (37)

A. The partners were assisted in differentiating between unassertive (i.e., not standing up for one's wishes or rights), assertive (i.e., appropriately asserting one's wishes or rights without infringing on the rights of others), and aggressive (i.e., asserting one's wishes and rights without regard to the rights of others).

B. The partners' use of unassertive, assertive, and aggressive patterns were identified and reviewed.

C. The partners were provided with positive feedback for their increase in assertive responses.

D. Additional feedback was provided to the partners as they struggled to identify the differences between unassertive, assertive, and aggressive actions.

38. Practice Assertive Communication (38)

A. The partners were directed to practice assertive communication skills, such as "I" statements in "get-something" situations.

B. The partners reported practicing assertive communication and were provided with positive feedback.

39. Reinforce Assertiveness (39)

A. The partners were reinforced for using assertive behaviors during the session.

B. The partners were questioned about their use of assertiveness between sessions. Provided the partners with positive feedback about these successes.

C. The partners were unable to identify healthy use of assertiveness between sessions and were redirected to use these skills.

40. Elicit Agreement Not to Capitulate (40)

A. The partners were directed not to give in to the angry wishes of the other during "get-something" situations.

B. Both partners were asked to verbally agree that neither partner is obligated to give in to the angry wishes of the other.

C. The partners were encouraged to maintain their commitment against giving in to the angry wishes of the other.

41. Practice Identifying Focus on Outcome versus Affect (41)

A. The partners were directed to have the listener paraphrase the speaker's message, focusing on the speaker's implicit or explicit desired outcome and not the angry affect.

B. The listener was assisted in paraphrasing the speaker's message.

C. The listener was reinforced for paraphrasing accurately the speaker's desired outcome and not the angry affect.

D. The listener was provided with tips and other feedback to more accurately understand and reflect the speaker's message, but not focus on the affect.

42. Direct Assertive Communication Regarding Independence (42)

A. The partners were directed to practice assertive communication skills for "assert independence" desired outcomes.
B. The partners were encouraged to identify the specific behaviors that trigger the perceptions of being controlled.
C. The partners were reinforced for understanding the specific behaviors that trigger the perceptions of being controlled and for making assertive communication about those behaviors.
D. Additional direct feedback was provided to the partners regarding identifying specific behaviors that trigger the perception of being controlled and how to assertively express this.

43. Focus on Speaker's Message (43)

A. The listener was directed to paraphrase the speaker's message, focusing on the speaker's perceptions and not the listener's desire to defend actions.
B. Positive feedback was provided to the partners as they focused on the "assert independence" situation and perceived control, and asserted healthy communication about these issues.
C. The listener was provided with additional feedback regarding the correct paraphrasing of the speaker's message, and the tendency to focus on defending one's own actions.

44. Identify Anger as Protection Emotions (44)

A. The partners were asked to identify the emotions that precede anger (e.g., hurt, fearful, or vulnerable) during a "protection" desired outcome.
B. Positive feedback was provided as the partners identified emotions that precede anger (e.g., hurt, fearful, or vulnerable).
C. The partners were urged to identify the emotions preceding anger during "protection" desired outcomes.

45. Practice "I" Statements (45)

A. The partners were directed to practice assertive communication skills, such as "I" statements in "protection" situations.
B. The partners reported practicing assertive communication and were provided with positive feedback

46. Practice Non-Attacking Protection (46)

A. For "protection" desired outcomes, the speaker was directed to practice taking responsibility for self-protection in a manner that does not attack the other partner.
B. The speaker was reinforced for protecting self in a manner that does not attack the partner.
C. The speaker was provided with specific examples of how to improve self-protection in a manner that does not attack the partner.

47. Practice Making Requests for Support (47)

A. During a "protection" desired outcome, the speaker was directed to practice making requests for support and caring from the other partner when hurt, fearful, or vulnerable.

B. The speaker was provided with positive feedback regarding requests for support.

C. The speaker was provided with specific directions regarding how to improve requests for support and caring for the other partner.

48. Search for Underlying Emotion (48)

A. During a "protection" desired outcome, the listener was directed to search for and reflect the underlying emotional content that the speaker is experiencing when feeling hurt or vulnerable.

B. The listener was assisted in identifying specific underlying emotions felt by the speaker when hurt or vulnerable.

C. Positive feedback was provided as the listener correctly identified the partner's underlying emotions.

D. The speaker was encouraged to critique the listener's assessment of the underlying emotions.

49. Direct Review of Defensiveness (49)

A. As the listener responded defensively to the speaker's communication when needing "protection," the partners were asked to switch places and the listener was asked to verbalize the other partner's perspective and feelings.

B. The listener was reinforced for displaying an increased understanding of the partner's perspective and feelings.

C. The listener responded defensively and was asked to switch places and verbalize the partner's feelings.

D. Positive feedback was provided when both partners exhibited being able to verbalize and identify their perspectives and feelings.

ANXIETY

CLIENT PRESENTATION

1. **Excessive Worry (1)***

A. The client described symptoms of preoccupation with worry that something dire will happen.

B. The client showed some recognition that his/her excessive worry or perceived threat is beyond the scope of rationality, but he/she is unable to control it.

C. The client described that he/she worries about issues related to family, personal safety, health, and employment, among other things.

D. The client reported that his/her worry about life's circumstances has diminished, and he/she is living with more of a sense of peace and confidence.

2. **Poor Role Fulfillment (1)**

A. The client's experience of perceived threat and worry impede his/her fulfillment of important roles.

B. The client has failed to complete typical tasks within the relationship due to his/her worry and anxiety.

C. As the client's anxiety level has decreased, he/she has experienced increased capability in important roles.

D. The client is less anxious and is able to normally fulfill important role tasks.

3. **Diagnosable Anxiety Disorder (2)**

A. The client's anxiety has been disruptive enough to meet the criteria of an anxiety disorder diagnosis (e.g., excessive and unwanted worry, motor tension, autonomic hyperactivity, and hypervigilance).

B. The client's partner anxiety has been disruptive enough to meet the criteria of an anxiety disorder diagnosis (e.g., excessive and unwanted worry, motor tension, autonomic hyperactivity, and hypervigilance).

C. Both partners' anxiety has been disruptive enough to meet the criteria of an anxiety disorder diagnosis (e.g., excessive and unwanted worry, motor tension, autonomic hyperactivity, and hypervigilance).

D. As treatment has progressed, the anxiety disorder has been resolved.

4. **Arguments about Anxiety (3)**

A. The partners have had arguments related to the anxiety problems.

B. The partners report persistent arguments over the adaptations that the anxiety has forced both partners to make.

C. The partners have frequently been at odds with each other over issues related to the anxiety.

*The numbers in parentheses on Client Presentation pages correlate to the number of the Behavioral Definition statement in the companion chapter with the same title in *The Couples Psychotherapy Treatment Planner* (Jongsma, O'Leary, and Heyman) by John Wiley & Sons, 1998. The numbers in parentheses on the Interventions Implemented page correspond to the number of the Therapeutic Intervention statement in the companion chapter in the same book.

D. As the anxious partner's pattern of anxiety has been eliminated, the arguments between the partners have decreased.

5. Social Isolation (4)

A. The couple described having no close friends or confidants outside of first-degree relatives.
B. The anxious partner has experienced symptoms that led to an inability to build and maintain a social network of friends and acquaintances.
C. The level of social isolation experienced by the partners is distressing to one or both partners.
D. The partner without the anxiety concerns has begun to reach out socially and to respond favorably to the overtures of others.
E. Both partners reported enjoying contact with friends and sharing personal information with them.

6. Fruitless Discussions about Worry (5)

A. The partners have engaged in lengthy, repetitive discussions regarding the anxiety and worry, without reduction of the anxiety.
B. The fruitless, repetitive discussions have become irritating to the partner without the anxiety disorder.
C. The partners have discontinued discussions or arguments regarding the worry.
D. As treatment has progressed, the anxiety levels have decreased and have become less of an issue between the partners.

INTERVENTIONS IMPLEMENTED

1. Identify Anxiety Symptoms (1)

A. The anxious partner was asked to describe the anxiety and avoidance symptoms that are being experienced.
B. Support and encouragement were provided to the anxious partner as the avoidance symptoms were described.
C. The anxious partner was assisted in clarifying the fears and anxieties that are experienced.

2. Review Development of Anxiety Problems (2)

A. The anxious partner was asked to describe the developmental course of the anxiety problems.
B. Support and encouragement were provided to the anxious partner as the developmental causes of the anxiety problems were uncovered.
C. Positive feedback was provided to the anxious partner, who was able to display significant insight regarding the developmental course of the anxiety problem.
D. The anxious partner was provided with assistance and suggestions in helping to identify the developmental course of the anxiety problem.

3. Ask Partner's Perspective (3)

A. The nonanxious partner was asked to provide another perspective of the other partner's anxiety and avoidance symptoms.

B. The nonanxious partner provided significant information regarding the partner's anxiety or avoidance symptoms that had not been previously mentioned; these were processed.
C. The partner provided similar information about the anxiety concerns that the anxious partner experiences.

4. Identify Anxiety Effects on Self (4)

A. The anxious partner was asked to describe the personal effects of the anxiety problems.
B. Support and encouragement were provided to the anxious partner as the personal effects of the anxiety problems were described.
C. The anxious partner was gently confronted regarding minimizing the effects of the anxiety problems.

5. Identify Anxiety Effects on Relationship (5)

A. The anxious partner was asked to describe the effects of the anxiety problems on the relationship.
B. Support and encouragement were provided to the anxious partner as the effects of the anxiety problems on the relationship were described.
C. The anxious partner was gently confronted regarding minimizing the effects of the anxiety problems.

6. Identify Anxiety Effects on Self by Nonanxious Partner (6)

A. The nonanxious partner was asked to describe the personal effects of the partner's anxiety problems.
B. Support and encouragement were provided to the nonanxious partner as the personal effects of the partner's anxiety problems were described.
C. The nonanxious partner was gently confronted regarding minimizing the personal effects of the partner's anxiety problems.

7. Identify Anxiety Effects on Relationship by Nonanxious Partner (7)

A. The nonanxious partner was asked to describe the effects of the partner's anxiety problems on the relationship.
B. Support and encouragement were provided to the nonanxious partner as the effects of the partner's anxiety problems on the relationship were described.
C. The nonanxious partner was gently confronted regarding minimizing the effects of the anxiety problems on the relationship.

8. Identify Coping Strategies (8)

A. Both partners were asked to describe how they currently are attempting to cope with the anxiety problem.
B. Supportive, attentive listening was used as the anxious partner identified how he/she copes with the anxiety symptoms.
C. Support and encouragement were used as the nonanxious partner described how he/she copes with the anxious partner's level of anxiety.
D. Feedback was provided to both partners as they described how they are currently attempting to cope with the effects of the anxiety on their relationship.

9. Review Supportiveness (9)

A. The nonanxious partner was asked to describe how the level of supportiveness has changed over time.

B. Attentive listening and encouragement were used to help the nonanxious partner described how the level of supportiveness has changed over time.

C. The couple was supported and guided as they processed the information about how supportiveness has changed across time.

10. Discuss Anxiety Precipitating Conflicts (10)

A. The couple was guided in a discussion about the ways in which the anxiety problem may precipitate relationship conflicts.

B. Positive feedback was provided as the couple identified a variety of ways in which the anxiety problems may precipitate relationship problems.

C. The couple displayed poor insight into the effect that the anxiety problems have on relationship conflicts and were provided with tentative interpretations in this area.

11. Inquire about Roles (11)

A. The partners were asked to describe how the anxiety problem has affected their current role arrangement.

B. Attentive listening was used as the partners described the effects of the anxiety problems on their current role arrangement.

C. It was reflected to the partners that the current role arrangements have been significantly modified by the anxiety problems.

D. The partners had a poor understanding of the ways in which the anxiety has led to changes in roles and were given tentative examples of these types of changes.

12. Discuss Etiology of Role Arrangement (12)

A. The couple was guided in the discussion about how the current role arrangements came about.

B. The couple was asked about whether the current responsibility allocations were made overtly, or if the current arrangement evolved implicitly.

C. Positive feedback was provided to the partners as they displayed significant insight regarding the etiology of their current role arrangement.

D. The partners have poor insight into their current role arrangement and were provided with tentative interpretations about the etiology of their current role arrangement.

13. Educate about Anxiety (13)

A. The partners were educated about how anxiety motivates the body's general response to fight or flee perceived threats.

B. The partners were educated about how anxiety responses can either help or hurt oneself and the relationship.

C. Feedback was provided as the partners reviewed examples in which anxiety motivates the body's general response to fight or flee perceived threats.

14. Educate about Negative Effects of Anxiety (14)

A. The partners were taught that while anxiety can serve a useful, protective function, overuse of this defense mechanism can exhaust both an individual and a relationship.

B. Feedback was provided as the partners provided examples of how anxiety has been overused as a defense mechanism, and the effects on both the individual and their relationship.

C. As the partners described the negative effects of anxiety on themselves and the relationship, they were directed to use this as a motivator for working together to overcome the anxiety problems.

15. Teach about How Anxiety Is Generalized and Can Be Overcome (15)

A. The partners were educated about how appropriate anxiety resulting from a specific, high-threat situation in the past often gets reapplied to new, low-threat situations.

B. The partners were educated about breaking anxiety habits by facing feared situations to test whether the feared consequences are real or overestimated.

C. The partners were provided with feedback as they gave examples of misapplied anxiety.

16. Explain about Maladaptive Coping Responses and Habituation (16)

A. The couple was taught that to truly break an anxiety habit, successful exposure to feared situations must prevent the client with the anxiety problem from using maladaptive coping responses (e.g., escape).

B. The partners were taught about exposure being long enough and regular enough for the anxiety to subside (i.e., the behavioral principle of habituation).

C. Positive feedback was provided as the partners verbalized an understanding of the principle that testing the accuracy of feelings and threats can break anxiety.

17. Encourage Exposure to Anxious Situation (17)

A. The anxious client was encouraged to face a specific anxiety-producing situation, gradually increasing the amount of time and the stimulus intensity, without using escape.

B. The anxious partner was directed to monitor actual versus imagined feelings of threat.

C. The nonanxious partner was directed to gently encourage the anxious partner.

D. Support and encouragement were provided to the partners as they gradually increased exposure to the anxious situation without using maladaptive coping techniques.

E. The partners have not increased exposure to the anxious situation and were redirected to do so.

18. Educate about Anxiety Channels (18)

A. The partners were educated about how anxiety operates through three channels—behavioral, cognitive, and affective/physiological.

B. Positive feedback was provided as the partners displayed an understanding of the concepts of behavioral, cognitive, and affective/physiological channels for anxiety.

C. The partners provided examples of how they have experienced behavioral, cognitive, and affective/physiological portions of anxiety, and these were processed.

D. Remedial information was provided as the partners labored to understand the concepts related to behavioral, cognitive, and affective/physiological channels for anxiety.

19. Assign Reading about Panic (19)

A. The partners were assigned to read material related to panic.
B. The partners were assigned to read *Mastering Your Anxiety and Panic-Patient's Workbook* (Barlow and Craske).
C. The partners have read the information about panic, and key concepts were reviewed.
D. The partners have not read the information about panic and were redirected to do so.

20. Assign Reading about Worry (20)

A. The partners were assigned to read material about worry.
B. The partners were assigned to read *Mastering Your Anxiety and Worry-Patient's Workbook* (Craske and Barlow).
C. The partners have read the material about worry, and key concepts were reviewed.
D. The partners have not read the material about worry and were redirected to do so.

21. Select Coach (21)

A. The anxious partner was asked whether he/she would feel comfortable with the nonanxious partner serving as coach.
B. Since both clients are anxious, each partner was asked to serve as coach for the other.
C. The anxious partner accepted the use of the nonanxious partner as coach and was provided with positive feedback for this decision.
D. The anxious partner felt uncomfortable having the nonanxious partner serve as coach, and this choice was accepted.
E. The anxious partner was supported for selecting another individual as the coach.

22. Direct Anticipation and Brainstorming about Problems (22)

A. With the nonanxious partner serving as coach, the couple was directed to anticipate potential problems and brainstorm ways to avoid them.
B. Both partners were contracted to use the relationship as a source of help and strength in conquering the problem.
C. Positive feedback was provided as the couple displayed healthy anticipation and brainstorming regarding problems.
D. Additional feedback was provided to improve the couple's use of anticipation and problem solving to avoid anxiety problems.

23. Educate about Gradations of Anxiety (23)

A. The partners were taught that anxiety is not an on/off phenomenon, but rather one of gradations.
B. The partners were provided with examples of gradations of anxiety.
C. The partners were supported for their understanding of the gradations of their anxiety.

24. Teach Subjective Units of Discomfort (SUDS) (24)

A. The couple was taught to use the Subjective Units of Discomfort (SUDS) scale, in which the anxious partner rates perceived anxiety on a 0–100 scale.

B. Positive feedback was provided as the partners displayed a clear understanding of the use of the SUDS scale.
C. Remedial information was provided when the partners failed to grasp the use of the SUDS scale.

25. Direct Discussion of SUDS Score (25)

A. The anxious partner was directed to describe for the nonanxious partner what his/her current SUDS score is.
B. The anxious partner was directed to identify the elements of the situation that are affecting the SUDS score, and what internal cues are being used to determine the SUDS score.
C. A discussion of the use of the SUDS score was facilitated.
D. The anxious partner was provided with feedback regarding the use of the SUDS score.

26. Contract for Discreet Signals (26)

A. The partners were contracted to discretely signal each other about SUDS scores being experienced in various situations.
B. The partners developed a specific, discreet signal that could be used to identify varying levels of SUDS scores in specific situations.

27. Identify Low-level Anxiety Cues (27)

A. The partners were assisted in identifying the behavioral, cognitive, and affective cues of being at low levels of anxiety (0–30 on a 0–100 scale).
B. The partners were provided with positive feedback as they identified a variety of behavioral, cognitive, and affective cues of low levels of anxiety.
C. The partners were provided with additional feedback regarding the common behavioral, cognitive, and affective cues of being at low levels of anxiety.

28. Identify Moderate-Level Anxiety Cues (28)

A. The partners were assisted in identifying the behavioral, cognitive, and affective cues of being at moderate levels of anxiety (31–50 on a 0–100 scale).
B. The partners were provided with positive feedback as they identified a variety of behavioral, cognitive, and affective cues of moderate levels of anxiety.
C. The partners were provided with additional feedback regarding the common behavioral, cognitive, and affective cues of being at moderate levels of anxiety.

29. Identify the High-Moderate Level of Anxiety Cues (29)

A. The partners were assisted in identifying the behavioral, cognitive, and affective cues of being at the high-moderate level of anxiety (51–70 on a 0–100 scale).
B. The partners were provided with positive feedback as they identified a variety of behavioral, cognitive, and affective cues of the high-moderate level of anxiety.
C. The partners were provided with additional feedback regarding the common behavioral, cognitive, and affective cues of being at the high-moderate level of anxiety.

30. Identify the Extreme Zone of Anxiety Cues (30)

A. The partners were assisted in identifying the behavioral, cognitive, and affective cues of being at the extreme zone of anxiety (71–100 on a 0–100 scale).

B. The partners were provided with positive feedback as they identified a variety of behavioral, cognitive, and affective cues of the extreme zone of anxiety.

C. The partners were provided with additional feedback regarding the common behavioral, cognitive, and affective cues of being at the extreme zone of anxiety.

31. Teach Diaphragmatic Breathing (31)

A. The partners were taught diaphragmatic breathing skills, including differentiating diaphragmatic breathing from chest breathing, taking deep breaths, inhaling slowly for five seconds while thinking the word "calm," and then exhaling for 10 seconds.

B. The nonanxious partner was taught diaphragmatic breathing to provide support to the anxious partner, as well as for personal tension management.

C. Positive feedback was provided as the partners displayed mastery of the diaphragmatic breathing skills.

D. The partners displayed and described less anxiety as they used diaphragmatic breathing skills and the benefits of this were processed.

E. The partners did not display mastery over diaphragmatic breathing skills and were provided with redirection in this area.

32. Assign Breathing Practice (32)

A. Both partners were assigned to individually practice diaphragmatic breathing for three 10-minute sessions each day.

B. The partners were assigned to record the time, date, their SUDS score prior to the practice session and their score following their practice session.

C. The partners have regularly practiced diaphragmatic breathing, and the changes in SUDS were analyzed and reviewed.

D. The partners have not regularly practiced diaphragmatic breathing and were redirected to do so.

33. Assign Anxiety Journal (33)

A. A written journal was assigned to identify the situations that trigger anxiety, as well as the thoughts and behaviors that occur during anxiety-eliciting situations,

B. The anxiety journal was reviewed, and the pattern of situations, thoughts and behaviors were processed.

C. Positive feedback was provided as the partners showed increased insight regarding anxiety-eliciting situations.

D. The anxiety-tracking homework has not been completed, and the partners were redirected in this area.

34. Develop Hierarchy of Feared Situations (34)

A. The anxious partner was asked to identify feared situations.

B. The anxious partner was asked to generate estimated SUDS scores for each feared situation.

C. A hierarchy of situations feared by the anxious partner was generated.

35. Conduct Imagined Exposure (35)

A. Within the session, imagined exposure was conducted regarding the feared situations for the anxious partner, beginning at the lower end of the hierarchy.
B. The nonanxious partner was taught how to ask for SUDS ratings every several minutes.
C. Encouragement for the anxious partner was modeled to the nonanxious partner.
D. Positive feedback was provided to the partners as they displayed comfortability moving through the hierarchy of anxious situations.
E. The anxious partner displayed significant difficulties while practicing exposure to the anxiety-eliciting situations and was taught more coping skills to enhance relaxation.

36. Assign *In Vivo* Exposure (36)

A. The couple was assigned to complete *in vivo* desensitization contact with the anxiety-producing stimulus object or situation.
B. The partners were taught the principles of desensitization and encouraged to have the anxious partner encounter the anxiety-producing stimulus in gradual steps, utilizing relaxation to counterattack any anxiety response.
C. Positive feedback was provided as the partners described successful use of the *in vivo* exposure and coping techniques.
D. The partners reported failure when they tried to use *in vivo* techniques and were provided with additional coping skills for this task.
E. The partners did not practice the *in vivo* desensitization techniques, and the reasons for this failure were brainstormed and redirection was given.

37. Define Probability Overestimation (37)

A. Probability overestimation was defined as the belief that the relatively rare, feared events happen more frequently than they actually do.
B. The couple was reinforced for displaying an understanding of probability overestimation and providing examples of how this has occurred.
C. The partners denied any pattern of probability overestimation for the anxious partner and were provided with additional feedback in this area.

38. Model Challenges to Probability Overestimation (38)

A. The partners were provided with a model to challenge probability overestimation.
B. The anxious partner was asked to estimate the probability of a feared event happening.
C. Evidence to support the estimated probability of a feared event happening was examined.
D. Positive feedback was provided to the partners when they were able to successfully use challenges to probability overestimation.
E. Additional feedback was provided to the partners when they struggled to appropriately address probability overestimation.

39. Practice Review of Probability Overestimation (39)

A. The nonanxious partner was directed to calmly discuss probability overestimation with the anxious partner in a manner similar to that previously modeled by the therapist.

B. Positive feedback was provided to the nonanxious partner as probability overestimation was calmly discussed with the anxious partner.

C. Additional direction was provided to the nonanxious partner to help increase the ability to discuss probability overestimation.

40. Define Catastrophizing (40)

A. Catastrophizing was defined as magnifying insignificant consequences out of proportion.

B. Examples of catastrophizing were provided, such as thinking a tornado will occur because of one dark cloud on the horizon.

C. The couple was asked to identify their own examples of catastrophizing to test their understanding of this concept.

D. The partners did not have a complete understanding of the concept of catastrophizing and were provided with remedial information in this area.

41. Model Self-Talk to Challenge Catastrophizing (41)

A. Self-talk techniques were modeled to the anxious partner to help challenge the pattern of catastrophizing.

B. The anxious partner was asked to imagine the worst-case scenario and discuss how the couple would cope with such an event.

C. The partners were directed to use partner dialogue to challenge the anxious partner's catastrophizing.

D. Reinforcement was provided to the anxious partner for successful challenges to the pattern of catastrophizing.

E. Feedback was provided to the couple as they used couple dialogue/self-talk techniques to challenge catastrophizing.

42. Practice Discussion of Catastrophizing (42)

A. The nonanxious partner was directed to calmly discuss the pattern of catastrophizing with the other partner in a manner similar to that previously modeled by the therapist.

B. Positive feedback was provided to the nonanxious partner as catastrophizing was identified and discussed with the anxious partner.

C. Additional direction was provided to the nonanxious partner to help increase the ability to discuss the anxious partner's catastrophizing.

43. Require Stress-Reducing Activities (43)

A. Both partners were asked to commit to regularly engaging in individual stress-reducing activities (e.g., diaphragmatic breathing, deep muscle relaxation techniques, exercise, music, or hobbies).

B. The partners were asked to specifically schedule regular individual stress-reducing activities.

C. The partners have regularly scheduled stress-reducing activities, and the benefits of these were reviewed.

D. The partners have not used stress-reducing activities on a scheduled basis, and the barriers to this practice were identified and resolved.

44. Identify Ways to Support (44)

A. Each partner was asked to identify actions that he or she could take to be a source of support and anxiety-reduction to the other partner.

B. The partners have identified ways to be a source of support for each other and were asked to regularly schedule couple anxiety-reducing activities.

C. The partners were provided with examples of how to help each other reduce stress and anxiety (e.g., foot rubs, back rubs, social engagements, walks, sex, or shared hobbies).

D. The partners were reinforced for regularly using stress-reducing activities.

45. Discuss Future Positively (45)

A. The couple was asked to engage in confident discussions about the future.

B. The couple was provided with feedback about their confident discussions about the future and were redirected when anxiety-producing messages began.

C. The partners were directed to continue confident discussions about the future at home, focusing on planning and coping for future events.

46. Assign "Worry Meetings" (46)

A. The couple was assigned to schedule set times for brief "worry meetings" to discuss the anxious partner's concerns.

B. The anxious partner was directed to air anxieties only during the limited times of the "worry meetings."

C. The couple reported appropriate implementation of the "worry meetings," and the benefits of this were reviewed.

D. The partners have not used the "worry meetings" and were redirected to do so.

BLAME

CLIENT PRESENTATION

1. Blaming for Relationship Problems and Dissatisfaction (1)*

A. One partner repeatedly blames the other for the relationship problems.
B. One partner repeatedly blames the other partner for dissatisfaction with the relationship.
C. One partner often makes comments about how the marriage would be better if the other partner would make certain changes.
D. As treatment has progressed, the partners have ceased blaming each other.

2. Dissatisfaction with the Relationship (2)

A. One partner has expressed dissatisfaction with the relationship.
B. Both partners expressed dissatisfaction with the relationship.
C. The partners often blame each other for the level of dissatisfaction that each experiences with the relationship.
D. As communication has increased, dissatisfaction within the relationship has been decreased for both partners.
E. Both partners expressed satisfaction with the relationship.

3. Resistance to Examining Role in Conflict (3)

A. The blaming partner does not see any personal contributions to the conflict.
B. The blaming partner is resistant to examining the contributors to the conflict.
C. The blaming partner often makes comments about how the marriage difficulties are the other partner's problem.
D. As treatment has progressed, the blaming partner has become more accepting of the fact that both partners contribute to the relationship problems.
E. The blaming partner has become more open to examining personal contributions to the conflict.

4. Projection of Responsibility (4)

A. Responsibility is often projected onto the other partner for the blaming partner's behavior.
B. Responsibility is often projected onto the other partner for the blaming partner's thoughts.
C. Responsibility is often projected onto the other partner for the blaming partner's feelings.
D. The blamed partner has refused to take responsibility for the blaming partner's thoughts, feelings, or behavior.
E. The blaming partner has terminated the projection of responsibility onto the other partner regarding thoughts, feelings, and behavior.

*The numbers in parentheses on Client Presentation pages correlate to the number of the Behavioral Definition statement in the companion chapter with the same title in *The Couples Psychotherapy Treatment Planner* (Jongsma, O'Leary, and Heyman) by John Wiley & Sons, 1998. The numbers in parentheses on the Interventions Implemented page correspond to the number of the Therapeutic Intervention statement in the companion chapter in the same book.

5. Blame Replaces Honest Self-Examination (5)

A. Virtually all discussions result in a pattern of blaming rather than honest, open self-examination.

B. One partner reacts to perceived shortcomings with blaming rather than honest, open self-examination.

C. As communication has increased, the partners are more open to honest self-examination.

6. Lack of Assertiveness (6)

A. The blamed partner lacks consistent assertiveness.

B. The blamed partner tends to terminate communication in a show of helplessness and frustration.

C. The partners experience a cycle of blaming, frustration, and termination of communication, which leads to more blaming.

D. As the partners have progressed in treatment, the blamed partner is more assertive and responds with healthy communication rather than with helplessness and frustration.

7. Low Self-Esteem (7)

A. The blamed partner verbalizes feelings of low self-esteem.

B. The blamed partner does not feel valued by the other partner.

C. As the blaming has decreased, the blamed partner verbalizes increased self-esteem and a sense of being valued by the other partner.

INTERVENTIONS IMPLEMENTED

1. Describe Relationship Problems (1)

A. An individual session was held with each partner to describe the problems in the relationship.

B. The partners were confronted about blaming and discouraged from placing blame solely on one partner.

C. When the partners described problems as having a basis in both partners' behavior, reinforcement was provided.

D. Paraphrasing was used to review each partner's description of the problems in the relationship.

2. Assess for Other Problems (2)

A. The couple was assessed for the presence of other problems that might be the basis of most of the blaming in the relationship.

B. Evidence of chemical dependence was uncovered, and treatment focus was switched to this concern.

C. Evidence of physical abuse was uncovered, and treatment focus was switched to this concern.

D. Evidence of sexual abuse was uncovered, and treatment focus was switched to this concern.

E. Evidence of an extra-marital affair was identified as the basis for most of the blaming in the relationship, and treatment was focused on this area.
F. It was reflected to the partners that alternative bases for the blaming in the relationship were assessed, but none were uncovered.

3. Model and Reframe Respectful Describing of Problem (3)

A. Modeling techniques were used to show the partners how to respectfully state problems in a noncondemning manner.
B. The partners' description of the problem areas tended to be quite blaming, so reframing techniques were used to express these same concerns in a respectful, noncondemning manner.
C. Positive feedback was provided for the partners for stating problems in a respectful, noncondemning manner.
D. The partners continued to state problems in a blaming manner and were provided with remedial assistance in this area.

4. Encourage/Reinforce Taking Responsibility (4)

A. The partners were encouraged to take personal responsibility for how each contributes to the problems rather than projecting all blame onto the other partner.
B. Reinforcing comments were made each time a partner took responsibility for personal contributions to the problems.
C. It was reflected to the partners that they have increased taking responsibility for their personal contributions to the problem, rather than projecting all blame onto the other partner.

5. Sign Therapeutic Agreement (5)

A. Each partner was directed to sign a therapeutic agreement indicating partial responsibility for satisfaction and/or dissatisfaction in the relationship.
B. The partners were reinforced for taking written responsibility for the satisfaction and/or dissatisfaction in the relationship.
C. The partners declined to sign a therapeutic agreement indicating at least partial responsibility for the satisfaction and/or dissatisfaction in the relationship and were asked to reconsider this refusal.

6. Direct Description of Responsibility for a Problem (6)

A. Each of the partners was directed to separately present some problems, however minor, for which they can admit partial responsibility and can agree to make constructive changes.
B. Active listening techniques were used to support both partners as they presented on problems for which they feel they can admit partial responsibility.
C. Positive reinforcement was provided as the partners agreed to make constructive changes.
D. The blaming partner failed to identify even minor problems for which partial responsibility can be accepted and was provided with tentative examples in this area.

7. Support Focus on Current Problem (7)

A. Modeling techniques were used to encourage both partners to focus on current problems rather than fixating on the distant past.

B. Praise was provided to encourage and reinforce both partners for focusing on current problems rather than fixating on the past.
C. As treatment has progressed, it was noted that the partners are more capable of focusing on current problems, and do not fixate on the distant past very often.
D. The partners continue to fixate on the distant past and this replaces the efforts to focus on current problems; this was reflected to them and they were encouraged to maintain a more present focus.

8. Encourage Forgiveness (8)

A. It was uncovered that the blaming partner has remained angry about a hurt from the distant past, causing divisive bitterness.
B. The blaming partner was encouraged to give up anger about a hurt from the distant past.
C. The blaming partner was encouraged to practice forgiveness that heals, rather than bitterness that divides.
D. As treatment has progressed, the blaming partner has significantly let go of anger about a hurt from the distant past, and the benefit of this change was emphasized.

9. Teach "I" Messages (9)

A. The clients were taught about the use of "I" messages (i.e., stating first what thoughts and feelings were experienced, before stating the partner's behavior that seemed to trigger those thoughts and feelings).
B. Role-playing and modeling were used to teach about the use of "I" messages.
C. The partners were reinforced for using "I" messages.
D. The partners have not used "I" messages and were redirected to do so.

10. Teach Assertiveness (10)

A. The partners were taught about the use of assertiveness versus passiveness or aggressiveness.
B. Role-playing and modeling techniques were used to teach the partners about how to use assertive means of expressing thoughts and feelings.
C. The partners were reinforced for the use of assertive communication of thoughts and feelings.
D. Redirection was provided when the partners did not express thoughts and feelings in an assertive manner.

11. Direct Increases in Satisfaction-Producing Behaviors (11)

A. Each partner was asked to identify two behaviors that would be appreciated by the other partner.
B. Each partner was asked to commit to engaging in two behaviors that would be appreciated by the other partner.
C. It was emphasized to the partners that engaging in behaviors that are appreciated by the other partner is a way to take responsibility for increasing satisfaction in the relationship.
D. The partners have engaged in behaviors to increase satisfaction in the relationship, and the benefits of this were reviewed.

E. The partners have not engaged in behaviors that would be appreciated by the other partner and would increase satisfaction in the relationship, and the reasons for this resistance were problem solved.

12. Reinforce Positive Interaction (12)

A. Each partner was asked to report on a positive interchange that reflected change and improvement in the relationship.

B. Each instance of positive interaction between the partners was reinforced through positive comments.

C. Emphasis was placed on the factors that contribute to the pleasantness of each positive interchange.

D. The partners were unable to identify any positive interchanges that reflect change and improvement in the relationship and were provided with tentative examples of situations that may have occurred.

13. Assign Expression of Appreciation (13)

A. Each partner was asked to express appreciation for two things each day that are pleasing about the other partner's behavior.

B. The partners' use of appreciative comments were reviewed and reinforced.

C. The benefits of appreciative comments were reviewed and emphasized.

D. The partners have not regularly expressed appreciation for two things each day that are pleasing about the other partner's behavior and were redirected to do so.

14. Teach about Responsibility for Own Behavior (14)

A. Each partner was taught to accept responsibility for personal behaviors, thoughts, and feelings.

B. Emphasis was placed on how each partner has a myriad of choices as a reaction to the other partner's behavior.

C. The partners were reinforced for acceptance of responsibility for own behaviors, thoughts, and feelings in the context of multiple choices as a reaction to the other's behavior.

15. List Desired Behaviors (15)

A. The blaming partner was assigned to list positive behaviors that the blamed partner could engage in to please the blaming partner (i.e., focus on the position that is desired rather than the negative that is criticized).

B. The list of positive, pleasing behaviors that the blamed partner is to engage in was reviewed, and feedback was provided.

C. The benefits of focusing on the position that is desired rather than the negative that is criticized was emphasized.

16. Solicit Agreement to Make Effort to Please (16)

A. An agreement was solicited from the blamed partner to make a reasonable, sincere effort to please the other partner.

B. Examples of reasonable, sincere efforts to please the other partner were reviewed within the session.

C. The blamed partner was supported for endorsing the need to make a reasonable, sincere effort to please the other partner.
D. The blamed partner has made a reasonable effort to please the other partner, and the benefits of this were reviewed.
E. The blamed partner has not made a sincere effort to please the other partner and was redirected to do so.

17. Review Compliments (17)

A. The blaming partner was asked to review occasions when compliments have been provided to the other partner.
B. The blaming partner was reinforced for shifting from a position of criticism to a position of praise.
C. The benefits of complimenting the blamed partner were reviewed.
D. The blaming partner has not shifted from a position of criticism to a position of praise and was redirected to do so.

18. Articulate "Basic Rules" of the Relationship (18)

A. Each partner was asked to articulate the "basic rules" of the couple's relationship.
B. The partners were provided with examples of "basic rules" of their relationship (i.e., that the husband should help to put the children to bed and the wife should assist in yard work).
C. The partners' perception of "basic rules" was reviewed and synthesized.
D. The partners have not listed the "basic rules" of the relationship and were redirected to do so.

19. Clarify Response to "Broken Rules" (19)

A. The partners were asked about how the "basic rules" of the relationship are being broken.
B. The negative feelings evoked by the rule violations were identified and processed.
C. The partners were reinforced for displaying a clear understanding of the connection between rule violations and negative feelings.

20. Renegotiate Rules and Roles (20)

A. The partners were assisted in renegotiating rules and roles within the relationship that are agreeable to each, as a means of reducing blaming behavior.
B. The partners were provided with feedback on their renegotiations of rules and roles.
C. An emphasis was placed on the reduced blaming behavior that occurs due to a renegotiated set of rules and roles.

21. List External Stressors (21)

A. Each partner was asked to list the external stressors that are putting pressure on the couple's relationship.
B. Active listening was provided as the couple described the external stressors that are putting pressure on the relationship.
C. The couple failed to identify external stressors putting pressure on their relationship, and they were provided with tentative examples in this area.

22. Use Problem-Solving Techniques (22)

A. The partners were assisted in using problem-solving techniques as a means of coping with external pressures as a team.

B. An emphasis was placed on using problem-solving techniques as a team rather than shifting all the responsibility to one partner.

C. The partners were reinforced for solving problems as a team, which has shifted blaming behaviors and responsibility away from each partner.

BLENDED-FAMILY PROBLEMS

CLIENT PRESENTATION

1. Discipline Arguments (1)*

A. The parent and stepparent often have arguments related to child-discipline differences.

B. The parent and stepparent display different child-discipline philosophies.

C. The parent and stepparent often disagree about how each disciplines the other's child.

D. As communication has increased, the parent and stepparent are more congruent in child-discipline techniques and able to tolerate differences.

2. Arguments over Favoritism (2)

A. The partners often have arguments regarding perceived favoritism or financial and gift supports for biological versus nonbiological children.

B. A pattern of parental favoritism for biological versus nonbiological children is evident and causes conflict within the relationship.

C. The partners have identified a pattern of financial and gift support that favors biological versus nonbiological children.

D. The partners have acknowledged a pattern of favoritism for biological versus nonbiological children and have committed to modifying this pattern.

E. The partners report a more balanced approach to the support of the biological and nonbiological children.

3. Financial Pressures of Previous Divorce (3)

A. The couple experiences financial pressures due to previous divorce settlements.

B. The couple often verbalizes resentment about the financial aspects of divorce settlements.

C. The partners are often at odds with each other regarding the financial aspects of previous divorce settlements.

D. As the partners have developed a more supportive approach to each other, financial pressures from divorce settlements have become a less important issue.

4. Jealousy Regarding Children (4)

A. A pattern of parental jealousy has developed due to the differences in the social and emotional development of the children from two different marriages.

B. Stepsiblings often experience rivalry stemming from the differences in the social and emotional development of the children from two different marriages.

C. The couple has taken a leadership role in decreasing jealousy and rivalry regarding the different social and emotional development of the children.

D. The children within the blended family have displayed a decreased pattern of sibling rivalry.

E. Parental jealousy regarding the children has abated.

*The numbers in parentheses on Client Presentation pages correlate to the number of the Behavioral Definition statement in the companion chapter with the same title in *The Couples Psychotherapy Treatment Planner* (Jongsma, O'Leary, and Heyman) by John Wiley & Sons, 1998. The numbers in parentheses on the Interventions Implemented page correspond to the number of the Therapeutic Intervention statement in the companion chapter in the same book.

5. **Sibling Sexual Concerns (5)**
A. The partners are reluctant about leaving stepsiblings alone together due to concerns about possible sexual abuse.
B. The partners are concerned about leaving stepsiblings alone together due to concerns about possible inappropriate sexual activity.
C. The family has developed appropriate supervision measures to eliminate concerns about sexual activity or sexual abuse between stepsiblings.
D. Concerns about leaving stepsiblings alone together have diminished.

6. **Suspicions of Inappropriate Sexual Attraction (6)**
A. The female partner has suspicions that the male partner is sexually attracted to her daughter.
B. One partner has suspicions that the other partner is sexually attracted to his/her child.
C. Suspicions about possible sexual attraction between stepparent and stepchild have been brought into the open.
D. As suspicions about possible sexual attraction between stepparent and stepchild have been processed, these suspicions have been significantly decreased.

7. **Conflicts Regarding Visitation (7)**
A. The partners have conflict regarding the dynamics of visitation with and transportation to and from the noncustodial ex-partner's home.
B. An ex-partner's failure to show up for visitation, lateness picking up a child, or entering the blended family's home to get the child has caused conflict between the partners.
C. As better limits have been set, the ex-partners failure to act appropriately regarding visitation and transportation has been decreased.
D. The partners have been more supportive of each other regarding visitation with and transportation issues to a noncustodial ex-partner's home.

8. **Distrust and Jealousy (8)**
A. The client has displayed a pattern of distrust and jealousy regarding his/her partner's suspected emotional and/or sexual connection to the ex-partner.
B. The client's partner has described a pattern of distrust and jealousy that the client continues to have an emotional and/or sexual connection to the ex-partner.
C. Frequent arguments have occurred due to the distrust and jealousy between the partners regarding the emotional and/or sexual connections with an ex-partner.
D. The ex-partner's actions have fueled the suspicions of emotional and/or sexual connection between the ex-partner and a current partner.
E. The partners have openly discussed their concerns about suspected emotional and/or sexual connection between one of the current partners and an ex-partner.
F. As the partners have processed suspected emotional and/or sexual connection between the current partner and an ex-partner, these issues have been resolved.

9. **Internalizing Child Behavior Problems (9)**
A. Both partners tend to internalize or feel overly responsible for their children's behavior problems.

B. The partners have supported each other in not taking the blame for a child's behavior problems.
C. Responsibility for a child's behavior rests clearly with the child, but both parents accept their role of guidance, discipline, and nurturance.

10. Externalizing Child Behavior Problems (9)

A. Parents tend to externalize or blame circumstances or others for their children's behavior problems.
B. Parents have agreed to place responsibility for their children's behavior choices on the child.
C. Conflicts between the parents have decreased as they focus on disciplining and guiding children who are held responsible for their behavior decisions.

INTERVENTIONS IMPLEMENTED

1. Ask about Emotions/Conflict with Ex-Partner (1)

A. Each partner was asked to describe his/her feelings about and conflicts with the ex-partner.
B. Support and encouragement were provided to each partner and feelings about and conflicts with an ex-partner were identified.
C. As one partner discussed feelings about and conflicts with an ex-partner, the other partner was directed to refrain from unsupportive or antagonistic comments.
D. The partners were provided with positive feedback as they were able to describe their feelings about and conflicts with ex-partners.

2. Describe Conflicts with Ex-Partner (2)

A. The partners were asked to relate the ways in which they experience conflict between themselves about dealing with their ex-partner.
B. The partners identified the ways in which dealing with an ex-partner causes problems within their current relationship, and these were processed.

3. Discuss "Failure" of Former Relationships (3)

A. The partners were encouraged to discuss their guilty feelings about the "failure" of the former relationships.
B. The partners were encouraged to discuss how their emotions about previous relationships affect their present relationship.
C. As the partners discussed their emotions related to former relationships, they were provided with support and encouragement.
D. The partners seemed to be very cautious about discussing their emotions related to previous partners and were encouraged to do this in an open, truly supportive manner.

4. Discuss Divorce/Separation Agreement (4)

A. The partners were encouraged to discuss their respective divorce and separation agreements.
B. The partners were directed to identify the short-term and long-term implications of the respective divorce and separation agreements.

C. The partners were provided with assistance in identifying the underlying or implicit agreements contained within the divorce or separation agreements.
D. The partners were provided with positive feedback as they came to a mutual understanding regarding the implicit and explicit implications of their divorce or separation agreements.

5. Guide Discussions about Legal/Financial Agreements (5)

A. The partners were guided in a discussion about how they will cope with the problems that may result from respective legal and/or financial agreements with an ex-partner.
B. The partners were provided with positive feedback as they displayed a clear understanding of the ways in which the family must cope with the respective legal and/or financial agreements.
C. The partners were provided with specific ways with which to cope with the problems that result from the respective legal and/or financial agreements.

6. Discuss Higher Education (6)

A. The partners were directed to discuss how they expect to deal with the expenses of the children's higher education.
B. The partners were praised for their healthy understanding regarding issues related to paying for the children's higher education.
C. The partners were provided with feedback as they gave rather unrealistic expectations regarding how to deal with expenses of the children's higher education.

7. Discuss Additional Expenses (7)

A. The partners were directed to discuss issues related to who will pay for expenses not covered in the divorce agreement (e.g., music and athletic lessons, team uniforms, camp).
B. The partners were provided with positive feedback, as they developed a realistic, mutual agreement regarding payment of costs not covered within the divorce or separation agreement.
C. The partners were provided with more direct feedback as they developed unrealistic expectations for how to pay costs not covered within the divorce agreement.

8. Encourage Discussion/Problem Solving (8)

A. The partners were encouraged to openly discuss how to provide financially and emotionally fair support of the children.
B. The partners were guided in problem-solving techniques regarding how to provide financially and emotionally fair support for the children.
C. The partners were provided with positive feedback as they displayed a healthy understanding of how to meet the emotional and financial needs of the children.
D. The partners displayed a poor understanding of how to provide financially and emotionally fair support of the children and were provided more specific direction in this area.

9. Make Agreements Explicit (9)

A. The partners were asked to explicitly identify the implicit agreements that have evolved between them and ex-partners (e.g., who is to pick up the children for visitation).

B. The partners were provided with specific examples of the implicit agreements that must be made explicit.
C. The partners were provided with positive feedback when they clearly identified the implicit agreements and made them more explicit.

10. Develop Time-Line for Action (10)

A. An ex-partner was identified as having violated the divorce agreement regarding child-support and/or maintanance.
B. The partners discussed how long they would allow an ex-partner to violate a divorce agreement before taking some action (e.g., having the financial matters handled directly by the court).
C. The partners were provided with conflict resolution techniques to reach an agreement regarding how long to wait before pursing additional action related to violation of a divorce agreement.
D. The partners were provided with positive feedback for developing realistic expectations about how to react to violations of the divorce agreement.

11. Review Visitation Issues (11)

A. The parents were reminded that visitation is commonly viewed by courts as a privilege, not as a legal responsibility.
B. The parents were asked to verbalize the difficulties and pain that they may experience about an ex-partners infrequent or nonexistent visits with the child.
C. The parents were provided with emotional support as they described the emotional effects of an ex-partner's infrequent or nonexistent visits with the child.

12. Develop Discipline Agreement (12)

A. An agreement was solicited from the nonbiological parent to support the biological parent's discipline behaviors.
B. An agreement was solicited from the nonbiological parent to defer discipline behaviors to the biological parent whenever practical.
C. The parents were provided with positive feedback as they were able to identify specific examples of when the nonbiological parent should take responsibility for parenting or should defer to the biological parent.
D. The nonbiological parent continues to fail to defer appropriate parenting issues to the biological parent and was redirected to do so.

13. Discuss Issues That Generate Disagreement (13)

A. The partners were directed to discuss within the session the disciplinary and financial matters that generate disagreement.
B. Reinforcement was provided to the partners regarding their ability to openly discuss matters that cause conflict in a fair, respectful manner.
C. The partners were directed to continue discussions regarding disciplinary and financial matters as private homework (e.g., not in the presence of the children).
D. The couple has honestly discussed disciplinary and financial matters as private homework and their experience with this was processed.

E. The couple has not discussed disciplinary and financial matters as private homework and was redirected to do so.

14. Develop Relationship-Building Activities with the Nonbiological Child (14)

A. The partners were directed to facilitate involvement in relationship-building activities between the stepparent and the nonbiological child.

B. The nonbiological parent was directed to refrain from significant involvement in discipline until an appropriate relationship has been developed with that child.

C. The partners reported that the nonbiological parent has developed a more involved relationship with the child, and this was reviewed within the conjoint session.

D. The nonbiological parent has struggled to develop a relationship with the child, and the focus of the session was on how to increase this involvement.

15. Encourage Development of Respect for the Stepparent (15)

A. The partners were encouraged to help each child demonstrate acceptance of the new stepparent via cordial, respectful, and civil interactions.

B. The partners reviewed and problem-solved ways in which they can increase their child's demonstration of the acceptance of the new stepparent.

C. The stepparent reported an improved relationship with the child due to support from the biological parent, and this support was reinforced within the session.

16. Discourage Blame (16)

A. The partners were discouraged from blaming their ex-partner for the "dissolution of the family."

B. The partners were discouraged from blaming their ex-partner's new love interest for the "dissolution of our family."

C. It was noted that the negative comments about the ex-partner develop a pattern of disrespect for all parents/stepparents.

17. Remind Partners That Instant Love Is a Myth (17)

A. The partners were reminded of the myth of "instant love" between new family members.

B. The partner's expectations of instant love and connections between blended family members were confronted with the reality that time is necessary for relationships to grow.

C. The couple has become more realistic regarding the time necessary for meaningful relationships to develop between family members.

18. Develop Realistic Expectations for Siblings (18)

A. The partners were assisted in accepting the position that siblings from different biological families need not like or love one another, but must be mutually respectful and kind.

B. The partners displayed an understanding of the expectations for the emotional relationship between stepsiblings and were assisted in developing the parameters for respect between stepsiblings.

19. Plan Separate Outings (19)

A. Since the children from the two different biological families do not get along well, the partners were directed to plan separate outings with each set of children.

B. The partners have used the separate outings to develop a better relationship between the stepchildren and the stepparent, and the benefits of this were reviewed.

C. The partners were provided with support as they reviewed the emotionally difficult experience of the stepchildren not getting along.

20. Encourage Positive Comments about the Ex-Partner (20)

A. The partners were encouraged to model identifying positive qualities about an ex-partner in front of the children.

B. Modeling and role-play were used to help the partners practice how to say positive comments about an ex-partner.

C. Positive feedback was provided to the couple regarding their ability to make positive comments about the ex-partner in front of the children.

D. The partners continue to make negative comments about ex-partners in front of the children and were redirected to discontinue this practice.

21. Assign Conversations about Activities with Ex-Partner (21)

A. The partners were assigned to talk with their children about some of the nice things the children experienced during visitation or vacation with the ex-partner.

B. Within the session, a review and discussion was held regarding the attempts that the partners have made to talk positively about the ex-partner.

C. The healthier relationship between the children, the partners, and the ex-partners was reviewed within the session.

D. The partners have failed to review the child's involvement with the ex-partner, and this process was role-played and problem-solved within the session.

22. Develop Agreement Regarding Communication with Ex-Partners (22)

A. The partners were assisted in reaching an agreement about the need for open communication with ex-partners about matters pertaining to the children.

B. The partners were assisted in developing boundaries for communication with ex-partners about matters pertaining to the children.

C. The partners were reinforced for reporting that they have engaged in a healthier pattern of open communication with ex-partners.

D. The partners were in conflict about the level of communication necessary between ex-partners, and this was reviewed and problem-solved within the session.

23. Rehearse Avoidance of Problems with Ex-Partner (23)

A. The partners rehearsed ways that they can avoid arguments and hostile interactions during problem-solving meetings with their ex-partners.

B. The partners were reinforced as they displayed a clear understanding of the techniques to use to avoid hostile interactions during problem-solving meetings with their ex-partners.

COMMUNICATION

CLIENT PRESENTATION

1. Frequent Arguments (1)*

A. The client reported frequent or continual arguing with his/her partner.

B. The frequency of conflict between the partners has diminished.

C. The partners report decreased arguments due to the implementation of conflict resolution skills.

D. The client reported that his/her relationship with his/her partner has significantly improved and arguing has become very infrequent.

2. Poor Problem-Resolution Skills (2)

A. The client and his/her partner often have continuing arguments because they have poor problem-resolution skills.

B. The partners described unresolved conflicts that have led to sustained periods of distrust and alienation from each other.

C. As the partners have progressed in therapy, problem-resolution skills and communication have increased.

3. Frequent Misunderstandings (3)

A. The client reported a repeated pattern of misunderstandings during discussions.

B. The client and his/her partner have often been involved in encounters that resulted in misunderstandings and ongoing unresolved issues.

C. As the partners have progressed in therapy, their pattern of misunderstanding has decreased.

4. Disagreements Become Global Problems (4)

A. The couple has a pattern of viewing disagreements as symbols of global problems (e.g., core themes such as love and respect) rather than as specific problems.

B. The partners described unresolved conflicts that led to sustained, long periods of distrust and alienation from each other.

C. The partners have learned to limit disagreements to the specific problems, rather than expanding each disagreement to larger issues.

5. Failure to Acknowledge Positive Actions (5)

A. The client reported a consistent failure of his/her partner to verbally acknowledge the positive actions that he/she does for the partner.

B. The client's partner indicated a consistent failure of the client to acknowledge the positive actions that are done for the client.

C. The partners displayed difficulty verbally acknowledging the positive actions of the other partner in the session.

*The numbers in parentheses on Client Presentation pages correlate to the number of the Behavioral Definition statement in the companion chapter with the same title in *The Couples Psychotherapy Treatment Planner* (Jongsma, O'Leary, and Heyman) by John Wiley & Sons, 1998. The numbers in parentheses on the Interventions Implemented page correspond to the number of the Therapeutic Intervention statement in the companion chapter in the same book.

D. The partners acknowledged their pattern of poor communication within the family.
E. As the partners have progressed in therapy, they have increased their communication, often acknowledging the positive actions of the other partner.

INTERVENTIONS IMPLEMENTED

1. Assess Communication (1)

A. The couple was directed to attempt to solve a major problem within the session.
B. The couple was observed in their communication styles, with specific skills and deficits noted.
C. Feedback was provided to the couple regarding communication skills and deficits.

2. Provide Feedback (2)

A. The couple was positively reinforced for the communication tasks that they do well.
B. The partners were provided with direct feedback regarding communication skills that needed improvement.
C. The feedback regarding the couple's communication skills was processed.

3. List Communication Solutions and Problems (3)

A. The partners were requested to list actions each can take to help solve communication problems.
B. The partners were requested to list actions that tend to make communication worse.
C. The partners identified a variety of actions that each can take to help solve communication problems, as well as actions that tend to make matters worse, and these were processed within the session.
D. The partners were provided with positive feedback for their ability to identify specific communication needs.
E. The partners failed to correctly identify specific communication needs and were provided with tentative examples in this area.

4. Practice Pinpointing (4)

A. The partners were directed to take turns pinpointing problems.
B. The partners were directed to make requests for change that are specific, observable, and ask for increases in positive behaviors rather than decreases in the other partner's negative behavior.
C. The partners were taught how pinpointing leads to an understandable, positive pattern of communication.
D. The partners have failed to master the skill of pinpointing and were provided with remedial assistance in this area.

5. Practice "I" Statements (5)

A. Role-playing techniques were used to help the partners practice making "I" statements.
B. The partners were directed to use the following form for "I" statements: "When _____ happens, I feel _____ I would like _____."

C. The couple was provided with feedback about their role-play of "I" statements.
D. The couple was reinforced for their mastery of the use of "I" statements.
E. The couple was provided with remedial information about the use of "I" statements.

6. Rephrase Mind-Reading (6)

A. One of the partners was identified as mind-reading the other partner.
B. When a partner was identified as mind-reading the other partner, the mind-reading partner was requested to rephrase statements in a manner that speaks only for one's self and expressing one's own perceptions.
C. The partners were provided with positive feedback as they decreased the tendency to mind-read.
D. The partners continued to focus on the internal thoughts of the other partner and were provided with additional feedback and direction in this area.

7. Teach Paraphrasing (7)

A. While one partner was serving as the speaker, the other partner was directed to paraphrase, rephrasing the speaker's major point.
B. The speaking partner was asked to acknowledge whether the paraphrasing partner had accurately described the intended message.
C. The partners were provided with positive feedback as they appropriately paraphrased each other's comments.

8. Identify Underlying Emotions (8)

A. While one partner was serving as the speaker, the other partner was directed to paraphrase, by rephrasing the speaker's underlying emotions.
B. The speaking partner was asked to acknowledge whether the paraphrasing partner had accurately described the underlying emotions.
C. The partners were provided with positive feedback as they produced several examples of appropriately paraphrasing each other's emotions.
D. The partners needed additional feedback and redirection as they strove to learn how to paraphrase each other's emotional content.

9. Practice Validation Skills (9)

A. The listening partner was directed to use validation skills with the speaking partner.
B. The listening partner was directed to convey that he/she understands and can empathize with the speaker's feelings even if not agreeing with them.
C. The partners were supported for displaying a healthy understanding, validation, and empathy for each other.
D. The partners were provided with feedback to improve their validation skills.

10. Switch Perspectives (10)

A. Understanding and problem solving seemed to be at an impasse, so partners were requested to switch places and discuss the issue from the other's perspective.
B. Positive feedback was provided as the partners reviewed the situation from the other partner's perspective.

C. The partners were redirected when they slipped back into their own perspective while trying to view the problem from the other's perspective.

D. The benefits gained from focusing on the issue from the other partner's perspective were reviewed and highlighted.

11. Emphasize Emotion Cues (11)

A. The partners were requested to share their feelings regarding conflictual issues.

B. The partners were provided with a list of emotion words to cue each partner to the subtleties of words expressing feelings (e.g., using *frustrated* rather then *mad*).

C. The partners were supported as they expressed and identified their feelings regarding conflictual issues.

D. Positive feedback was provided when the partners were able to identify the subtleties of words expressing feelings.

E. The partners were given additional feedback to help them identify feeling words as they discussed conflictual issues.

12. Teach "Measured Truthfulness" (12)

A. The partners were taught the speaker skill of "measured truthfulness" (i.e., the speaker balances the need to comment about the other against a concern for the other's feelings).

B. Within the session, the partners practiced the skill of "measured truthfulness" on areas of conflict.

C. Positive feedback was provided regarding the couple's successful use of "measured truthfulness."

D. The partners were provided with more specific feedback regarding situations in which they can use "measured truthfulness."

13. Teach Communication Purposes (13)

A. The partners were taught that communication tends to serve one of two purposes, venting (i.e., sharing feelings) or problem solving.

B. The partners were requested to identify how they feel when one person is pursuing venting and the other is problem solving.

C. The partners were supported for displaying an understanding of the purposes of communication and the problems that occur when the purposes of communication are not aligned.

14. Role-Play Communication Outcome (14)

A. Role-play was used to teach the speaker how to ask which purpose is intended—venting or problem solving.

B. The partners were asked to role-play having the listener ask the speaker which purpose is intended—venting or problem solving.

C. The partners displayed insight into how to identify the purpose of the communication, and the benefits to their communication were processed.

D. The partners failed to grasp the use of communication outcomes and were provided with additional information in this area.

15. Practice Making and Accepting Suggestions (15)

A. One partner was asked to practice making suggestions for enjoyable activities together.

B. The partner being invited to do an activity was requested to practice accepting the suggestions by making eye contact, reinforcing the person for asking and planning when to do the activity.

C. Feedback was provided to the partners regarding their use of communication skills while making and accepting suggestions.

16. Practice Making and Rejecting Suggestions (16)

A. One partner was asked to practice making suggestions for enjoyable activities together.

B. The other partner was requested to practice rejecting the suggestions by using the positive-negative-positive "sandwich" method (e.g., reinforcing the partner for asking, identifying the specific element being rejected, and making a countersuggestion).

C. Positive feedback was provided as the partners displayed the use of the positive-negative-positive "sandwich" method for rejecting suggestions.

D. The partners were provided with additional feedback to help practice rejecting suggestions.

17. Assign Couple Meeting (17)

A. The partners were assigned to set aside 10 to 15 minutes two or three times per week for a couple meeting to discuss suggestions or complaints in a constructive manner.

B. The partners have used the couple meeting, and the positive benefits were processed.

C. The partners have used the couple meeting technique, but have engaged in more arguments, and this technique was problem-solved.

D. The partners have not used the couple meeting technique and were redirected to do so.

18. Teach Editing (18)

A. The partners were taught the listener skill of editing (i.e., responding to a provocation in a manner that is in one's long-term best interest, rather than engaging in retaliation or debate).

B. The partners were directed to practicing editing on areas of conflict.

C. The positive benefits of editing were processed.

D. The partners have failed to appropriately use editing and this resistance was processed.

19. Teach Metacommunication (19)

A. The partners were taught the listening skills of metacommunication (i.e., commenting on the *process* rather than the *content* of the speaker statement).

B. The partners were directed to use metacommunication to overtly correct dysfunctional communication, rather than acting out anger over negative communication behaviors.

C. The partners were directed to practice metacommunication.

D. The partners were provided with feedback on their use of metacommunication to correct dysfunctional communication.

E. The partners have failed to properly understand metacommunication and were provided with additional feedback in this area.

20. Identify Soothing/De-Escalating Behaviors (20)

A. Each partner was asked to identify the behaviors that each employs during discussions to self-sooth.

B. Each partner was asked to identify techniques employed to de-escalate the conflict.

C. The partners were assisted in identifying self-soothing and de-escalating behaviors.

21. Review Interpretation of Soothing/De-Escalating Behaviors (21)

A. Each partner was asked to confirm whether the other partner's supposed soothing/de-escalating behaviors were interpreted as such.

B. Each partner was asked to confirm whether the other partner had correctly interpreted soothing/de-escalating behaviors.

C. The partners regularly agree that soothing and de-escalation behaviors are interpreted accurately and were directed to increase these types of behaviors.

D. The partners do not agree on their interpretations of each other's supposed soothing/de-escalation behaviors and were directed to discuss their opposing interpretations of the behavior.

22. Identify Impending Argument (22)

A. The partners were assisted in identifying cues that an argument is impending (e.g., behaviors, thoughts, feelings, bodily sensations).

B. The partners identified a variety of cues that tell them that an argument is impending, and these were processed within the session.

C. The partners were directed to contract with each other the actions that they will take to cool off before talking further.

D. The partners have used the identification of cues that an argument is impending, and contracted actions to cool off. The benefits of this were processed within the session.

E. The partners have not paid attention to cues that an argument in impending and have not used techniques to cool off before talking further. They were redirected to do so.

23. Track Arguments (23)

A. The partners were assigned to track times and places that trigger arguments.

B. The partners have tracked times and places that regularly trigger arguments, and these were processed within the session.

C. The partners have identified patterns of arguments that occur, and this was processed within the session.

D. The partners have not tracked times and places that often trigger arguments and were redirected to do so.

24. Identify Times for Discussing/Problem Solving (24)

A. The partners were asked to identify times that are conducive to discussing and/or solving problems (e.g., after the children are in bed) and times that are not conducive (e.g., when dinner is being prepared).

B. The partners' list of identified times that are conducive to discussing and/or solving problems and times that are not conducive was processed.

C. The partners agreed to discuss or solve problems during times that are more conducive for this and were provided with positive feedback in this area.
D. The benefits of discussing problems during more conducive times were reviewed.

25. Identify Cues to Receptivity (25)

A. The partners were directed to identify the cues that indicate that either partner is receptive to discussing and/or resolving problems.
B. The partners were assisted in identifying cues to receptivity, such as the partner being awake, alert, and not too tired; no distractions are present; no alcohol has been consumed; enough time is available for closure.
C. The partners were directed to review the cues for receptivity prior to initiating discussion and/or problem solving.

26. Practice Approaching Partner (26)

A. Each partner was directed to practice approaching the other partner during the session to discuss a problem.
B. The couple was given homework to practice approaching each other to discuss a problem.
C. The partners' practice of approaching each other to discuss a problem was reviewed and critiqued.

27. Develop Agenda/Time Limits (27)

A. The partners were introduced to the idea of having an agenda and a time limit for having problem-solving discussions.
B. The partners were asked to role-play setting an agenda and a time limit for problem-solving discussions within the session.
C. The partners were directed to practice setting agendas and time limits for problem-solving discussions in real-life situations.
D. The partners' use of an agenda and time limits for problem-solving discussions was reviewed and processed.

28. Teach about Pinpointing Problems (28)

A. The partners were taught to agree to their mutual satisfaction that a problem has been correctly pinpointed, before actually trying to solve the problem.
B. The partners were directed to practice correctly pinpointing problems within the session.
C. The partners were directed to practice correctly pinpointing problems between sessions.
D. The partners' use of correctly pinpointing problems prior to attempting to solve them was reviewed, processed and problem solved.

29. Maintain Focus on One Problem (29)

A. The partners were directed to agree to discuss only one problem during problem-solving discussions.
B. The partners were monitored during in-session practice to maintain their focus on only one problem during the problem-solving discussion.
C. The partners reported that they regularly focus on only one problem, and the positive effects of this were reviewed.

D. The partners reported difficulty focusing on only one problem during problem-solving discussions, and this was problem-solved within the session.

30. Model Brainstorming (30)

A. Modeling and role-playing were used to display brainstorming techniques that produce at least two solutions to a problem before trying to solve that problem.
B. The partners were directed to practice brainstorming techniques within the session on areas on conflict.
C. As the partners practiced brainstorming techniques, they were provided with feedback and redirection.

31. Teach Evaluation of Pros and Cons (31)

A. The partners were taught the process of evaluating the pros and cons of the brainstormed solutions.
B. The partners were directed to practice the evaluation of pros and cons within the session on specific areas on conflict.
C. The partners were provided with feedback about their evaluation of the pros and cons of their brainstormed solutions.

32. Teach Planning and Reviewing of Solutions (32)

A. The partners were taught how to select a specific plan for attaining a solution.
B. The partners were directed to include a time in the future to evaluate the progress of the solution.
C. The partners were asked to practice selecting a specific plan and a time for evaluation of the plan within the session.
D. The partners displayed significant skill regarding selecting a plan for attaining a solution and planning for evaluation of the solution, and they were provided with positive feedback in this area.
E. The couple struggled to select a specific plan for attaining a solution, or to plan for future evaluation and was provided with redirection in this area.

33. Identify Core Themes (33)

A. The partners were assisted in identifying core themes (e.g., love, respect, power differential) that underlie their most affectively charged arguments.
B. The partners were provided with feedback as they identified the core themes that underlie their most affectively charged arguments.
C. The partners failed to identify the core themes that underlie their arguments and were provided with tentative suggestions about what these themes may be.

34. Discuss Core Themes Overtly (34)

A. The partners were directed to discuss the core themes of their arguments as part of their problem-solving discussions.
B. The partners were assisted in discussing the core themes of their arguments as part of their problem-solving discussion.

C. The partners reported a decrease in arguments and communication problems as they have begun to resolve the core themes of their relationship.

D. The partners tend to avoid facing the core themes of their arguments and were provided with feedback about this defense mechanism.

35. Track How Partner Pleases (35)

A. Both partners were directed to track on paper the "catch your partner pleasing you" exercise, including at least one positive behavior they noticed the partner do each day and at least one positive behavior that they did themselves that day.

B. The partners have completed the "catch your partner pleasing you" exercises, and the positive behaviors were reviewed and processed.

C. The partners have not completed the "catch your partner pleasing you" exercises and were redirected to do so.

36. Elicit Appreciation for Partners' Behaviors (36)

A. Each partner was directed to use "I" statements to express appreciation for the other partner's behaviors noted on the "catch your partner pleasing you" tracking sheet.

B. As the partners used the "I" statements to express their appreciation, the positive benefits of each partner's pleasing actions and each partner's appreciation were supported.

C. The partners were provided with feedback about their lack of use of "I" statements to express appreciation for other partner's behaviors.

DEPENDENCY

CLIENT PRESENTATION

1. Relationship-Based Self-Worth (1)*

A. Nearly all of the dependent partner's feelings of self-worth, happiness, and fulfillment have been derived from the relationship with the partner.
B. The dependent partner consistently uses direct and indirect means to solicit feedback from the partner regarding self-worth.
C. The dependent partner lacks an inner sense of identity and self-worth that is independent from the other partner's opinion of him/her.
D. The dependent partner has come to realize that self-worth is not dependent on relationships with others, but is inherent to one's own identity.
E. The dependent partner has decreased the incessant solicitation of feedback from the nondependent partner regarding self-worth.

2. Abandonment Fears (2)

A. The client described a history of being very anxious whenever there is any hint of abandonment in an established relationship.
B. The client's hypersensitivity to abandonment has caused him/her to desperately cling to destructive relationships.
C. The client has begun to acknowledge his/her fear of abandonment as excessive and irrational.
D. Conflicts within the relationship have been reported by the client, but he/she has not automatically assumed that abandonment will be the result.
E. The client's fear of abandonment has been resolved, and he/she is more confident in himself/herself.

3. Reluctance to Make Decisions (3)

A. The client has been unable to make decisions or initiate actions without excessive advice, support, and reassurance from others.
B. The client's dependency on others is reflected in his/her seeking out their approval before he/she can take any action.
C. The client has shown the ability to make decisions on a small scale without seeking approval from others.
D. The client has shown confidence in implementing problem-solving techniques to enhance his/her decision-making skills.

4. Avoids Disagreements (4)

A. The dependent partner has consistently avoided disagreement with the partner out of fear of being rejected.

*The numbers in parentheses on Client Presentation pages correlate to the number of the Behavioral Definition statement in the companion chapter with the same title in *The Couples Psychotherapy Treatment Planner* (Jongsma, O'Leary, and Heyman) by John Wiley & Sons, 1998. The numbers in parentheses on the Interventions Implemented page correspond to the number of the Therapeutic Intervention statement in the companion chapter in the same book.

B. The dependent partner's fear of rejection is lessening, and the dependent partner is becoming somewhat more assertive.
C. The dependent partner has begun to verbalize mild disagreement with others and has managed to cope with the insecurity surrounding that behavior.
D. The dependent partner has become quite comfortable at expressing thoughts and opinions that are contrary to the other partner's, without fear of rejection.

5. Assumes Servant Role for Approval (5)

A. The partners described a history of the dependent partner performing services for others that are strongly influenced by a desire to please them.
B. A strong need for approval from others has dominated the dependent partner's motivation.
C. The dependent partner has become more aware of his/her people-pleasing pattern and has begun to become more assertive and honest in relationships with others.

6. Sequential Intimate Relationships (6)

A. The dependent partner described a history of multiple, sequential intimate relationships with little, if any, space between the ending of one relationship and the start of the next.
B. The dependent partner acknowledged a fear of being alone and a strong need for having a companion.
C. Acknowledging the unhealthy dependence that was present in previous relationships, the dependent partner has begun to feel more comfortable with a more independent role in the current relationship.

7. Initiates Contact in Diverse Settings (7)

A. The dependent partner has displayed a pattern of seeking out the partner in diverse settings (e.g., when the partner is at work, driving, or at the gym).
B. The dependent partner contacts the partner in diverse settings because of the need for reassurance and a fear of being alone.
C. The dependent partner has begun to understand the inappropriateness of seeking out the partner in diverse settings.
D. The dependent partner has decreased his/her pattern of initiating contact with the partner numerous times a day.

8. Jealousy (8)

A. The dependent partner described feelings of jealousy about the time the other partner spends with work colleagues.
B. The dependent partner described jealousy due to the suspicion that the nondependent partner has another sexual partner.
C. The dependent partner has become less suspicious of the nondependent partner's loyalty and faithfulness.
D. The dependent partner's pattern of jealousy has decreased, and the dependent partner is comfortable with the time that the nondependent partner spends at work.

9. Anxiety (9)

A. The dependent partner acknowledged strong feelings of panic, fear, and helplessness when faced with situations in which the other partner is not available for support or encouragement.
B. The dependent partner described a pattern of avoidance of situations in which the other partner is not available for support or encouragement.
C. The dependent partner has begun to overcome feelings of anxiety associated with situations in which support and encouragement are not available at the level desired.

INTERVENTIONS IMPLEMENTED

1. Identify Anxiety that Leads to Dependency (1)

A. The dependent partner was asked to list the situations that lead to anxiety which triggers making contact with the nondependent partner unnecessary.
B. The dependent partner was provided with feedback as anxiety situations were listed.
C. The dependent partner was provided with assistance to identify how irrational anxiety leads to contacting the other partner unnecessarily.
D. The dependent partner had difficulty identifying how anxiety leads to contacting the other partner unnecessarily and was provided with tentative feedback in this area.

2. List Effects of Intrusiveness (2)

A. The nondependent partner was asked to provide feedback about the effects of the dependent partner's intrusiveness.
B. The partners were provided with support and feedback as the nondependent partner identified the effects of the dependent partner's intrusiveness.
C. Both partners were assisted in processing the effects of the dependent partner's intrusiveness on the nondependent partner.

3. Assign Reading on Dependency (3)

A. The dependent partner was assigned to read specific materials on dependency.
B. The dependent partner was assigned to read *Co-Dependent No More* (Beattie).
C. The dependent partner has read the assigned material, and key points of this reading material were processed.
D. The dependent partner has not read the assigned material and was redirected to do so.

4. Discuss Reading Material Conjointly (4)

A. The reading material on dependency was discussed within the conjoint session.
B. The partners were directed to discuss the salient points of *Co-Dependent No More* (Beattie).
C. The dependent partner was asked to identify patterns of dependency within the relationship.
D. The dependent partner was provided with positive feedback for identification of the dependent patterns within the relationship.
E. The dependent partner was unable to identify patterns of dependency within the relationship, and the nondependent partner was asked to provide feedback in this area.

F. The partners were unable to identify patterns of dependency within the relationship and were offered tentative feedback in this area.

5. Set Behavioral Goals for Independence (5)

A. The dependent partner was assisted in setting graduated behavioral goals for increasing independence in the relationship.

B. The dependent partner was provided with positive feedback for making progress toward specific, graduated behavioral goals for increasing independence in the relationship.

C. As the dependent partner has gradually increased independence in the relationship, the graduated goals have been appropriately reset.

D. The dependent partner had great difficulty in identifying graduated behavioral goals for increasing independence in the relationship and was provided with specific examples in this area.

6. Review Crossed Boundaries (6)

A. The dependent partner was asked to identify privacy boundaries that have been crossed in the past week with the partner.

B. The dependent partner was provided with positive feedback for identification of privacy boundaries that have been crossed in the past week.

C. The dependent partner showed significant insight into privacy boundary intrusion and was provided with positive feedback.

D. The dependent partner failed to identify privacy boundaries that have been crossed in the past week with the partner, so the nondependent partner was assisted in explaining these broken boundary areas to the dependent partner.

7. Elicit Description of Independence (7)

A. The dependent partner was asked to describe to the other partner the ways in which the level of dependency has lessened.

B. The dependent partner was reinforced for describing to the other partner situations that demonstrated change from dependent behavior to independence, self-confidence, and freedom from fear of rejection or disapproval.

8. Request Feedback about Boundary Progress (8)

A. The nondependent partner was asked to provide feedback to the dependent partner about progress that is being made in observing privacy boundaries.

B. The nondependent partner was provided with support and clarification of the progress that is being made in observing boundaries.

C. The dependent partner was congratulated for the progress that the nondependent partner has noted regarding being able to observe boundaries.

9. Encourage Noncontingent Reassurance (9)

A. The nondependent partner was encouraged to tell the dependent partner noncontingently about the care and love that is felt.

B. The nondependent partner was directed to give reassurance only when the dependent partner is *not* asking for it.

C. The nondependent partner has consistently provided reassurance and caring comments only in noncontingent situations, and was provided with positive feedback in this area.

D. The nondependent partner has not focused on reassuring the dependent partner on a non-contingent basis, and was redirected to do so.

10. Explore/Resolve Fear of Rejection (10)

A. The dependent partner's fear of rejection was explored.

B. It was noted that the dependent partner's fear of rejection originated in a lack of acceptance from the family of origin.

C. The dependent partner was assisted in taking the early fear and anger regarding a lack of acceptance experienced in the family of origin and separating it from the current relationship.

D. As the dependent partner has gained insight into the fear of rejection that originated in a lack of acceptance from the family of origin, the level of dependency has decreased, and positive feedback was provided in this area.

E. The dependent partner displayed poor insight into the fear of rejection that originated in a lack of acceptance from the family of origin and was provided with additional feedback in this area.

11. Discuss Balancing Dependence and Independence (11)

A. In a conjoint session, it was discussed how both independence and dependence could be positive for a relationship.

B. The partners were taught about how a balance between independence and dependence can encourage mutual respect for personal traits and abilities, as well as allowing each partner to give support to the other.

C. The partners were provided with positive feedback as they identified examples of a healthy balance between independence and dependence for both partners.

12. Identify Boundaries (12)

A. The dependent partner was asked to list what boundary behaviors must be instilled in nonintimate relationships (e.g., keeping certain thoughts and feelings private, allowing others privacy and time alone, and making personal decisions without anxiety or seeking approval).

B. Positive feedback was provided to the dependent partner for identifying the boundaries needed for self and relationships.

C. The dependent partner failed to identify significant boundary behaviors for nonintimate relationships and was provided with feedback in this area.

13. Identify Extent of Boundary Issues (13)

A. The dependent partner was asked to identify whether boundary issues are restricted to the other partner or generalized (i.e., occur with coworkers, other family members, or peers).

B. The nondependent partner was asked to provide the dependent partner with feedback about the level of boundary issues that occur outside their relationship.

14. Review Crossed Boundaries (14)

A. The dependent partner was asked to identify the boundaries that have been crossed in the past week with coworkers or family members.

B. The dependent partner was provided with positive feedback for identification of boundaries that have been crossed in the past week.

C. The dependent partner was reinforced for showing significant insight into problematic boundary areas.

D. When the dependent partner failed to identify boundaries that have been crossed in the past week with the coworkers or family members, the nondependent partner was assisted in explaining these broken boundary areas to the dependent partner.

15. Apply Fear of Rejection Issues to Other Relationships (15)

A. The dependent partner was assessed regarding the understanding of how fear of rejection or disapproval influences relationships with others beyond the nondependent partner.

B. The dependent partner was taught about how fear of rejection or disapproval influences relationships with others.

C. The dependent partner was encouraged to work toward increased confidence and assertiveness.

16. List Benefits of Privacy in Casual Relationships (16)

A. The dependent partner was assisted in listing the benefits of being more private in casual relationships.

B. Positive feedback was provided as the dependent partner identified the benefits of being more private in casual relationships (e.g., less alienation of self from others, more pride and respect for self, projection of an image of more competence and less neediness).

C. As the dependent partner has experienced the increased benefits of being more private in casual relationships, a greater commitment to this privacy has been developed; these benefits were highlighted.

17. Review Family of Origin Dependency (17)

A. The couple was directed to discuss the dependency patterns in their families of origin.

B. The partners' experiences in the family of origin were interpreted as having led to feelings of insecurity and eagerness to please others.

C. The partners were assisted in discussing the differences and similarities between their families of origin dependency patterns.

18. Explore Abandonment Experiences (18)

A. The partners were assisted in exploring abandonment experiences in the family of origin.

B. The partners were assisted in exploring abandonment experiences with significant others in adulthood.

C. Abandonment experiences in the past were identified as fueling the current fears of abandonment.

D. The partners were reinforced for their insight into how abandonment experiences with the family of origin and significant others are fueling current fears of abandonment.

E. The partners failed to make the connection between abandonment experiences and the current fear of abandonment and were provided with additional feedback and tentative interpretations in this area.

19. Review Benefits of Outside Support (19)

A. The partners were requested to list three reasons why affirmations from others outside the relationship are good for building self-esteem.
B. A discussion was held regarding how support from others outside the relationship can actually benefit the relationship.
C. The partners were assisted in identifying specific reasons for support from others outside the relationship, such as decreasing the need for partner support, broadening the support network, and affirming self in ways that cannot or will not be satisfied by partner.
D. The partners were unable to clearly identify the benefits of support from outside the relationship and were provided with specific examples of these benefits.

20. Review Benefits of Independence (20)

A. The dependent partner was requested to set goals for independence.
B. The dependent partner was reminded about how independence builds self-esteem and makes the relationship more interesting.
C. The dependent partner was assisted in identifying specific goals for independence and was provided with feedback on the goals were set.

21. Reinforce Progress in Independence (21)

A. The dependent partner's course of progress in independence, decision making, assertiveness, and resilience in the face of disapproval was reviewed.
B. The dependent partner was provided with positive feedback for progress in independence, decision making, assertiveness, and resilience in the face of disapproval.

22. Encourage Increasingly Larger Levels of Independence (22)

A. The dependent partner was encouraged to take increasingly larger ventures alone outside the home (e.g., the store, gym, social outing, and overnight trips).
B. The dependent partner's experience on independent ventures was reviewed and supported.
C. The dependent partner continues to be reluctant to increase the level of independence and was redirected in this area.

23. Assign Increased Time Alone (23)

A. The dependent partner was assigned the task of spending increased time at work or recreation without partner contact.
B. The dependent partner was assisted with developing a specific plan for how to successfully spend increased time at work or recreation without partner contact.
C. The dependent partner was provided with support and positive feedback for increasing the periods of time at work or recreation without partner contact.
D. The dependent partner has not increased time spent at work or recreation without partner contact and redirection was provided in this area.

24. Encourage Solo Decision Making (24)

A. The dependent partner was assigned the task of making decisions alone, without support from the partner.

B. The dependent partner was assisted with developing a specific plan for making decisions alone, without support from the partner.

C. The dependent partner was provided with support and positive feedback for increasing the frequency of making decisions alone, without support from the partner.

D. The dependent partner has not increased the frequency of making decisions alone and redirection was provided in this area.

25. Develop Feedback Regarding Decisions (25)

A. The partners were asked to list decisions that the dependent partner has made without consulting others for reassurance or agreement.

B. The nondependent partner was directed to reinforce good decisions made unilaterally by the dependent partner.

C. The nondependent partner was provided with encouragement regarding the positive support provided to the dependent partner for independent decision making.

D. Both partners reported an increased comfort level with the decisions made by the dependent partner.

26. List Rights and Needs (26)

A. Each partner was asked to list the legitimate rights that each has in the relationship.

B. Each partner was asked to list the needs that could be fulfilled by the other partner.

C. Each partner has listed legitimate rights, also the needs to be filled by the other partner, and these were reviewed and processed within the session.

D. The partners have not listed the legitimate rights or the needs to be fulfilled by the other partner and were redirected to do so.

27. List Others' Rights (27)

A. Each partner was asked to list the legitimate rights that each partner has in relationship with others.

B. Each partner was asked to list the needs that could be fulfilled by those outside of the relationship (i.e., friends or coworkers).

C. Each partner has listed legitimate rights each has in relationship with others and the needs to be filled by the friends, coworkers, or others outside of their relationship; these were reviewed and processed within the session.

D. The partners have not listed the needs to be fulfilled by those outside the relationship and were redirected to do so.

28. List Others Rights and Needs (28)

A. A discussion was held regarding the rights and needs of each partner that can impact the relationship with the other partner, as well as relationships outside of the couple.

B. The couple was supported for displaying an understanding of the legitimate rights that each partner has.

C. The partners were assisted in identifying how some of the dependent partner's needs can be fulfilled by others, such as coworkers or family.

D. The nondependent partner was encouraged to describe personal experiences of having needs met by coworkers, family, or others outside of the couple.

29. Explore Automatic Thoughts (29)

A. The dependent partner's automatic thoughts regarding assertiveness, being alone or not meeting other's needs were explored.

B. The dependent partner was assisted in clarifying and verbalizing the negative thoughts experienced when contemplating assertiveness, being alone or refusing to meet the other's needs.

C. The dependent partner failed to identify automatic thoughts associated with assertiveness, being alone, or not meeting other's needs and was provided with tentative examples in this area.

30. Model Positive Self-Talk (30)

A. Through modeling, the dependent partner was assisted in developing positive self-talk to replace negative thoughts that precipitate fear and desperation.

B. Role-playing was used to teach positive self-talk techniques.

C. The dependent partner was reinforced for implementing positive self-talk to replace negative thoughts that precipitate fear and desperation.

D. The dependent partner has failed to grasp the use of the positive self-talk and was provided with remedial direction in this area.

31. Refer to Assertiveness Training Class (31)

A. The dependent partner was referred to an assertiveness-training class.

B. The dependent partner has attended the assertiveness-training class, and the positive benefits of these techniques were reviewed.

C. The dependent partner has not attended the assertiveness-training class and was redirected to do so.

DEPRESSION DUE TO RELATIONSHIP PROBLEMS

CLIENT PRESENTATION

1. Feeling Blue (1)*

A. The client reported feeling deeply sad and has periods of tearfulness on an almost daily basis.
B. The client's depressed affect was clearly evident within the session because tears were shed on more than one occasion.
C. The client has begun to feel less sad and can experience periods of joy.
D. The client appeared to be happier within the session, and there is no evidence of tearfulness.
E. The client reported no feelings of depression.

2. Lack of Concentration (2)

A. The client reported an inability to maintain concentration and is easily distracted.
B. The client reported an inability to read material with good comprehension because of being easily distracted.
C. The client reported an increased ability to concentrate as the depression has lifted.

3. Lack of Sexual Interest (3)

A. The client reported a diminished interest in, or enjoyment of, sexual activities that were previously found pleasurable.
B. The client has begun to be more involved with sexual activity.
C. The client has returned to a normally active interest in, and enjoyment of, sexual activities.

4. Sleeplessness/Hypersomnia (4)

A. The client reported periods of inability to sleep and other periods of sleeping for many hours without the desire to get out of bed.
B. The client's problem with sleep disturbance has diminished as the depression has lifted.
C. Medication has improved the client's problems with sleep disturbance.
D. The client reported a normal sleep routine resulting in feeling rested.

5. Decreased Energy Level (5)

A. The client reported feeling a very low level of energy.
B. It was evident within the session that the client has low levels of energy as demonstrated by slowness of walking, minimal movement, lack of animation, and slow responses.
C. The client's energy level has increased as the depression has lifted.
D. It was evident within the session that the client is demonstrating normal levels of energy.

6. Lack of Activity Enjoyment (6)

A. The client reported a diminished interest in or enjoyment of activities that were previously found pleasurable.

*The numbers in parentheses on Client Presentation pages correlate to the number of the Behavioral Definition statement in the companion chapter with the same title in *The Couples Psychotherapy Treatment Planner* (Jongsma, O'Leary, and Heyman) by John Wiley & Sons, 1998. The numbers in parentheses on the Interventions Implemented page correspond to the number of the Therapeutic Intervention statement in the companion chapter in the same book.

B. The client is less involved in social activities.
C. The client has begun to be more involved with activities that he/she previously found pleasurable.
D. The client has returned to an active interest in and enjoyment of activities.

7. Low Self-Esteem (7)

A. The client described a very negative self-perception.
B. The client's low self-esteem was evident within the session because many self-disparaging remarks were made, and very little eye contact was maintained.
C. The client's self-esteem has increased as he/she is beginning to affirm his/her self-worth.
D. The client verbalized positive feelings about himself/herself.

8. Feeling of Hopelessness/Worthlessness (8)

A. The client has reported feelings of hopelessness and worthlessness that began as the depression deepened.
B. The client's feelings of hopelessness and worthlessness have diminished as the depression is beginning to lift.
C. The client expressed hope for the future and affirmation of self-worth.

9. Suicidal Ideation (9)

A. The client reported experiencing suicidal thoughts but has not taken any action on these thoughts.
B. The client reported strong suicidal thoughts that have resulted in suicidal gestures or attempts.
C. Suicidal urges have been reported to have diminished as the depression has lifted.
D. The client denied any suicidal thoughts or gestures and is more hopeful about the future.

10. Inappropriate Guilt (10)

A. The client described feelings of pervasive, irrational guilt.
B. The client identified feelings of guilt about how the marital relationship has been affected by the depression.
C. Although the client verbalized an understanding that his/her guilt was irrational, it continues to be prominent.
D. The depth of irrational guilt has lifted as the depression has subsided.
E. The client no longer expresses feelings of irrational guilt.

11. Movement Retardation (11)

A. The client displayed a pattern of movement retardation.
B. The client presents as having little energy and slow patterns of movement.
C. As the client has begun to recover from the depression, activity levels have returned to normal.

12. Accelerated Movement (11)

A. The client displayed an abnormally increased movement pattern.
B. The client displays pacing or other agitated patterns of movement.

C. The client's movement acceleration has begun to diminish.
D. As the client has begun to recover from the depression, activity levels have returned to normal.

13. Recurrent Sadness and Crying Spells (12)

A. The client reports a pattern of recurrent feelings of sadness and crying spells.
B. The client cried often within the session.
C. The client reports an inability to improve his/her mood or keep himself/herself from crying.
D. As the client has progressed in treatment, he/she displays a decreased pattern of sadness.
E. The client reports that his/her crying has greatly diminished to appropriate levels, and he/she feels more upbeat.

14. Nonresponsive to Medication (13)

A. The client has been maintained on antidepressant medication, but has not displayed any significant benefit from the medication.
B. Despite an extended period of time on antidepressant medication, the client's depression symptoms persist.
C. The antidepressant medication appears to be providing a greater benefit recently.

15. Declines Antidepressant Medication (14)

A. The client has been prescribed antidepressant medication and found this to be helpful in controlling the depression symptoms, but chooses not to take such medication due to the negative side-effects that have been experienced.
B. As the client has discontinued the use of antidepressant medication, the depression symptoms seem to have increased.
C. The client has returned to using the antidepressant medication, with changes in the medication regimen to decrease the pattern of side effects.
D. The client has agreed to continue taking the antidepressant medication despite the side effects.

16. Poor Grief Resolution (15)

A. The client described a history of personal losses and his/her inability to resolve the grief associated with these losses.
B. The client's ability to resolve grief issues has improved.
C. The client has accepted the losses and no longer is hampered by grief.

17. Blames Relationship for Depression (16)

A. The client reported the belief that the relationship problems are the cause of the depression.
B. The client has identified additional life circumstances and biochemical problems as the causes for the depression.
C. The client acknowledged that the relationship problems are just one cause of the depression.
D. The client endorsed a reciprocal relationship between the depression and relationship problems.
E. As the relationship problems have been resolved, the depression has lifted.

18. History of Relationship Problems (17)

A. The client reported a history of relationship problems prior to the onset of the depression.
B. The client acknowledged that the relationship problems existed prior to the depression.
C. As the depression has lifted, the relationship problems have diminished.

19. Precipitating Relationship Event (18)

A. The client identified events within the relationship that have been very destructive (e.g., verbal abuse, physical abuse, discovery of action by other partner that led to distrust).
B. The client related how the precipitating events within the relationship have led to the depression that he/she experiences.
C. As the client has begun to resolve his/her issues related to the precipitating events within the relationship, he/she has also experienced decreased depression symptoms.

INTERVENTIONS IMPLEMENTED

1. Explore Relationship (1)

A. Each partner was asked to describe thoughts and feelings concerning the relationship.
B. Each partner was asked to identify an overall level of satisfaction with the relationship.
C. The partners were supported as each provided honest thoughts and feelings regarding the relationship.
D. When partners were reluctant to provide honest thoughts and feelings regarding the relationship, they were encouraged to be more open.

2. Administer Standardized Assessment (2)

A. Each partner was asked to complete a standardized assessment of relationship satisfaction.
B. Each partner was requested to complete the Locke Wallace Marital Adjustment Test.
C. Each partner was asked to complete the Spanier Dyadic Adjustment Scale.
D. Each partner has completed a standardized assessment scale of relationship satisfaction, and the results were reviewed within the session.
E. The partners have not completed the standardized assessment scale of relationship satisfaction and were redirected to do so.

3. Assess Commitment (3)

A. Each partner was asked to describe a level of commitment to the relationship.
B. Each partner was asked to complete a standardized assessment of commitment to the relationship.
C. Each partner was asked to complete the Commitment Scale (Broderick and O'Leary).
D. The partners have completed descriptions or assessments of commitment to the relationship, and the results were reviewed with both partners.
E. The partners have not completed a standardized commitment to relationship scale and were redirected to do so.

4. Assess Love/Caring (4)

A. Each partner was asked to describe a level of love and caring within the relationship.

B. Each partner was asked to complete a standardized assessment of love and caring within the relationship.

C. Each partner was asked to complete the Positive Feelings Questionnaire (O'Leary).

D. The partners have completed descriptions or assessments of love/caring, and the results were reviewed with both partners.

E. The partners have not completed a standardized scale assessing love and caring in the relationship and were redirected to do so.

5. Assess Relationship Problems Contributing to Depression (5)

A. The extent to which each partner believes relationship problems preceded the depression was assessed.

B. It was interpreted to the partners that the relationship problems seemed to have preceded the depression symptoms.

C. It was interpreted to the partners that the depression symptoms seem to precede the relationship problems.

D. It was noted that the partners tend to give variable information about the etiology of relationship problems and depression.

6. Connect Depression and Relationship Problems (6)

A. Each partner was asked to describe whether and why depression was caused by problems in the relationship.

B. The partners were assisted in explaining the relationship between the depression and the problems the couple experiences.

C. It was interpreted to the partners that they are in significant agreement regarding how the depression and relationship problems are connected.

D. It was interpreted to the partners that they have little agreement regarding how the depression and relationship problems are connected, and additional processing of these types of concerns was provided.

7. Identify Depression Causes (7)

A. The client was asked to verbally identify the source of the depressed mood.

B. The client listed several factors that he/she believes contribute to the hopelessness and sadness.

8. Administer Standardized Testing (8)

A. Objective psychological testing was administered to the client to assess the depth of his/her depression and monitor suicide potential.

B. The Beck Depression Inventory was administered to the client.

C. The Beck Hopelessness Scale was administered to the client.

D. The client cooperated with the psychological testing, and feedback about the results was given to him/her.

E. The psychological testing confirmed the presence of significant depression.
F. The psychological testing indicated no significant depression.

9. Develop Crisis Plan (9)

A. A plan of action was developed with information about whom the client should call when hopeless feelings are becoming magnified.
B. Twenty-four hour supervision was coordinated for the client with clear instructions about how to reach help.
C. The client was provided with positive feedback as he/she has used the crisis plan in difficult situations.
D. The client has not used the crisis plan as appropriate and was redirected to do so.

10. Teach Connection between Anger and Depression (10)

A. The client was taught about how individuals with depression often become angry quickly and make hostile comments to people that they love.
B. The client was assisted in identifying examples of how his/her depression has resulted in anger and hostile comments.
C. The client's partner identified examples of how the client's depression has led to anger and hostile comments, and this was processed within the session.

11. Minimize Hostile Comments (11)

A. The client with depression symptoms was asked to self-monitor and minimize hostile comments to the other partner.
B. Positive feedback and encouragement was provided to the depressed client regarding his/her ability to monitor himself/herself and minimize hostile comments to the other partner.
C. The client's partner was asked to share whether changes have occurred in the level of hostile comments to the other partner, and this was processed within the session.

12. Encourage Measured Sharing of Depressed Feelings (12)

A. The client was encouraged to share his/her depressed feelings within the therapy session.
B. The client was encouraged to share his/her depressed feelings with his/her significant other, but on a limited basis.
C. Support and feedback were provided as the client shared his/her depressed feelings.
D. The client was reinforced for sharing his/her depressed feelings with the significant other on a limited basis.
E. The client's partner indicated that the client has not shared feelings of depression on a limited basis, and the client was provided with additional feedback and direction in this area.

13. Outline Appropriate Reliance (13)

A. The client was assisted in outlining appropriate reliance on significant others (friends and family) to minimize the avoidance of the client.
B. The client was provided with positive feedback regarding his/her identified appropriate reliance on significant others.
C. The client has relied on significant others at an appropriate level, which has minimized the avoidance of the client, and this was processed within the session.

D. The client has not used an appropriate level of reliance on significant others, and they have tended to avoid him/her. This was processed within the session.

14. Encourage Spiritual Activities (14)

A. The client's history of involvement with religious services, spiritual writings, and prayer was investigated.
B. The client was encouraged to use religious services, spiritual writings, and prayer to alleviate depression.
C. The client's use of religious services, spiritual writings, and prayer was reviewed, and the benefits of these practices were identified.

15. Encourage Apologies for Nonsupport (15)

A. The client's partner was identified as being nonsupportive.
B. The client's partner was encouraged to apologize for being nonsupportive and to make some restitution for lack of support.
C. The client's partner was provided with positive feedback for acknowledging, apologizing for, and making restitution for the previous lack of support.
D. The client's partner denied any pattern of being nonsupportive and was provided with additional feedback in this area.

16. Assign Positive Comments (16)

A. Each partner was assigned to give positive, supportive comments to the other on a daily basis.
B. The partners reported regular use of positive, supportive comments to each other, and the benefits of this were reviewed.
C. The partners reported that they have not both regularly used positive, supportive comments to the other on a daily basis and were redirected to do so.

17. Develop Kind Acts (17)

A. Each partner was assisted in developing a list of thoughtful, kind acts that would be appreciated.
B. The partners were assigned to engage in at least one caring gesture for each other each day.
C. The partners have engaged in caring gestures on a frequent basis, and the benefits of these interactions were reviewed.
D. The partners have not engaged in caring gestures on a frequent basis and were redirected to do so

18. Assign Verbal/Physical Affection (18)

A. The couple was assessed for the level of anger and hostility experienced.
B. As the couple's level of anger and hostility has subsided, they were assigned to be verbally and physically affectionate to each other each day.
C. A review was conducted of the positive effects of being verbally and physically affectionate with each other.
D. The partners have not practiced verbal and physical affection with each other each day, and the reasons for this were brainstormed and problem-solved.

19. Discontinue Comments Due to Frustration (19)

A. The partner without depression was directed to refrain from making hostile, counterproductive comments to the other partner out of frustration with the partner's depression.
B. The partner without depression was assessed for changes in the pattern of hostile, counterproductive comments.
C. The partner without depression was directed to other outlets to express frustration with the partner's depression.
D. As hostile, counterproductive comments have decreased, the partner's level of depression has also decreased.

20. Review Communication (20)

A. The couple's pattern of communication was assessed to identify the extent of negativity and hostility.
B. Positive reinforcement was given to both partners regarding the low level of negativity and hostility that exists within their communication.
C. The couple was provided with direct feedback regarding the high levels of negativity and hostility that exists in their communication.
D. The couple was asked to make a commitment to decrease the level of negativity and hostility that exists in their communication.

21. Provide Audio/Video Feedback (21)

A. When the therapist's requests to avoid negativity proved ineffective, the couple was provided with audiotaped feedback to illustrate the hostility displayed in the session.
B. When the therapist's requests to avoid negativity proved ineffective, the couple was provided with videotaped feedback to illustrate the hostility displayed in the session.
C. The couple has gained a greater understanding of the level of negativity within their communication, and this was processed within the session.
D. The couple persists in their denial regarding the negativity within their communication and was provided with additional feedback in this area and a request to continue to review it.

22. Assign Individual Therapy (22)

A. When the therapist's requests to avoid negativity were ineffective, individual adjunctive sessions were encouraged to address the anger and hostility.
B. The partners have used individual sessions to address their anger and hostility.
C. The couple has declined the use of individual sessions to address anger and hostility and was redirected to use these.
D. The couple has failed to follow through on individual sessions to address their anger and hostility and was redirected to do so.

23. Refer for Medication Evaluation (23)

A. A referral to a physician was made for the purpose of evaluating the client for a prescription of psychotropic medications.

B. The client has followed through on a referral to a physician and has been assessed for a prescription of psychotropic medications, but none were prescribed.
C. The client has been prescribed psychotropic medications.
D. The client declined evaluation by a physician for a prescription of psychotropic medication and was assisted in reconsidering this option.

24. Monitor Medications (24)

A. The client was monitored for compliance with his/her psychotropic medication regimen.
B. The client was provided with positive feedback about his/her regular use of psychotropic medication.
C. The client was monitored for the effectiveness and side effects of his/her prescribed medications.
D. Concerns about the client's medication effectiveness and side effects were communicated to the physician.
E. Although the client was monitored for medication side effects, he/she reported no concerns in this area.

25. Review Side Effects of Medication (25)

A. The possible side effects related to the client's medication were reviewed with the client.
B. The client identified significant side effects, and these were reported to the medical staff.
C. Possible side effects of the client's medication were reviewed, but he/she denied experiencing side effects.

26. Review Medication Responsiveness and Changes (26)

A. The client was assessed regarding his/her response to antidepressant medication.
B. The client was noted to have had a lack of response to the medication and was redirected to discuss this with his/her physician and to raise the issue of changing the dosage and/or medication.
C. The client has been maintained on his/her current medication.
D. The client's dosage of his/her medication has been changed.
E. The client's antidepressant medication has been modified.

27. Review Negative Self-Talk (27)

A. The client's pattern of negative, pessimistic self-talk was assessed.
B. The client was confronted and his/her pattern of pessimistic self-talk regarding self, partner, and the future was highlighted.
C. The client was provided with positive feedback as he/she displayed increased insight into his/her pessimistic self-talk and displayed a commitment to decrease this pattern.
D. The client continues with a pattern of negative self-talk and was provided with further redirection in this area.

28. Teach Positive Messages (28)

A. The client was taught to replace negative self-talk with positive messages regarding self, partner, and the future of their relationship.

B. The client was directed to write down positive messages to replace negative self-talk and review these at least twice per day.
C. The client's depression was noted to be lessening, as evidenced by the client replacing negative self-talk with positive messages regarding himself/herself, the partner, and the future of their relationship.
D. The client has not regularly used positive messages regarding self, partner, and the future of their relationship and was redirected to do so.

29. Reinforce Positive Thoughts and Verbalizations (29)

A. The client was noted to be making more positive verbalizations of hope and reporting more self-esteem-enhancing thoughts.
B. The client was reinforced for his/her use of hopeful verbalization and self-esteem-enhancing thoughts.

DEPRESSION INDEPENDENT OF RELATIONSHIP PROBLEMS

CLIENT PRESENTATION

1. Pervasive Sadness (1)*

A. The client reported feeling deeply sad and having periods of tearfulness on an almost daily basis.

B. The client's depressed affect was clearly evident within the session as tears were shed on more than one occasion.

C. The client has begun to feel less sad and can experience periods of joy.

D. The client appeared to be happier within the session and there is no evidence of tearfulness.

E. The client reported no feelings of depression.

2. Lack of Concentration (2)

A. The client reported an inability to maintain concentration and is easily distracted.

B. The client reported an inability to read material with good comprehension because of being easily distracted.

C. The client reported an increased ability to concentrate as the depression is lifting.

3. Lack of Sexual Interest (3)

A. The client reported a diminished interest in or enjoyment of sexual activities that were previously found pleasurable.

B. The client has begun to be more involved with sexual activity.

C. The client has returned to a normally active interest in and enjoyment of sexual activities.

4. Sleeplessness/Hypersomnia (4)

A. The client reported periods of inability to sleep and other periods of sleeping for many hours without the desire to get out of bed.

B. The client's problem with sleep disturbance has diminished as the depression has lifted.

C. Medication has improved the client's problems with sleep disturbance.

D. The client reported a normal sleep routine resulting in feeling rested.

5. Decreased Energy Level (5)

A. The client reported feeling a very low level of energy.

B. It was evident within the session that the client has low levels of energy as demonstrated by slowness of walking, minimal movement, lack of animation, and slow responses.

C. The client's energy level has increased as the depression has lifted.

D. It was evident within the session that the client is demonstrating normal levels of energy.

*The numbers in parentheses on Client Presentation pages correlate to the number of the Behavioral Definition statement in the companion chapter with the same title in *The Couples Psychotherapy Treatment Planner* (Jongsma, O'Leary, and Heyman) by John Wiley & Sons, 1998. The numbers in parentheses on the Interventions Implemented page correspond to the number of the Therapeutic Intervention statement in the companion chapter in the same book.

6. Lack of Activity Enjoyment (6)

A. The client reported a diminished interest in or enjoyment of activities that were previously found pleasurable.

B. The client is less involved in social activities.

C. The client has begun to be more involved with activities that he/she previously found pleasurable.

D. The client has returned to an active interest in and enjoyment of activities.

7. Low Self-Esteem (7)

A. The client described a very negative self-perception.

B. The client's low self-esteem was evident within the session as many self-disparaging remarks were made, and very little eye contact was maintained.

C. The client's self-esteem has increased as he/she is beginning to affirm his/her self-worth.

D. The client verbalized positive feelings about himself/herself.

8. Feeling of Hopelessness/Worthlessness (8)

A. The client has reported feelings of hopelessness and worthlessness that began as the depression deepened.

B. The client's feelings of hopelessness and worthlessness have diminished as the depression is beginning to lift.

C. The client expressed hope for the future and affirmation of self-worth.

9. Suicidal Ideation (9)

A. The client reported experiencing suicidal thoughts but has not taken any action on these thoughts.

B. The client reported strong suicidal thoughts that have resulted in suicidal gestures or attempts.

C. Suicidal urges have been reported as diminished as the depression has lifted.

D. The client denied any suicidal thoughts or gestures and is more hopeful about the future.

10. Inappropriate Guilt (10)

A. The client described feelings of pervasive, irrational guilt.

B. The client identified feelings of guilt about how the marital relationship has been affected by the depression.

C. Although the client verbalized an understanding that his/her guilt was irrational, the feelings of guilt continue to be prominent.

D. The depth of irrational guilt has lifted as the depression has subsided.

E. The client no longer expresses feelings of irrational guilt.

11. Movement Retardation (11)

A. The client displayed a pattern of movement retardation.

B. The client presents as having little energy and slow patterns of movement.

C. As the client has begun to recover from the depression, activity levels have returned to normal.

12. Recurrent Depression (12)

A. The client's pattern of depression symptoms has remained chronic, with no significant alleviation for an extended period of time.
B. The client has experienced a recurrent pattern of depression symptoms, gaining some relief, and then experiencing a recurrence of the depression symptoms.
C. The client's chronic or recurrent experience of depression has been alleviated.
D. The client has been able to maintain his/her freedom from depression for an extended period of time.

13. Nonresponsive to Medication (13)

A. The client has been maintained on antidepressant medication, but has not displayed any significant benefit from the medication.
B. Despite an extended period of time on antidepressant medication, the client's depression symptoms persist.
C. The antidepressant medication appears to be providing a greater benefit recently.

14. Declines Antidepressant Medication (14)

A. The client has been prescribed antidepressant medication and has found this to be helpful in controlling the depression symptoms, but chooses not to take such medication due to the negative side-effects that have been experienced.
B. As the client has discontinued the use of antidepressant medication, the depression symptoms seem to have increased.
C. The client has returned to using the antidepressant medication, with changes in the medication regimen to decrease the pattern of side effects.
D. The client has agreed to continue taking the antidepressant medication despite the side effects.

15. Lack of Grief Resolution (15)

A. The client described a history of personal losses and his/her inability to resolve the grief associated with these losses.
B. The client's ability to resolve grief issues has improved.
C. The client has accepted the losses and no longer is hampered by grief.

INTERVENTIONS IMPLEMENTED

1. Identify Depression Causes (1)

A. The client was asked about the factors that he/she believes cause him/her to be depressed
B. The client identified a variety of factors that have contributed to his/her depression, and these were summarized and processed.
C. The client was unable to determine the factors that contribute to the depression and was provided with tentative examples of these concerns.

2. Rank Depression Causes (2)

A. The client was asked to verbally identify the source of the depressed mood.
B. The client was supported as several factors that he/she believes contribute to the hopelessness and sadness were discussed.
C. The client was asked to rank the factors that are making him/her depressed.
D. Active listening and reflection skills were used while the client described his/her ranking of the depression causes.

3. Explore Positive Factors/Interpretations (3)

A. The factors causing the client's depression symptoms were explored for possible changes that can be made to result in an improved mood.
B. The client identified a variety of changes that he/she is able to implement to improve and develop a positive mood.
C. The client's pattern of negative interpretations of the causative factors was investigated to identify different interpretations.
D. The client identified a variety of interpretations that can be changed to improve his/her mood, and these were processed.
E. The client failed to identify significant causative factors, negative interpretations, or changes that could be made in these areas and was redirected to focus in this area.

4. Administer Standardized Testing (4)

A. Objective psychological testing was administered to the client to assess the depth of his/her depression and monitor suicide potential.
B. The Beck Depression Inventory was administered to the client.
C. The Beck Hopelessness Scale was administered to the client.
D. The client cooperated with the psychological testing, and feedback about the results was given to him/her.
E. The psychological testing confirmed the presence of significant depression.
F. The psychological testing indicated no significant depression.

5. Develop Crisis Plan (5)

A. A plan of action was developed, with information about whom the client should call when hopeless feelings are becoming magnified.
B. Twenty-four-hour supervision was coordinated for the client with clear instructions about how to reach help.
C. The client was provided with positive feedback as he/she has used the crisis plan in difficult situations.
D. The client has not used the crisis plan as appropriate and was redirected to do so.

6. Develop Family Tree (6)

A. The client was assigned to make a family tree with brief descriptions of the mental health of each family member and notations about whether they experienced depression.
B. The client was assisted in identifying possible family-of-origin factors that relate to a vulnerability to depression.

C. A significant pattern of family history of depression was identified.
D. No specific family pattern of depression has been identified.

7. Review Genetic Vulnerability for Depression (7)

A. A discussion of the client's family risk and genetic vulnerability for depression was held.
B. A significant genetic vulnerability for depression was identified.
C. A strong emphasis was placed on the equally important roles that psychological and environmental factors play in preventing and coping with depression, despite hereditary risk factors.

8. Teach Connection between Anger and Depression (8)

A. The client was taught about how individuals with depression often become angry quickly and make hostile comments to people that they love.
B. The client was assisted in identifying examples of how his/her depression has resulted in anger and hostile comments.
C. The client's partner identified examples of how the client's depression has led to anger and hostile comments; this was processed within the session.
D. The client with depression symptoms was asked to self-monitor and minimize hostile comments to the other partner.
E. Positive feedback and encouragement was provided to the depressed client regarding his/her ability to monitor himself/herself and minimize hostile comments to the other partner.
F. The client's partner was asked to share whether changes have occurred in the level of hostile comments to the other partner, and this was processed within the session.

9. Encourage Measured Sharing of Depressed Feelings (9)

A. The client was encouraged to share his/her depressed feelings in the therapy session.
B. The client was encouraged to share his/her depressed feelings with his/her significant other, but on a limited basis, with an emphasis on understanding the factors that support the depression.
C. Support and feedback were provided as the client shared his/her depressed feelings.
D. The client was reinforced for sharing his/her depressed feelings with the significant other on a limited basis.
E. The client's partner indicated that the client has not shared feelings of depression on a limited basis, and the client was provided with additional feedback and direction in this area.

10. Outline Appropriate Reliance (10)

A. The client was assisted in outlining appropriate reliance on significant others (friends and family) to minimize the avoidance of the client.
B. The client was provided with positive feedback regarding his/her identified appropriate reliance on significant others.
C. The client has relied on significant others at an appropriate level, which has minimized the avoidance of the client; this was processed within the session.
D. The client has not used an appropriate level of reliance on significant others, and they have tended to avoid him/her; this was processed within the session.

11. Encourage Spiritual Activities (11)

A. The client's history of involvement with religious services, spiritual writings, and prayer was investigated.

B. The client was encouraged to use religious services, spiritual writings, and prayer to alleviate depression.

C. The client's use of religious services, spiritual writings, and prayer was reviewed, and the benefits of these practices were identified.

12. Refer for Medication Evaluation (12)

A. A referral to a physician was made for the purpose of evaluating the client for a prescription of psychotropic medications.

B. The client has followed through on a referral to a physician and has been assessed for a prescription of psychotropic medications, but none were prescribed.

C. The client has been prescribed psychotropic medications.

D. The client declined evaluation by a physician for a prescription of psychotropic medication, and was assisted in reconsidering this decision.

E. The client was encouraged to take the antidepressant medication on a regular basis.

13. Review Side Effects of Medication (13)

A. The possible side effects related to the client's medication were reviewed with the client.

B. The client identified significant side effects, and these were reported to the medical staff.

C. Possible side effects of the client's medication were reviewed, but he/she denied experiencing side effects.

D. The client was advised that many of the side effects of medication go away after the first few weeks of medication use.

14. Report Side-Effects/Effectiveness of Medications (14)

A. The client was monitored for the effectiveness and side effects of his/her prescribed medications.

B. Concerns about the client's medication effectiveness and side effects were communicated to the physician.

C. Although the client was monitored for medication side effects, he/she reported no concerns in this area.

D. The client was directed to inform the prescribing physician about the medication effectiveness and side effects.

15. Review Medication Responsiveness and Changes (15)

A. The client was assessed regarding his/her response to antidepressant medication.

B. The client was noted to have had a lack of response to the medication and was redirected to discuss this with his/her physician and raise the issue of changing the dosage and/or medication.

C. The client has been maintained on his/her current medication.

D. The client's dosage of his/her medication has been changed.

E. The client's antidepressant medication has been modified.

16. Review Medication Responsiveness and Changes (16)

A. The client was assessed regarding his/her response to antidepressant medication.

B. The client was noted to have had a lack of response to the medication and was taught about the use of electroconvulsive shock therapy.

C. The client declined any involvement in electroconvulsive shock therapy.

D. The client is willing to talk over the use of electroconvulsive shock therapy with his/her physician.

E. The client has been administered electroconvulsive shock therapy, and the benefits of this were reviewed.

17. Assign Social Contacts (17)

A. The client was assigned to make a certain number of social contacts (phone calls, visits, letter writing, e-mail) per week.

B. The client was reinforced for making a number of social contacts each week.

C. The client has made a number of social contacts in the preceding week, and the experiences were processed.

D. The client has not made social contacts over the past week, and the reasons for this were identified and problem-solved.

18. Obtain Daytime Support from Partner (18)

A. The client was assigned to make a certain number of contacts with the other partner per week, at the partner's work site (provided that the employer permits such contacts and the partner is supportive).

B. The partners have identified a specific number of contacts that should be made that allow for the depressed partner to feel supported, without overwhelming the nondepressed partner.

C. The client has used the contacts with the other partner to maintain support through daytime periods of depression, and this was processed.

D. The partners have not coordinated daytime support, and the problems with this were identified and resolved.

19. Coordinate Physical Activities (19)

A. The client was assisted in planning regular physical activities (e.g., walking, jogging, working out at the gym).

B. Where appropriate, the client's partner was encouraged to be involved in the regular physical activities.

C. The client has reported a minimal use of physical activities, but does endorse some lessening of the depression symptoms.

D. The client has regularly used physical activities and reports a gradual decrease in his/her depression symptoms; this was processed during the session.

E. The client has not used regular activities, and the difficulties with this were problem-solved.

20. Encourage Positive Self-Talk (20)

A. The client was taught to replace negative self-talk with positive messages regarding self, partner, and the future of their relationship.

B. The client was directed to write down positive messages to replace negative self-talk and review these at least twice per day.
C. The client's depression was noted to be lessening, as evidenced by the client replacing negative self-talk with positive messages regarding self, the partner, and the future of their relationship.
D. The client has not regularly used positive messages regarding self, partner, and the future of their relationship and was redirected to do so.

21. Educate Partner about Symptoms of Depression (21)

A. The client's partner was informed about how the depressed partner's mood and aversive behaviors are symptomatic of clinical depression.
B. The client's partner was provided with support as the frustration experienced with the client's depression symptoms was reviewed.
C. As the client's partner has developed a better understanding and sympathy for the client's depression symptoms, their relationship has improved, and they were directed to continue this pattern.

22. Encourage Adjustment of Expectations (22)

A. The partner without depression was encouraged to adjust expectations due to the severity of the partner's depression/impaired functioning.
B. The partner without depression was asked to identify examples of the adjustment in expectations due to the severity of the partners depression/impaired functioning.
C. The partners reported that the adjustment in expectations due to the severity of the partner's depression/impaired functioning has assisted in a more realistic understanding, and the benefits of this were processed.
D. The partner without depression was confronted regarding the failure to adjust expectations due to the severity of the partner's depression/impaired functioning.

23. Assign Reading on Depression (23)

A. The client was assigned material to read regarding depression.
B. The client was assigned to read *Feeling Good* (Burns).
C. The client has read the assigned material, and key ideas were processed in session.
D. The client has not read the assigned material on depression and was redirected to do so.

DISILLUSIONMENT WITH RELATIONSHIP

CLIENT PRESENTATION

1. Out of Touch (1)*

A. The client identified increased feelings of being out of touch with his/her partner.

B. The client's partner has experienced a sense of distance in the relationship with the client.

C. As treatment has progressed, the partners identified a closer bond.

D. The partners are sharing time, thoughts, and feelings with each other.

2. Going One's Own Way (2)

A. The client identified a pattern of decreased interaction with his/her partner.

B. The partners identified a sense that each is going his or her own way.

C. The partners have a decreased pattern of sharing of activities, interests, and communication with each other.

D. The partners have begun to develop mutual interests, activities, and communication.

E. As treatment has progressed, the partners have identified the sense that they are "going the same way" within the relationship.

3. Fear of Separation or Divorce (3)

A. The client identified concerns that his/her relationship will deteriorate to the point of separation or divorce.

B. The client's partner has identified concerns about the specter of separation or divorce.

C. Both partners have indicated that separation or divorce is a distinct possibility due to their disillusionment with the relationship.

D. The partners have begun to identify other solutions to the relationship problems instead of separation or divorce.

E. The partners have indicated that the idea of separation or divorce has become less likely.

4. Failed Attempts to Resolve Relationship (4)

A. The partners have experienced failed attempts at jointly attending to the needs of the relationship.

B. Failed attempts to attend to the needs of the relationship have caused arguments and increased distance within the relationship.

C. As attempts to jointly attend to the needs of the relationship have been more successful, arguments have decreased and the couple feels closer to each other.

5. Blaming (5)

A. The client blames the other partner for past personal or relationship disappointments.

B. The client's partner blames the client for past personal or relationship disappointments.

*The numbers in parentheses on Client Presentation pages correlate to the number of the Behavioral Definition statement in the companion chapter with the same title in *The Couples Psychotherapy Treatment Planner* (Jongsma, O'Leary, and Heyman) by John Wiley & Sons, 1998. The numbers in parentheses on the Interventions Implemented page correspond to the number of the Therapeutic Intervention statement in the companion chapter in the same book.

C. Through counseling, the pattern of blaming the other partner for past personal or relationship disappointments has decreased.

6. **Uncertain Future (6)**

A. The client reported difficulties in planning for his/her future because of arguments or distance in the relationship.

B. The client's partner is uncertain about how to plan for the future because of arguments or distance in the relationship.

C. Both partners talk in a tentative manner about the future of the relationship.

D. As counseling has progressed and the couple has grown closer, they look forward to the future with mutual anticipation.

7. **Negative Effect of Unmet Expectations (7)**

A. The partners identified expectations of each other, themselves, and the relationship that have not been met.

B. The unmet expectations of the self, partner, or relationship have led to negative outcomes (e.g., frustrations, disappointments, depression, anxiety, and anger).

C. The partners have developed more realistic expectations for each other and the relationship.

D. The partners identified that although expectations are not always met, the negative outcomes (e.g., frustrations, disappointments, depression, anxiety, anger) have not been as prevalent.

8. **Preoccupation with Disappointments (8)**

A. The client identified a pattern of preoccupation with past personal and relationship disappointments.

B. The client's partner is often focused on past personal and relationship disappointments.

C. The preoccupation with past personal and relationship disappointments has led to additional conflict within the relationship.

D. As the partners become more fulfilled with the relationship, preoccupation with past personal and relationship disappointment has decreased.

INTERVENTIONS IMPLEMENTED

1. **Administer Relationship Dissatisfaction Questionnaire (1)**

A. The couple was administered a questionnaire/survey to identify each partner's current approach to the relationship dissatisfaction.

B. The partners were administered the Stages of Change questionnaire (Prochaska et al.)

C. The couple was identified as being in one of the four stages of change (e.g., precontemplation, contemplation, action, or maintenance).

D. The results of the questionnaire/survey regarding the approach to the relationship dissatisfaction were reviewed in a conjoint session.

2. **Identify Strengths (2)**

A. Each partner was asked to describe the strengths of the current relationship.

B. The client was provided with feedback when he/she identified the strengths of the current relationship.

C. The client's partner was provided with feedback regarding the identified strengths of the current relationship.

D. The partners struggled to identify strengths of their current relationship and were provided with some tentative examples in this area.

3. Identify Relationship Areas for Improvement (3)

A. Each partner was asked to describe the elements of the current relationship that they would like to improve.

B. Active listening was used as the client identified a variety of elements of the current relationship that he/she would like to improve.

C. Active listening was used as the client's partner identified elements of their relationship that can be improved.

D. The partners were confronted when they identified only areas in which the other partner should make improvements.

E. The partners were reinforced as they described elements of the relationship that they can take personal responsibility for improving.

4. List Personal Changes to Improve Relationship (4)

A. The client was asked to list three ways in which he/she could change to cause improvements in the relationship.

B. The client's partner was asked to list three personal changes that would cause improvements in the relationship.

C. Each partner has listed ways to improve the relationship, and these were processed with the couple.

5. Identify Developmental Influences on Interpersonal Style (5)

A. The partners were asked to identify important events in their individual developmental history that may relate to their current style of interacting.

B. Each partner identified important events in their development that relate to their current style of interacting; these were processed, with an emphasis on helping the partners understand each other.

C. As the partners have gained more understanding of each other's developmental influences on current styles of interacting, they have become more supportive of each other, and the benefits of this were processed within the session.

6. Identify Relationship Development Influences on Interpersonal style (6)

A. The partners were asked to identify important events in their relationship history that may relate to their current style of interacting.

B. Each partner identified important events in their relationship development that relate to their current style of interacting; these were processed, with an emphasis on the partners understanding each other.

C. As the partners have gained more understanding of how relationship developments have influenced current styles of interacting, they have become more supportive of each other, and the benefits of this were processed within the session.

7. Identify Explicit Relationship Contract (7)

A. The partners were asked to describe what their stated expectations of each other were at the start of the relationship.

B. It was noted that the partners agreed on the stated expectations of each other within the relationship.

C. It was noted that the partners were in disagreement of the stated expectations of the explicit relationship contract at the start of the relationship.

8. Describe Implicit Relationship Contract (8)

A. The partners were asked to describe what their unspoken expectations of each other were at the start of the relationship.

B. The partners were taught about the implicit relationship contract that they have developed.

C. The partners were reinforced for a greater understanding of each other as they were able to identify unspoken expectations of each other and the implicit relationship contract.

D. The partners failed to identify their unspoken expectations of each other and were provided with tentative examples of implicit relationship contracts.

9. Explore Benefits of Relationship Contract (9)

A. The clients were focused onto the ways in which the original relationship contract (both implicit and explicit) has benefited each partner.

B. The partners identified a variety of ways in which the original relationship contract has benefited each of them.

C. The partners reported little significant benefit from the original relationship contract; they were provided with tentative examples of benefits to each partner.

10. Explore Contract Negatives (10)

A. The partners were focused on the negative aspects of the original relationship contract.

B. The couple was assisted in identifying negative aspects of their original relationship contract that have led to conflict, disappointment, or frustration.

C. The partners identified negative aspects of the original relationship contract, and these were processed within the session.

11. Encourage Elimination of Frustrating Expectations (11)

A. The partners were encouraged to eliminate expectations that have been a source of conflict, disappointment, or frustration.

B. The partners agreed to eliminate expectations that have been sources of conflict, disappointment, or frustration and were assisted in developing a clearer understanding of this concept.

C. The partners were encouraged to express their feelings related to expectations that they were giving up to help decrease conflict, disappointment, or frustration.

D. The clients did not endorse the need to eliminate expectations that have been sources of conflict and were requested to reconsider this need.

12. Explore Evolution of Relationship Contract (12)

A. The partners were asked to identify how their relationship contract has evolved over time.

B. The pattern of changes in the partners' relationship contract was explored and processed.

C. The partners were supported as they identified several implicit and explicit changes that have occurred in their relationship contract.

D. The partners failed to understand how their relationship contract has evolved over time and were provided with additional feedback in this area.

13. Explore Needed Changes (13)

A. The partners were asked to reflect on how their relationship contract might have needed to change although it did not.

B. The partners were directed to review how one partner's understanding of the relationship contract had changed, even though the other partner's understanding had not changed in a similar manner.

C. The partners were provided with positive feedback regarding their insight into the ways in which their relationship contract needed to change but has not changed.

D. The partners were supported as they committed to making significant changes in the relationship contract.

E. The partners were unable to identify specific ways in which their relationship contract needed to change and were provided with additional feedback in this area.

14. Elucidate Personal Dreams (14)

A. Each partner was asked to identify personal dreams.

B. Each partner identified how their dreams have been fulfilled, and this was processed within the session.

C. A discussion was held regarding how dreams have not been fulfilled.

D. As a discussion about fulfillment of personal dreams was held, the partners displayed increased insight into each other's level of fulfillment within the relationship.

15. Identify Relationship Dreams (15)

A. The partners were asked to identify dreams for how the relationship would fulfill their needs.

B. Each partner identified how their dreams for the relationship have been fulfilled, and this was processed within the session.

C. A discussion was held regarding how dreams for the relationship have not been fulfilled.

D. As discussions about fulfillment of dreams for the relationship were held, the partners displayed increased insight into each other's level of fulfillment within the relationship.

16. Explore Reactions to Realized and Unfilled Dreams (16)

A. Each partner was directed to express gratitude to the other partner for dreams that were realized.

B. Each partner was directed to let go of the resentment over dreams that have remained unfulfilled.

C. The partners were provided with feedback as they expressed gratitude and let go of resentment regarding their dreams.

D. The benefits of letting go of unrealistic relationship dreams were reviewed.

E. The partners were noted to have difficulty letting go of the unrealistic dreams for the relationship and were urged to work on this over the time between sessions.

17. Tell Life Stories (17)

A. The partners were requested to tell their life stories.

B. The partners told their life stories, and an emphasis on the predictabilities and continuities of their shared life was noted.

C. As the partners' life stories were reviewed, they displayed an increased level of understanding and acceptance of the predictability and continuities of their shared life.

18. Retell Life Story (18)

A. The partners were requested to retell their life story, emphasizing the surprises, choices, sacrifices, and unpredictability of their shared life.

B. As the partners retold their story, areas of surprises, choices, sacrifices, and unpredictability within their shared life were emphasized.

C. The partners reported an increased acceptance of their shared life.

19. Contrast Life Stories (19)

A. The partners were requested to compare and contrast the predictable and unpredictable versions of their past lives and relationships.

B. The partners were asked to identify how their emotional and coping responses have impacted the predictable and unpredictable parts of their shared life.

C. The partners identified significant differences in their view on their life as predictable versus unpredictable.

20. Add Chapters to Life Story (20)

A. Each partner was asked to add chapters to each version of their life story, envisioning their future.

B. As the partners described the future chapters of their life story, they were assisted in summarizing their expectations.

21. Discuss Future Chapters (21)

A. Discussion was held regarding the pros and cons of both versions of their future chapters.

B. An emphasis was placed on the security and predictability in the relationship.

C. The need for each other during times of unpredictability was emphasized.

D. The partners endorsed the need for the security of predictability as well as the need for each other during times of unpredictability and were provided with positive feedback about this healthy relationship.

22. Reframe Past Decisions (22)

A. Past decisions were reviewed considering contextual factors that influence the choices.

B. Past decisions were reframed into " the best decisions that could be made."

C. The partners were reinforced for accepting the reframing and reducing the blame on each other.

D. The partners rejected the reframing on decisions as "the best that could be made at the time" and were urged to contemplate this concept further.

23. Direct Taking of Responsibility (23)

A. Each partner was directed to take personal responsibility for disappointing decisions, thereby reducing blame on the other partner.

B. Each partner was reinforced for taking personal responsibility for disappointing decisions.

C. The partners reported a decreased pattern of blame as they took personal responsibility for disappointing decisions, and the benefits of this were reviewed.

D. The partners failed to take personal responsibility for disappointing decisions and were redirected to do so.

24. Reframe Current Problems (24)

A. Current problems were reframed as a natural outgrowth of the partners' individual attempts to cope with changes forced on them by life's circumstances.

B. The partners were asked to identify specific examples of how current problems are a result of individual attempts to cope with changes.

C. The partners were unable to identify any examples of how attempts to cope with changes have contributed to current problems and were given tentative examples of this dynamic.

25. Discuss Life's Circumstances (25)

A. The partners were directed to review the life circumstances that have forced them to cope in a certain manner (e.g., changing social expectations, changing gender roles, and family life-cycle changes).

B. As the partners described the life circumstances that have forced them to cope, an emphasis was placed on the need to foster acceptance of each other.

C. The partners have described their life's circumstances and have developed a better acceptance of each other, and the benefits of this were processed with them.

D. The partners have not been accepting of each other; they have discussed their life's circumstances and were urged to review these concepts.

26. Discuss Coping Measures (26)

A. The partners were directed to review the ways in which they have coped with their life circumstances (e.g., changing friendships, becoming more assertive, and spending time with family in a different manner).

B. As the partners described the ways in which they have coped with changing life circumstances, an emphasis was placed on the need to foster acceptance of each other.

C. The partners have described their adaptive coping to life's circumstances and have developed a better acceptance of each other, and the benefits of this were processed with them.

D. The partners have not been accepting of each other as they have discussed the manner of coping with life's circumstances and were urged to review these concepts.

27. Focus on Empathy (27)

A. The listening partner was directed to empathize with the speaker's point of view regarding coping.

B. Positive feedback was provided as the listening partner empathized with the speaking partner's point of view regarding coping.

C. The partners verbalized empathy regarding each other's coping attempts and were supported for this progress.

D. The listening partner did not empathize with the speaking partner and was redirected on how to be more empathetic.

28. Process Reaction to Coping (28)

A. After the listening partner had empathized, that partner was directed to explain the impact that the speaker's coping had, and how the listener was forced, in turn, to cope with those changes.

B. The listening partner was directed to identify how the speaker's coping attempt elicited further coping skills.

C. Through reviewing the interchange of coping needs, both partners were able to increase their empathy for each other.

D. The partners failed to grasp the interactions of each other's coping styles and were provided with specific feedback in this area.

29. Reframe Current Problems (29)

A. The partners' current problems were reframed as a result of the partners being out-of-sync with each other in coping.

B. The partners were supported as they identified examples of how current problems are a result of being out-of-sync with each other in coping.

C. The partners identified the need to become more in-sync with each other, and this was processed.

30. Emphasize Working as a Team (30)

A. The need for the partners to begin working on coping as a team was emphasized.

B. The partners agreed that they would need to begin working on coping as a team to get more in-sync with each other, and they were supported for this understanding.

C. The partners identified specific ways in which they can work together as a team to resolve problems.

31. Remediate Communication Problems (31)

A. The partners were provided with specific skills to help remediate communication problems.

B. The partners were reinforced for using specific skills for remediating communication problems and reporting an increased level of functioning in their relationship.

C. The partners continue to have poor communication skills and were provided with additional assistance in this area.

32. Hold a "Constitutional Convention" (32)

A. The partners were directed to hold a "Constitutional Convention" to reevaluate their relationship contract, specifying what expectations, rights, and responsibilities each agrees to.

B. The partners have held their "Constitutional Convention," and the benefits of this were reviewed.

C. The partners have not held a "Constitutional Convention" and were redirected to do so.

33. Identify Current Needs (33)

A. Each partner was asked to identify his or her own current needs.

B. As each partner identified their own current needs, they were supported and encouraged in this area.

34. Identify What to Give in a Relationship (34)

A. Each partner was asked to identify what he or she is willing to give to the relationship.

B. The partners were reinforced for identifying what each would give within the context of their relationship.

C. The partners are reluctant to commit their personal resources to the relationship and were provided with additional feedback in this area.

35. Identify Needs Met In or Out of Relationship (35)

A. The partners were asked to identify the needs that each would like to have met within the relationship.

B. The partners were asked to identify the needs that each would like to have met outside of the relationship.

C. The partners displayed realistic expectations regarding the relationship needs that can be met within the relationship and were provided with positive feedback.

D. The partners displayed realistic expectations regarding those needs that can be met outside of the relationship and were provided with positive feedback.

E. The partners displayed unrealistic expectations regarding needs that should be met inside the relationship and were redirected in this area.

F. The partners displayed unrealistic expectations regarding needs that should be met outside the relationship and were redirected in this area.

36. List Challenges (36)

A. The partners were asked to generate a list of future challenges that they anticipate having to contend with.

B. The partner's list of challenges that they expect to contend with in the future was reviewed.

C. The partners displayed an adequate understanding of the challenges that they will have for the future and this was reflected to them.

D. The partners made an obviously incomplete list of the challenges that they may have in the future and were redirected in this area.

37. Plan Future as a Team (37)

A. Using the agreements detailed in the new relationship contract, the couple was directed to plan for their future as a team.

B. The couple has developed specific plans for their future, and these were reviewed within the session.

C. The partners have not developed a plan for the future, and they were redirected to do so.

38. Discuss Support Systems Already in Place (38)

A. The support systems outside of the relationship that are already in place were identified and discussed.

B. Emphasis was placed on how the present support systems can help the partners renew the vitality of their relationship (e.g., friends, self-help and support groups, the religious community).

C. The partners reported limited support systems available to them and were redirected to find more in this area.

39. Discuss Support Systems to Be Added (39)

A. The partners were directed to identify support systems outside of the relationship that can be added to help the partners renew the vitality of their relationship.

B. The partners identified a variety of support systems that can help then renew the vitality of their relationship, and these were reviewed and processed.

C. The partners struggled to identify support systems that can be added to help renew the vitality of their relationship, and they were provided with examples, such as friends, self-help, support groups, and religious community.

EATING DISORDER

CLIENT PRESENTATION

1. Chronic Rapid Overeating (1)*

A. The client described a history of chronic, rapid consumption of large quantities of high carbohydrate food.

B. The client has engaged in binge eating on almost a daily basis.

C. The frequency of binge eating of non-nutritious foods has begun to diminish.

D. The client reported that there have been no recent incidents of binge eating.

2. Self-Induced Vomiting (1)

A. The client has engaged in self-induced vomiting out of a fear of gaining weight.

B. The client's purging behavior with self-induced vomiting has occurred on almost a daily basis.

C. The client has increased his/her control over the self-induced vomiting, and the frequency of this behavior has decreased.

D. The client reported no recent incidents of self-induced vomiting.

3. Laxative Abuse (1)

A. The client has a history of the abuse of laxatives to purge his/her system of food intake.

B. The frequency of laxative abuse has begun to diminish.

C. The client reported no recent incidents of laxative abuse as a purging behavior for food intake.

4. Extreme Weight Loss (2)

A. The client's eating disorder has resulted in extreme weight loss and a refusal to consume enough calories to increase his/her weight to more normal levels.

B. The extreme weight loss has resulted in amenorrhea in the client.

C. The client's weight loss has plateaued, and he/she is beginning to acknowledge the need for weight gain.

D. The client has begun to gain weight gradually and endure the anxious feelings associated with that experience.

E. The client is now at the lower end of normal in terms of his/her weight and has been able to maintain that weight level.

5. Body Image Disturbance (3)

A. The client has a history of preoccupation with his/her body image and perceives himself/herself as overweight, even when thin.

*The numbers in parentheses on Client Presentation pages correlate to the number of the Behavioral Definition statement in the companion chapter with the same title in *The Couples Psychotherapy Treatment Planner* (Jongsma, O'Leary, and Heyman) by John Wiley & Sons, 1998. The numbers in parentheses on the Interventions Implemented page correspond to the number of the Therapeutic Intervention statement in the companion chapter in the same book.

B. The client is beginning to acknowledge that his/her body image is grossly inaccurate, and that some weight gain is necessary.
C. As the client has begun to gain some weight, his/her anxiety level has increased, and the fear of obesity has returned.
D. The client has been able to gain weight to normal levels without a distorted fear of becoming overweight overwhelming him/her.

6. Irrational Feeling of Becoming Overweight (4)

A. The client has developed a predominating, intense fear of becoming overweight.
B. The client's fear of becoming overweight has caused him/her to control his/her food intake to an extreme level.
C. The client has used purging methods to control his/her weight.
D. The client's fear of becoming overweight has diminished.
E. The client has not reported any fear of becoming overweight

7. Electrolyte Imbalance (5)

A. An electrolyte imbalance resulting from the client's eating disorder is compromising his/her health.
B. The client has accepted the fact that his/her eating disorder has resulted in a fluid and electrolyte imbalance.
C. The client has agreed to terminate the bingeing/purging behavior that has resulted in the electrolyte imbalance.
D. The client has agreed to increase his/her nutritious food intake and terminate purging behaviors to correct a fluid and electrolyte imbalance.
E. The client's fluid and electrolyte imbalance has been corrected as he/she has increased food intake and terminated purging behavior.

8. Avoidance of Affection (6)

A. The client described a desire to avoid expressive affection with his/her partner.
B. The client's partner described that the client persistently avoids expressions of affection with his/her partner.
C. As the client's eating disorder has improved, he/she expressed an increased desire to share affection with his/her partner.
D. The client has become appropriately comfortable in expressing affection toward his/her partner.

9. Avoidance of Sexual Contact (7)

A. The client described a desire to avoid sexual contact with his/her partner.
B. The client's partner described that the client persistently avoids sexual contact with his/her partner.
C. As the client's eating disorder has improved, he/she expressed an increased desire to share sexual contact with his/her partner.
D. The client has become appropriately comfortable in having sexual contact with his/her partner.

10. Arguments about Dieting, Bingeing, and Purging (8)

A. The partners have had arguments related to the eating disorder problems.

B. The partners report persistent arguments over the adaptations that the eating disorder has forced both partners to make.

C. The partners have frequently been at odds with each other over issues related to the eating disorder.

D. As the partner's pattern of eating disorder symptoms has been eliminated, the arguments between the partners have decreased.

11. Depression (9)

A. The client presents with a recurrent pattern of depression.

B. The client displays current symptoms of depression, including sleep and appetite changes; irritability; sadness; lack of energy; and feelings of worthlessness, hopelessness, and helplessness.

C. As treatment has progressed, the client's pattern of depression symptoms has been significantly decreased.

D. The client reports experiencing no symptoms of depression.

12. Partner's Depression (10)

A. The client's partner presents with a recurrent pattern of depression.

B. The client's partner displays current symptoms of depression, including sleep and appetite changes; irritability; sadness; lack of energy; and feelings of worthlessness, hopelessness, and helplessness.

C. As treatment has progressed, the client's partner's pattern of depression symptoms has been significantly decreased.

D. The client's partner reports experiencing no symptoms of depression.

13. Poor Communication (11)

A. The client and his/her partner describe a pattern of poor communication with each other.

B. There is very limited communication between the client and his/her partner.

C. As the client's eating disorder concerns have begun to resolve, he/she reports an increased pattern of communication with his/her partner.

14. Explosive Interchanges (12)

A. The client reported an intermittent pattern of explosive interchanges between the partners.

B. The partners' discussions regarding eating disorder concerns have often led to explosive interchanges between the partners.

C. As treatment has progressed, the discussions between partners have been less explosive.

INTERVENTIONS IMPLEMENTED

1. Describe Eating Patterns (1)

A. The clients were asked to describe the eating patterns of the partner with the eating disorder.

B. The partners described a pattern of eating that is consistent with a diagnosable eating disorder.

C. The partners' descriptions of the eating pattern of the partner with an eating disorder were noted to be inconsistent with each other.

2. Describe Purging Patterns (2)

A. The clients were asked to describe the purging patterns of the partner with the eating disorder.
B. The partners described a pattern of purging that is consistent with a diagnosable eating disorder.
C. The partners' descriptions of the purging pattern of the partner with an eating disorder were noted to be inconsistent with each other.

3. List Contributory Factors (3)

A. The partners were asked to list factors that they believe are causing the eating problems.
B. Feedback was provided to the partners as they listed factors that they believe are causing the eating problems.
C. The partners displayed significant insight regarding the factors that are contributing to the eating patterns.
D. The partners failed to identify significant factors that are causing the eating problems and were provided with feedback in this area.

4. Identify Partner's Exacerbation/Maintenance of Eating Problems (4)

A. The partner without the eating disorder was asked to identify personal behaviors that may exacerbate or maintain the other partner's eating problems.
B. The partner without the eating disorder was supported for listing personal examples of exacerbation and /or maintenance of the other partner's eating problems.
C. The partner without the eating disorder was unable to identify personal behaviors that contribute to the exacerbation and/or maintenance of the other partner's eating problems and was provided with additional feedback in this area.

5. Assign Treatment-Related Reading (5)

A. The partners were assigned reading related to the treatment of eating disorders.
B. The partners were assigned to read *Eating Disorders* (brochure #94-3477 from NIMH).
C. The partners have read the treatment-related information, and this was processed in the session.
D. The partners have not read the treatment-related information and were redirected to do so.

6. Refer to Physician (6)

A. The client was referred to a physician for a complete physical examination.
B. The client has followed through on a referral to a physician for an examination and reported that negative consequences of the eating disorder were discovered.
C. The client's physical examination ruled out any serious negative consequences resulting from the eating disorder.
D. The client's evaluation indicated that he/she has developed an electrolyte imbalance that resulted from the eating disorder.

7. Educate Regarding Self-Esteem (7)

A. The partners were taught the central role that low self-esteem plays in the development and maintenance of an eating disorder.

B. The partners were provided with specific examples of how low self-esteem contributes to the development and maintenance of an eating disorder.

C. The partners reviewed how the partner with the eating disorder may have experienced low self-esteem issues.

8. Emphasize Supportive Feedback (8)

A. The partner without the eating disorder was directed to provide the other partner with supportive feedback to enhance his/her self-esteem.

B. The partner with the eating disorder identified that the other partner has increased the use of supportive feedback; reinforcement was given for this increase.

C. Positive feedback from the partner without the eating disorder has not increased, and redirection was provided in this area.

9. Review Use of Appetite Suppressant (9)

A. The current evidence regarding the role of appetite suppressant medication in treating eating disorders was reviewed with the client and his/her partner.

B. The partners verbalized an understanding of the risks and potential benefits of appetite-suppressant medication to treat the eating disorder, and any additional questions were answered.

C. The partners have indicated a desire to use appetite suppressant medication for the eating disorder and were provided with a referral for an evaluation from a physician.

D. The partners have decided against the use of appetite suppressant medication and this decision was accepted.

10. Review Use of Psychostimulant as Treatment (10)

A. The current evidence regarding the role of psychostimulant medication in treating eating disorders was reviewed with the client and his/her partner.

B. The partners verbalized an understanding of the risks and potential benefits of psychostimulant medication to treat the eating disorder, and any additional questions were answered.

C. The partners have indicated a desire to use psychostimulant medication for the eating disorder and were provided with a referral for an evaluation from a physician.

D. The partners have decided against the use of psychostimulant medication and this decision was accepted.

11. Review Use of Antidepressant (11)

A. The current evidence regarding the role of antidepressant medication in treating eating disorders was reviewed with the client and his/her partner.

B. The partners verbalized an understanding of the risks and potential benefits of antidepressant medication to treat the eating disorder, and any additional questions were answered.

C. The partners have indicated a desire to use antidepressant medication to treat the eating disorder and were provided with a referral for an evaluation from a physician.
D. The partners have decided against the use of antidepressant medication and this decision was accepted.

12. Refer for Medication Evaluation and Monitor Medications Used (12)

A. A referral to a physician was made for the purpose of evaluating the client for a prescription of psychotropic medications.
B. The client has followed through on a referral to a physician and has been assessed for a prescription of psychotropic medications, but none were prescribed.
C. The client has been prescribed psychotropic medications and he/she was urged to comply with the prescription.
D. The client declined an evaluation by a physician for a prescription of psychotropic medication and was encouraged to reconsider this decision.
E. The client was monitored for compliance with and effectiveness of the psychotropic medication regimen.
F. Concerns about the client's medication effectiveness and side effects were communicated to the physician.
G. Although the client was monitored for medication side effects, none were reported.

13. Address Partner's Conflict/Anger (13)

A. The partner without the eating disorder was directed to describe the experience of conflict and anger regarding the other partner's eating disorder.
B. As the partner without the eating disorder described his/her experiences of conflict and anger toward the other partner's eating disorder, support and empathy were provided.
C. The partner without the eating disorder indicated no conflict or anger over the other partner's eating disorder, and this was reflected as a possible defense mechanism.

14. Obtain Commitment to Accept Responsibility (14)

A. The partner with the eating disorder was asked to commit to accepting responsibility for changing problematic eating patterns and attitudes.
B. Positive feedback was provided to the partner with the eating disorder for accepting responsibility for changing problematic eating patterns and attitudes.
C. The partner with the eating disorder was reluctant to accept responsibility for changing problematic eating patterns and attitudes and was provided with additional feedback and encouragement in this area.
D. As the partner with the eating disorder accepted responsibility for changing problematic eating patterns and attitudes, an emphasis was placed on the other partner minimizing attempts to control eating behaviors.

15. Gain Commitment to Minimize Control (15)

A. The partner without an eating disorder was requested to minimize attempts to control the eating behavior of the other partner.
B. The partner without an eating disorder agreed to minimize attempts to control the eating behavior of the other partner.

C. As the partner without the eating disorder made a commitment not to control the eating behavior of the other partner, an emphasis was placed on the partner with the eating disorder to take responsibility for changing problematic eating patterns and attitudes.

16. Discuss Role of Perfectionism (16)

A. The role that high standards and perfectionism play in the life of the partner with the eating disorder was discussed.

B. The partners were reinforced for identifying and understanding the roles that high standards and perfectionism play in continuing an eating disorder.

C. The partners could not identify ways in which high standards and perfectionism have played a role in the development of the eating disorder and were given feedback in this area.

17. Review Effects of Perfectionism on the Relationship (17)

A. The clients were asked to identify how perfectionism may interfere with various aspects of their relationship.

B. The partners were asked about how perfectionism affects their communication.

C. The clients were asked about how perfectionism affects their sexual functioning.

D. The partners identified a variety of ways in which perfectionism affects their relationship, and these were processed within the session.

E. The partners did not identify significant effects of perfectionism on their relationship and were provided with additional feedback in this area.

18. Identify Specific Feedback Desired (18)

A. The partner with the eating disorder was requested to describe in detail the specific positive feedback that is most desired from the other partner.

B. The partner with the eating disorder was reinforced for identifying specific positive feedback that is desired to help build self-esteem efforts to overcome the eating disorder.

FINANCIAL CONFLICT

CLIENT PRESENTATION

1. **Arguments over Amounts Spent (1)***

A. The couple described multiple arguments over the issue of how much one partner is spending.

B. The partners hold different viewpoints about the amount of money spent by one partner and the necessity for these expenditures.

C. The partners have begun to talk constructively about spending and saving guidelines.

D. An agreement has been reached between the spouses regarding the amount of money to be spent by each partner.

E. There have been no recent disagreements over the amount of money spent.

2. **Arguments over How to Spend (2)**

A. The partners reported that they often conflict about how they should use their financial resources.

B. One partner is more conservative about the use of finances and the other partner is more liberal, causing frequent arguments.

C. The partner's have begun to develop healthy communication about spending and saving habits.

D. The partners have developed a healthy compromise about how to allocate their financial resources.

3. **Critical Comments about Earnings (3)**

A. One partner reports that the other partner often makes critical comments about his/her earnings capabilities.

B. One partner complained that the other partner does not make enough money.

C. The partners have agreed not to make critical comments about each other's earning potential.

D. The partners have formed a specific plan to develop greater earning potential.

4. **Arguments about Saving (4)**

A. The partners described a pattern of conflict over savings goals and practices.

B. The partners have begun to talk constructively about savings guidelines.

C. Agreement has been reached between the partners regarding a savings goal and practices.

5. **Feeling Left Out of Financial Decisions (5)**

A. One partner identified feelings of being left out of decision making regarding money.

B. The partners described that one partner does most of the decision making, spending, and bill paying.

*The numbers in parentheses on Client Presentation pages correlate to the number of the Behavioral Definition statement in the companion chapter with the same title in *The Couples Psychotherapy Treatment Planner* (Jongsma, O'Leary, and Heyman) by John Wiley & Sons, 1998. The numbers in parentheses on the Interventions Implemented page correspond to the number of the Therapeutic Intervention statement in the companion chapter in the same book.

C. The partners have developed a more involved role for both partners regarding making financial decisions.

D. The partners both report a sense of involvement regarding making financial decisions.

6. Suspicions of Secretive Spending (6)

A. One partner identified suspicions that the other partner is secretly spending money.

B. One partner made vague, indirect comments about how the other partner may be secretly spending money.

C. As finances have been reviewed, one partner acknowledged secretly spending money, and more guidelines regarding spending were developed.

D. As finances were reviewed, suspicions that one partner is secretly spending money were found to be incorrect.

E. Both partners reported an increased level of trust of each other regarding spending.

7. Arguments over Retirement Needs (7)

A. The partners described arguments over the need to save money for retirement.

B. The partners have developed helpful guidelines about how much money to save for retirement.

C. The partners have agreed on the best ways to save money for retirement.

D. The partners reported no longer arguing over the need to save money for retirement.

8. Arguments about Income Tax Reporting (8)

A. The couple described frequent arguments over "legitimate" methods of reporting income for tax purposes.

B. One partner believes the other to be acting in an immoral or illegal manner regarding reporting income for tax purposes.

C. The couple has begun to develop constructive communication regarding income tax issues.

D. Agreement has been reached between the couple regarding accurate reporting of income for tax purposes.

9. Arguments over Price Shopping (9)

A. The couple reported frequent arguments over the need to shop for the best possible price on an item.

B. One partner described that the other partner tends to spend a great deal of time shopping for additional savings.

C. One partner described that the other partner does not sufficiently comparison shop, often paying a higher price than is needed.

D. The partners have developed a healthy compromise regarding how to price shop, and that they no longer argue about this.

INTERVENTIONS IMPLEMENTED

1. Facilitate Expression of Anger (1)

A. Each partner was asked to describe their angry feelings about how money is spent.

B. When each partner expressed angry feelings about how money is spent, these feelings were processed in the session.

C. The partners hesitated to express their angry feelings about how money is spent and were encouraged to do this within the confines of the safe, clinical setting.

2. Express Disappointment Regarding Money (2)

A. Each partner was asked to describe disappointments regarding the family finances.

B. When each partner expressed feelings of disappointment about the financial problems the couple faces, these feelings were processed in the session.

C. The partners hesitated to express their feelings of disappointment about their finances, and were encouraged to do this within the confines of the safe, clinical setting.

3. Prioritize Spending (3)

A. Each partner was asked to prioritize how money should be spent.

B. As each partner described how money should be spent, support and encouragement were provided.

C. Emphasis was placed on the commonalities between the partners' priorities about how money should be spent.

D. Differences between the partners regarding how money should be spent were identified and processed.

4. Discuss Presence of Different Priorities (4)

A. A discussion was held regarding whether there are basic differences between partners over priorities in the use of money.

B. It was noted that the partners had significant differences in their priorities regarding the use of money.

C. The partners indicated that there was very little difference between their priorities regarding the use of money, and this was accepted.

5. Describe Family of Origin Influences (5)

A. The clients were directed to describe the use of money in their families of origin.

B. The clients were assisted in identifying how their families of origin have influenced their current attitudes about finances.

C. The partners displayed insight into the effect that the use of money in their family of origin has on their current attitudes about finances and were provided with positive feedback in this area.

D. The partners failed to identify significant connections between the use of money in their families of origin and their current patterns and were provided with additional feedback in this area.

6. Inquire about Early Financial Expectations (6)

A. The partners were asked to describe the income, savings, and spending expectations that existed when the relationship began.

B. The partners were asked to describe the expectations that they had in the beginning of their relationship regarding the amount of money that they would have.

C. As the partners described their financial expectations at the beginning of their relationship, these were processed.

7. Identify Parental Influence (7)

A. Each partner was asked to explain whether there is any parental influence on current financial decisions.

B. As the partners identified parental influence on current financial decisions, the effects of this influence were processed.

C. The partners described many situations in which a partner's parents have influenced one or both partners, insisted on certain financial decisions, or disparaged and ridiculed the couple for certain financial decisions.

D. Money has been lent to the partners by one of the partner's parents, and since that time the parent has believed that this is an entitlement to unduly influence the couple's financial decisions.

E. The partners denied any parental influence of current financial decisions, and this was accepted.

8. Discourage Family Influence (8)

A. The couple was encouraged to engage in cooperative, partnership-based financial planning.

B. The partners were discouraged from permitting undue extended family influence over their financial plans.

C. The partners were reinforced for advising the over-involved family members that their involvement is no longer needed.

D. As the partners have developed cooperative, partnership financial planning (free from undue family influence), their conflicts over financial concerns have decreased, and the benefits of this were reviewed.

E. The partners continue to allow significant family influence on financial issues and were provided with additional feedback in this area.

9. Practice Listening without Interrupting (9)

A. Each client was asked to practice listening without interruption to the other partner's views about financial and budgetary goals.

B. As the partners practiced listening without interruption, they were given immediate feedback for listening in an open, patient manner.

C. As the partners practiced listening without interruption, they were given immediate feedback when interruptions occurred.

D. Each client took turns practicing the skill of listening without interruption, and the benefits of this were reviewed.

10. Practice Paraphrasing (10)

A. After one partner had listened without interrupting, the partner was asked to paraphrase what the other partner said.

B. After one partner had paraphrased, the other partner was asked to validate whether the paraphrasing was accurate.

C. The partners were given immediate feedback as they practiced paraphrasing and validating.

D. The partners often failed to paraphrase correctly, and the skill of withholding one's own opinion was emphasized.

11. Brainstorm Solutions (11)

A. After paraphrasing and validation, each partner was directed to offer a number of possible solutions to their conflicts about finances.

B. While each partner was offering a number of possible solutions to their conflicts about finances, the other partner was directed to refrain from interrupting.

C. The partners were provided with immediate feedback as solutions to financial conflicts were identified; interruptions were purposefully redirected.

D. The use of the brainstorming technique (listening without interrupting, paraphrasing, validating, and offering solutions) was emphasized as the process to be used in a variety of different discussions.

12. Evaluate Solutions (12)

A. Each partner was directed to validate their understanding of the other partner's suggested solutions to financial problems.

B. The partners were assisted in maintaining their focus on the suggested solutions to the financial problems.

C. As the partners evaluated the suggested financial solutions, specific solutions were noted to be acceptable to both partners.

13. Assign Implementation of One Solution (13)

A. The couple was assigned to implement at least one of the possible solutions during the next week.

B. The couple has identified one of the possible solutions to implement during the next week, and this solution will be reviewed at the next session.

C. The partners' implementation of one of the possible financial solutions was reviewed.

D. The partners have not implemented the identified solution and were redirected to do so.

14. Identify Employment History (14)

A. The partners were asked to describe their employment situations at the time that they first met.

B. The partners described their employment situation at the time they first met, and this was processed.

15. Explore Employment Expectations at Start of Relationship (15)

A. The partners' expectations regarding their own employment once they had become a couple were explored.

B. The partners' expectations regarding each other's employment were explored.

C. The partners' expectations for employment were identified as being roughly similar to each other.

D. A variety of differences regarding employment expectations were identified and processed.

16. Facilitate Agreement Regarding Each Partner Working (16)

A. The partners were asked to identify their values regarding the need for each partner to work outside the home versus one staying home to manage household and family responsibilities.

B. An agreement was facilitated regarding the amount of time for each partner to work outside of the home.
C. An agreement was facilitated regarding one partner staying home to manage household and family responsibilities.
D. The partners were unable to agree regarding one partner working versus staying home, and additional feedback was provided in this area.

17. Explore Employment Expectations Subsequent to Having Children (17)

A. The partners' expectations regarding their own employment subsequent to having children were explored.
B. Each partner's expectations regarding the other partner's employment subsequent to having children were explored.
C. The partners' expectations for employment subsequent to having children were identified as being roughly similar to each other.
D. A variety of differences regarding employment expectations subsequent to having children were identified and processed.

18. Facilitate Agreement Regarding Income and Child-Care Needs (18)

A. The partners were asked to identify their values regarding child-care needs and income needs.
B. An agreement was facilitated regarding the couple's expectations regarding child-care needs and income needs.
C. An agreement was facilitated regarding one partner staying home to manage household and family responsibilities.
D. An agreement was facilitated regarding both partners working and pursuing child-care elsewhere.
E. The partners were unable to agree regarding one partner working versus staying home, and additional feedback was provided in this area.

19. Review Bankruptcy, Welfare, and Credit Counseling (19)

A. The partners needs were reviewed regarding filing for bankruptcy, applying for welfare, and/or obtaining credit counseling.
B. The partners were assisted in deciding whether to file bankruptcy.
C. The partners were assisted in deciding whether to apply for welfare.
D. The partners were assisted in deciding to obtain credit counseling.

20. Refer to Financial Planner/Create Budget (20)

A. The couple was referred to a professional financial planner.
B. The couple has met with the financial planner, and the benefits of this were reviewed.
C. The couple has not met with the financial planner and was redirected to do so.
D. The partners were asked to write a current budget and a long-range savings and investment plan.
E. The couple has developed a budget, and the benefits of this were reviewed.
F. The couple has not developed a budget and was redirected to do so.

21. Review Budgeting Information (21)

A. The partners were provided with information regarding household expense allocations.

B. The partners were referred to *Family Economics Review* (U.S. Department of Agriculture) for information regarding household expense allocations.

C. The partners were reinforced for their increased understanding of appropriate budget allocations as a result of reviewing information on household expense allocations.

D. The partners have not read the information on household expense allocations and were redirected to do so.

22. Review Control Issues (22)

A. Each partner was asked to describe the ways in which the other partner seems to exert control in the relationship.

B. As each partner described the ways that the other partner seems to take control, attentive listening and support were provided.

C. It was reflected that one partner seems to exercise virtually exclusive control over the couple's finances and financial decisions.

D. The partners were provided with positive feedback regarding a more equal allocation of their control in the relationship.

23. Facilitate Mutual Agreement Regarding Financial Decisions (23)

A. The partners were assisted in developing a mutual agreement on how they can cooperatively make financial decisions.

B. An emphasis was placed on each partner's need to have his or her ideas regarding financial decisions respected.

C. The partners were supported for developing an agreement on how they can cooperatively make financial decisions that respect each partner's ideas.

D. The partners have not developed an agreement on how to cooperatively make financial decisions and were provided with additional feedback in this area.

24. Reinforce Planning, Compromise, and Cooperation (24)

A. The partners were reinforced as they made changes that reflected responsible planning for their financial needs.

B. Whenever the partners described a pattern of compromise regarding financial issues, they were provided with positive feedback in this area.

C. The partners exhibited respectful cooperation with each other and were reinforced for this.

D. The partners did not display changes that reflected responsible planning, compromise, or respectful cooperation and were redirected in these areas.

25. Assess Greater Control Issues (25)

A. An assessment was provided regarding how the one partner attempts to restrict the other partner regarding contact with family, friends, and/or enhancement of educational/vocational skills.

B. One partner was noted to be very restrictive in areas outside of finances, and this was reflected to the couple.

C. It was noted to the partners that they did not have a tendency to be overly restrictive of each other.

26. Treat Abuse (26)

A. Psychological abuse was noted to be occurring, and the partners were provided with direct treatment in this area.
B. Physical abuse was noted to be occurring, and the partner that was being abused was provided with options to create safety.
C. The treatment focus was switched to the abuse taking place within the relationship.

27. Explore Control of Finances and Emotions (27)

A. Specific areas of control that one partner has over the finances of the partnership were explored.
B. The partner who does not have control over the finances was asked to express emotions related to the financial control issues.
C. Support and feedback were provided as one partner described the degree of feelings about the other partner's control over finances.
D. The partner who does not have control over the finances was reluctant to express emotions over this lack of control and was encouraged to do this at a later time.

28. Assess Personality/Behavioral Disorder (28)

A. An individual session was held with each partner to assess whether a personality or behavioral disorder interferes with financial issues in the family.
B. A personality or behavioral disorder was identified as interfering with the financial issues of the family, and appropriate treatment was recommended.
C. The partners were assessed for personality or behavioral disorders, but none were noted.

29. Treat Individual Disorders (29)

A. Substance abuse was identified as interfering with financial solidarity, so the partner with the substance abuse problem was referred for treatment in that area.
B. Occupational problems were identified as interfering with financial solidarity, and the partner was referred for treatment in that area.
C. Another, separate disorder was identified as interfering with financial solidarity, so a referral for appropriate treatment was made.

INFIDELITY

CLIENT PRESENTATION

1. Explicit Relationship Expectations Violated (1)*

A. One partner has engaged in sexual behavior that violates the explicit expectations of the relationship.

B. One partner has engaged in intercourse, oral sex, or anal sex with someone outside of the relationship.

C. One partner has engaged in kissing or fondling with someone outside of the relationship, which violates the explicit expectations of the relationship.

D. The sexual behavior outside of the relationship has been discontinued.

2. Implicit Relationship Expectations Violated (1)

A. One partner has engaged in sexual behavior with someone outside the relationship that violates the implicit expectations of the relationship.

B. The sexual behavior with someone outside the relationship that violates the implicit expectations of the relationship has been discovered by the other partner.

C. The sexual behavior with someone outside the relationship that violates the implicit expectations of the relationship has been discontinued.

3. Sharing Intimate Feelings with Extra-Marital Partner (2)

A. Nonsexual behavior that involves sharing intimate feelings with an extra-marital partner has occurred.

B. The hurt partner has expressed feeling hurt by the other partner's sharing of intimate feelings with an extra-marital partner.

C. The sharing of intimate feelings with an extra-marital partner has been discontinued.

4. Secrecy (2)

A. The unfaithful partner has displayed a pattern of secrecy that violated the implicit and explicit expectations of the relationship.

B. The unfaithful partner has gone to significant lengths to cover up contact with the extra-marital partner.

C. As the affair has been uncovered, the pattern of secrecy has been discontinued.

D. The unfaithful partner is open about contact and activities with the extra-marital partner.

INTERVENTIONS IMPLEMENTED

1. Establish Type of Treatment (1)

A. A discussion was held to identify the type of treatment that will be conducted.

B. Relationship therapy was selected as the type of treatment to be conducted, focusing on the expectation that the affair will end; the goal will be to salvage the relationship.

*The numbers in parentheses on Client Presentation pages correlate to the number of the Behavioral Definition statement in the companion chapter with the same title in *The Couples Psychotherapy Treatment Planner* (Jongsma, O'Leary, and Heyman) by John Wiley & Sons, 1998. The numbers in parentheses on the Interventions Implemented page correspond to the number of the Therapeutic Intervention statement in the companion chapter in the same book.

C. Ambivalence therapy was identified as the appropriate treatment, with the goal to clarify the future of the relationship and the affair.
D. Separation therapy was identified as the appropriate treatment, with the focus on ending the relationship and separating under the best possible terms.

2. Negotiate Noncollusion Contract (2)

A. A noncollusion contract was presented to the partners, stipulating that the therapist will not agree to secrecy with either.
B. The therapist's role was emphasized as one of working for the mutual well-being of the couple.
C. The partners were supported for their acceptance of the noncollusion contract as presented by the therapist.

3. Contract for Number of Sessions (3)

A. A verbal contract was identified with the client for a specific minimum number of sessions.
B. One partner only reluctantly agreed to a specific minimum number of sessions to focus on the agreed therapeutic issues.

4. Discourage At-Home Discussions about the Affair (4)

A. The partners were directed to avoid deep discussions at home about the affair or the future of the relationship during the first month of treatment.
B. The partners agreed to avoid deep discussions at home about the affair or the future of the relationship during the first month of treatment.
C. The partners reported avoiding deep discussions about the affair and the future of the relationship outside of the treatment setting and were reinforced for this compliance with the therapeutic process.
D. The partners reported ongoing discussions about the affair or the future of the relationship during the first month of treatment and were redirected to discontinue this pattern.

5. Assess for Suicidality and Homicidality (5)

A. Each partner was asked independently about whether they have any thoughts, intent, or means to hurt themselves or others.
B. A partner identified concerns related to suicide, and appropriate steps were taken to assure that partner's safety.
C. A partner identified concerns related to homicidality, and appropriate steps were taken to ensure safety.
D. The partners were assessed, but no evidence of homicidality or suicidality was present.

6. Normalize Hurt Partner's Experience (6)

A. The partner hurt by the infidelity identified a variety of emotions related to the situation.
B. The partners were provided with handouts of common reactions to trauma (e.g., symptoms of major depressive disorder, and posttraumatic stress disorder).
C. The hurt partner's reaction to the infidelity was assessed as it relates to symptoms of reaction to trauma.

D. The hurt partner's emotional reaction to the infidelity was normalized as a common reaction to trauma.

7. Provide Hope (7)

A. Hope was provided to both partners by assuring them that many relationships do survive infidelity.

B. An emphasis was placed on how new assumptions can eventually replace shattered ones (i.e., promises of monogamy, trust, honesty, commitment, and emotional safety).

C. The couple was assigned to read materials relating to surviving infidelity.

D. The partners were assigned to read *After the Affair* (Spring) and *Private Lies* (Pittman).

E. The partners have read the assigned material, and the main points were processed.

F. The couple has not read the assigned material, and their reluctance was processed and redirected.

8. Educate about Course of Therapy (8)

A. The partners were educated regarding the common course of therapy for infidelity.

B. An expectation was identified that progress in therapy will involve emotional setbacks, and that setbacks frequently follow times of increased closeness and vulnerability.

C. The partners were provided with positive feedback as they displayed an understanding of the common course of therapy for infidelity.

9. Encourage Full Acceptance of Responsibility (9)

A. The unfaithful partner was encouraged to accept full responsibility for the decision to engage in the affair.

B. The unfaithful partner was encouraged to apologize directly for the pain that this decision caused to the hurt partner, family, and friends.

C. The unfaithful partner was reinforced for accepting full responsibility and apologizing for the pain caused by the decision to engage in an affair, and was provided with positive feedback for this.

D. The unfaithful partner was confronted for continuing to blame the other partner's behavior as the cause of the affair developing.

10. Encourage Acceptance of Apology (10)

A. The hurt partner was encouraged to verbalize directly an acceptance of the apology from the unfaithful partner.

B. The hurt partner has accepted the apology from the unfaithful partner, and this was interpreted to signify a beginning of the process of forgiveness, even though hurt and anger are understandably felt.

C. The hurt partner did not directly accept the apology from the unfaithful partner and was redirected to consider this next step.

11. Teach "Stop-and-Share" Technique (11)

A. The clients were taught the "Stop-and-Share" technique.

B. The unfaithful partner was directed to stop all contacts (including nonsexual contacts) with the lover.

C. Because it is impossible to discontinue all contact with the unfaithful partner's lover, the unfaithful partner agreed to stop all personal discussions with the lover.
D. The unfaithful partner was directed to share all incidents of contact with the hurt partner before being asked.
E. The unfaithful partner has not implemented the "Stop-and-Share" technique and was redirected to give this further reflection.

12. Assess Relationship Strengths and Needs (12)

A. The current strengths and needs of the relationship were assessed via interviews.
B. Psychological inventories were used to assess the strengths and needs of the relationship.
C. The results of the relationship strengths and needs evaluation were shared with the couple.

13. Assess Pre-Affair Functioning (13)

A. The partners' pre-affair functioning was assessed through taking a relationship history.
B. The partners were questioned about their pre-affair functioning, including how they met, why they were attracted to each other, the steps in the relationship, the postmarital adjustment, and the highs and lows during the relationship.
C. The partners' description of their pre-affair functioning was summarized and paraphrased to them.

14. Increase Caring Behaviors (14)

A. The partners were assigned to "catch your partner pleasing you," including recording at least one positive behavior for each day by the partner and at least one by self.
B. The partners have used the "catch your partner pleasing you" exercise, and the results of this were processed.
C. An increase in caring behaviors was noted.
D. A decrease in selective negative attention was noted.
E. The partners did not regularly record at least one positive behavior by the partner and by self and were redirected to do so.

15. Identify Specific Feedback Desired (15)

A. Each partner was requested to describe in detail the specific changes that are most desired from the other partner to feel more loved, respected, or committed.
B. An emphasis was placed on the partners to make requests from the other partner that are brief and ask for a positive behavior to increase rather than a decrease in negative behavior.
C. Each partner identified specific positive changes that are desired to help each feel more loved, respected, and committed.
D. When requested behaviors became more complicated, vague, or focused on decreasing negative behaviors, the partner was redirected.

16. List Changes (16)

A. Each client was assigned to list changes for self and the other partner that would improve the relationship.
B. A structured questionnaire, Areas of Change (Weiss and Birchler), was used to help the clients list the changes that would improve the relationship.

C. The partners have developed a list of changes for self and the other partner that would improve the relationship, and these were reviewed within the session.
D. The partners have not developed a list of changes for self and other partner and were redirected to do so.

17. Prioritize Behaviors to Benefit the Relationship (17)

A. Each client was assigned to list and prioritize behaviors that would benefit the relationship, from the *least* to the *greatest* in terms of effort, trust, and sacrifices that each behavior would require.
B. A Cost-Benefit Analysis (Birchler and Weiss) test instrument was used to prioritize behaviors helpful to the relationship.
C. The partners were directed to mutually enact the list of behaviors, starting with the *least* amount of trust and commitment first, following later with those of greater cost.
D. The partners were reinforced for implementing the lowest items on the priority list of behaviors that would benefit the relationship.
E. The partners have not implemented the lowest items on the priority list and were redirected to do so.

18. Teach Time-Out Techniques (18)

A. The partners were taught about the six components of time-out techniques (i.e., *self-monitoring* for escalating feelings of anger and hurt, *signaling* to the partner that verbal engagement should end, *acknowledging* the need of the partner to disengage, *separating* to disengage, *cooling down* to regain control of anger, and *returning* to controlled verbal engagement).
B. Positive feedback was provided as the partners displayed mastery of the time-out technique.
C. The partners were advised about the potential for misuse and manipulation of the time-out technique if used to avoid arguments or manipulate the other partner.
D. The partners have misused the time-out technique and were provided with additional feedback in this area.

19. Plan for Lover Contact (19)

A. A discussion was held with the couple regarding the need for a plan on what to do if the lover attempts to contact them.
B. The partners were directed in session to rehearse and role-play reaction scenarios to the lover contacting them.
C. Positive feedback was provided to the partners as they identified and rehearsed several reactions to the lover contacting them.
D. The couple declined to develop a plan for the lover attempting to contact them and were redirected in this area.

20. Assess and Remediate Communication (20)

A. The couple's current level of communication was assessed by having the partners conduct a short, naturalistic conversation about the affair, with the therapist observing but not interrupting.
B. The couple's specific communication deficits were identified.

C. Communication skills (e.g., "I" statements and empathetic listening) were taught to foster constructive, nonaccusatory, nondefensive exchanges.
D. The partners were reinforced for their clear understanding and healthy use of communication skills.
E. The partners did not display a clear understanding of communication skills and were provided with additional feedback and explanation in this area.

21. Identify Hurt Partner's Questions (21)

A. The hurt partner was asked to list questions about the affair.
B. The hurt partner was assisted in clarifying questions about the affair, although these were not immediately presented during a conjoint session.
C. The hurt partner has not listed questions about the affair and was redirected to do so.

22. Teach Anxiety Management Techniques (22)

A. The hurt partner was taught anxiety management techniques to help cope with intrusive thoughts.
B. The hurt partner was taught anxiety management techniques, such as setting aside worry times, keeping a journal, using diaphragmatic breathing, and thought-stopping techniques.
C. Anxiety management techniques were modeled to the hurt partner.
D. The hurt partner was reinforced for the reported use of anxiety management techniques.
E. The hurt partner has not used anxiety management techniques and was provided with remedial assistance in this area.

23. Identify and Share Intrusive Thoughts (23)

A. The hurt partner was asked to describe intrusive thoughts about the affair.
B. The unfaithful partner was directed to listen empathetically and supportively to the hurt partner.
C. The unfaithful partner was directed to use specific skills, such as paraphrasing the content of the hurt partner's statements, reflecting the emotional meaning of the hurt partner's statement, and taking responsibility for causing distress.
D. As the hurt partner described intrusive thoughts, empathetic support was modeled for the unfaithful partner.
E. Positive feedback was provided as the unfaithful partner listened empathetically and supportively.
F. The unfaithful partner did not listen empathetically and supportively and was given specific redirection in this area.

24. Teach about Re-Establishing Trust (24)

A. The hurt partner was taught to begin re-establishing trust by focusing on the unfaithful partner's current behavior.
B. The hurt partner was directed to focus away from catastrophic cognitions.
C. The hurt partner was directed to act as a detective, if necessary, to reduce worrying through verifying or fact checking.

D. The hurt partner was reinforced for beginning to re-establish trust by focusing on the unfaithful partner's current behavior.
E. The hurt partner has failed to re-establish trust, and the reasons for this were reviewed, processed, and problem-solved.

25. Review Life Events Preceding the Affair (25)

A. The partners were directed to discuss important life events that have taken place during the years immediately preceding the affair.
B. The partners discussed important life events that took place during the years immediately preceding the affair; a summarization of trends was provided.

26. Review Beliefs (26)

A. Each partner was asked to describe beliefs regarding monogamy, need for excitement, escapism, romantic love, admiration, and growth.
B. As the partners described beliefs about monogamy and other issues, patterns were summarized and reviewed.
C. The partners were directed to describe how these beliefs might have made an affair more likely.
D. The partners displayed insight into how beliefs played a role in making an affair more likely and were provided with positive feedback in this area.
E. The partners struggled to identify how beliefs made an affair more likely and were provided with feedback in this area.

27. Treat Specific Problems (27)

A. A treatment plan was developed to address specific relationship problems.
B. As treatment for their secondary problems has been enacted, the couple's secondary problems have decreased.

28. Model Questioning (28)

A. Modeling was used to show the hurt partner how to question the unfaithful partner.
B. Communication skills, such as making eye contact and asking questions in a calm, nonthreatening manner, were emphasized as the hurt partner questioned the unfaithful partner.
C. The hurt partner was reinforced for the use of healthy communication skills while questioning the unfaithful partner about the initiation and course of the affair.
D. Ongoing assistance was provided to the hurt partner for questioning the unfaithful partner about the initiation and course of the affair.

29. Contract Time Frames for Questioning (29)

A. The partners were contracted to agree to time frames for ending repeated questioning about the affair.
B. The partners have agreed to an appropriate period of time for questioning about the affair.
C. The partners have been unwilling to agree on an appropriate time frame for questioning about the affair and were encouraged to develop specific boundaries in this area.

30. Teach Asking of Factual Questions (30)

A. The hurt partner was taught to ask factual questions about the affair first, saving how and why questions for later.

B. The use of factual questions was modeled to the hurt partner, including questions of who, what, where, and when.

C. The hurt partner was reinforced for the use of factual questions while asking the unfaithful partner about the affair.

D. The hurt partner did not ask factual questions and was redirected in this area.

31. Teach "Take-Two" (31)

A. The partners were taught the "take-two" technique, in which the discussion of details of the affair were interrupted, and the questions repeated until the hurt partner could ask the questions in a calm, nonthreatening manner.

B. The partners were directed to use the "take-two" technique for discussion of the details of the affair, within the session.

C. The "take-two" technique was used until the unfaithful partner could answer questions directly and succinctly, without blaming the hurt partner.

32. Review Learning about Relationship (32)

A. The partners were asked to describe what has been learned about self that can be used to improve the relationship.

B. As the partners described what they have learned about themselves that can be used to improve the relationship, summarization and feedback was provided.

33. Discuss Learning Histories That Influence Susceptibility to Affair (33)

A. The unfaithful partner was asked about previous experiences or learning histories that may have influenced susceptibility to the affair.

B. The partners were asked about a variety of areas, including what they have learned about commitment and sensitivity from previous relationships, themes from early relationship, and how they learned about love from parents.

C. As the partners reviewed learning histories, themes and patterns were reflected to them.

34. Ask about Affairs in Family of Origin (34)

A. Each partner was asked about whether there is a history of affairs in the family of origin.

B. The unfaithful partner was asked about how affairs from the family of origin have affected feelings and behaviors related to the affair.

C. The hurt partner was asked about how affairs in the family of origin may have affected feelings and behaviors about learning about the affair.

D. As the partners reviewed the history of affairs in their families of origin, the information was objectively summarized and patterns were identified.

35. Brainstorm Closure Ritual (35)

A. Using brainstorming techniques, both partners were helped to devise an appropriate ritual to signify that the unfaithful partner takes responsibility for the affair and asks forgiveness, and that forgiveness is granted by the hurt partner.

B. Emphasis was placed on the need for the ritual to convey that the affair is forgiven but not forgotten, and that both partners now move forward.
C. The partners were provided with feedback as they develop an appropriate ritual to signify taking responsibility and giving forgiveness.
D. The partners did not develop a ritual to signify responsibility and forgiveness and were provided with redirection in this area.

36. Brainstorm Recommitment Ritual (36)

A. Brainstorming techniques were used to help the partners devise an appropriate ritual to identify their mutual recommitment to an explicitly monogamous relationship.
B. The partners were supported for their selection of an appropriate ritual to signify their mutual recommitment to an explicitly monogamous relationship.
C. The partners failed to identify an appropriate ritual to signify their mutual recommitment to an explicitly monogamous relationship and were provided with additional feedback and redirection.

37. Develop Plan to Decrease Effects of Affair (37)

A. The partners were assisted in devising a plan for reclaiming places, people, or events tarnished by the affair.
B. The partners have developed a plan for reclaiming places, people, or events tarnished by the affair, and this was reviewed.
C. The partners have used the plan for reclaiming people, places, or events tarnished by the affair, and the use of these techniques were reviewed.

INTOLERANCE

CLIENT PRESENTATION

1. Rigid Attitude (1)*

A. One or both partners display a rigid, consistent attitude that own behavior, beliefs, feelings, and opinions are right.

B. Rigid, consistent attitude by one partner that the other partner's behavior, beliefs, feelings, and opinions are wrong.

C. As the partners have become more open, the insistence on one's own behavior, beliefs, feelings, and attitudes has discontinued.

D. Both partners are much more open to discussion of each other's behaviors, beliefs, feelings, and opinions.

E. The partners have become much more tolerant of each other's behavior, beliefs, feelings, and opinions.

2. Frequent Arguments (2)

A. The partners reported frequent or continual arguing with each other.

B. The arguments have created an environment rife with tension.

C. The frequency of conflict between the partners has diminished.

D. The partners report a significantly decreased number of arguments due to the implementation of conflict resolution skills.

E. The client reported that his/her relationship with his/her partner has significantly improved and arguing has become very infrequent.

3. Disagreements Interpreted as Global Problems (3)

A. Disagreements are often not restricted to specific problems, but are interpreted as symbols of global problems.

B. Disagreements are often reflected as being caused by the partner's personality or lack of love or respect.

C. As treatment has continued, the couple has shown more tolerance for each other and disagreements have been limited to specific problem areas.

4. Problem Resolution Attempts Cause Increased Tension (4)

A. The couple described that their attempts to solve problems often cause more tension and problems than the original problem.

B. Within the session, the couple displayed increased tension and conflict as they attempted to resolve problems.

C. As the couple has learned to resolve problems, the level of tension and conflict during these discussions has decreased.

*The numbers in parentheses on Client Presentation pages correlate to the number of the Behavioral Definition statement in the companion chapter with the same title in *The Couples Psychotherapy Treatment Planner* (Jongsma, O'Leary, and Heyman) by John Wiley & Sons, 1998. The numbers in parentheses on the Interventions Implemented page correspond to the number of the Therapeutic Intervention statement in the companion chapter in the same book.

5. Coercive Blaming Cycles (5)

A. One partner has attempted to change the other partner's behavior, creating coercive responses in return.

B. The couple has become stuck in a blaming cycle.

C. The couple has learned to have disagreements without coercion.

D. As coercion has decreased, the couple is less likely to blame each other.

6. Anger and Vengeance (6)

A. Expressions of affect consist almost exclusively of protective emotions such as anger and vengeance.

B. Empathy-enhancing emotions, such as hurt and fear, are rarely expressed.

C. As the partners have become more tolerant and able to communicate better, they have focused on empathy-enhancing emotions rather than protective emotions.

INTERVENTIONS IMPLEMENTED

1. Administer Standardized Assessment (1)

A. Each partner was asked to complete a standardized assessment of relationship satisfaction.

B. Each partner was requested to complete the Locke Wallace Marital Adjustment Test.

C. Each partner was asked to complete the Relationship Satisfaction Questionnaire (Burns).

D. Each partner was asked to complete the Dyadic Adjustment Scale (Spanier).

E. Each partner has completed a standardized assessment scale of relationship satisfaction, and the results were reviewed within the session.

F. The partners have not completed the standardized assessment scale of relationship satisfaction and were redirected to do so.

2. Assess Relationship Strengths and Needs (2)

A. The current strengths and needs of the relationship were assessed via interviews.

B. Psychological inventories were used to assess the strengths and needs of the relationship.

C. The results of the relationship strengths and needs evaluation were shared with the couple.

3. Identify Strengths (3)

A. Each partner was asked to describe the strengths of the current relationship.

B. The client was provided with feedback as he/she identified the strengths of the current relationship.

C. The client's partner was provided with feedback regarding the identified strengths of the current relationship.

D. The partners struggled to identify strengths of their current relationship and were provided with some tentative examples in this area.

4. Assess Developmental Stage of Relationship (4)

A. The relationship was identified as currently being in the *early marriage* stage.

B. The relationship was identified as currently being in the *parents of young children* stage.

C. The relationship was identified as being currently in the *long-term marriage* stage.

5. Assess History of Relationship (5)

A. The partners' long-term pattern of functioning was assessed by taking a relationship history.

B. The partners were questioned about their long-term pattern of functioning, including how they met, why they were attracted to each other, the steps in the relationship, the postmarital adjustment, and the highs and lows during the relationship.

C. The partners' description of their long-term pattern of functioning in the relationship was summarized and paraphrased to them.

6. Assess Steps toward Divorce (6)

A. The couple's relationship was assessed in regard to steps each partner has taken toward divorce.

B. The Marital Status Inventory (Weiss and Cerreto) was used to help assess the degree of dissatisfaction with the marriage and steps taken toward breaking off the relationship.

C. Each partner was focused onto their sense of hope and vision for the future.

D. The partners were identified to be unlikely to divorce at this time, and this was reflected to them.

E. The partners were identified to be at significant risk for divorce, and this was reflected to them.

7. Identify Relationship Areas for Improvement (7)

A. Each partner was asked to describe the elements of the current relationship that they would like to improve.

B. Active listening was used as the clients identified a variety of elements of the current relationship that are problems within the relationship.

C. The partners were confronted when they identified only areas in which the other partner should make improvements.

D. The partners were reinforced as they described elements of the relationship that they can take personal responsibility for improving.

8. List Changes to Improve Relationship (8)

A. Each partner was assigned to list changes for self and the other that would improve their relationship.

B. The partners were administered the Areas of Change Questionnaire (Weiss and Birchler).

C. The list of changes for self and the other that would improve the relationship were reviewed within the session.

9. Identify Replacing Problem with Reaction (9)

A. The partners were assisted in identifying instances where their definition of, or reaction to, a problem became the main issue.

B. The details of how the argument moved from the problem to the definition of it or reaction to it were identified.

C. The partners were provided with examples of how the definition or reaction to a problem can become the main issue.

10. Provide Feedback on Coping Strengths and Weaknesses (10)

A. The partners were provided with feedback about their strengths and weaknesses.

B. The partners were provided with feedback about how strengths or tolerated weaknesses are now perceived as problems.

11. Teach Reactions as Understandable (11)

A. The partners were taught that the other's emotional and behavioral reactions are understandable, given their respective perceptions on the problem.

B. The partners were provided with examples of how understandable emotional and behavioral reactions can often cause further problems.

C. The partners were reinforced for seeing that the other partner is reacting in an understandable manner.

D. The partners were helped to see that their understandable emotional and behavioral reactions are ultimately self-defeating.

12. Emphasize Forced Solutions as Worsening the Relationship (12)

A. Emphasis was placed on how each partner forcing the other to change causes the problems to become worse.

B. The partners were provided with specific examples of how forcing the other to change can cause the problems to become worse.

C. Each partner was asked to provide their own perspective on how forcing the other to change causes more problems.

13. Suggest Need for Accepting and Tolerating Each Other (13)

A. It was suggested to the partners that healing will only occur when they return to where all couples start a relationship by accepting the other's strengths and tolerating the weaknesses.

B. Discussion was directed regarding the need to accept the other's strengths and tolerate the weaknesses.

C. The partners were reinforced for agreeing with the need to accept the other's strengths and tolerate the weaknesses.

D. The partners indicated little interest in accepting the other's strengths and tolerating weaknesses and they were encouraged to review this further.

14. Present Pain Equations (14)

A. The partners were presented with the following equation: Pain + Accusation = Relationship discord.

B. The partners were also presented with the following equation: Pain − Accusation = Acceptance.

C. The couple was asked to discuss the implication of the emotional pain equations for their relationship.

D. The partners applied the emotional pain equations to their relationship in a positive manner.

E. The partners did not see the relevance of the emotional pain equations to their relationship.

15. Discourage Speaking for Other (15)

A. Each partner was encouraged to express only his or her own thoughts and feelings and not to presume to know or speak for the other's thoughts and feelings.

B. The partners were encouraged to avoid blame and mind-reading of the other partner.

C. The partners were confronted when presuming to know or to speak for the other's thoughts and feelings.

D. Positive feedback was provided to the partners for focusing only on their own thoughts and feelings and not presuming to know or to speak for the other's thoughts and feelings.

E. The partners continued to mind-read each other, and were provided with additional feedback in this area.

16. Teach about Hard and Soft Emotions (16)

A. Hard emotions were defined as protective emotions such as anger, retribution, and resentment.

B. Soft emotions were defined as vulnerable emotions such as hurt, insecurity, and fear.

C. The partners were taught the different consequences of expressing hard versus soft emotions.

D. Positive feedback was provided as the partners displayed a clearer understanding of the difference between hard and soft emotions.

E. The partners struggled to identify the difference between hard and soft emotions and were redirected in this area.

17. Replace Hard Emotions with Soft Emotions (17)

A. When a partner expressed a hard emotion, redirection was provided to identify the soft emotion that underlies the hard emotion.

B. Positive feedback was provided to the partner for identifying the soft emotions that underlie the hard emotions.

C. The partner struggled to identify the soft emotions that underlie the hard emotions and were provided with tentative feedback in this area.

18. Direct Paraphrasing of Soft Emotions (18)

A. The listening partner was encouraged to paraphrase or reflect the other partner's disclosure of soft emotions.

B. The partner expressing emotions was asked to validate the other partner's paraphrasing of the emotions.

C. Positive feedback was provided to a partner for accurately paraphrasing the other partner's soft emotions.

D. The listening partner failed to correctly paraphrase the other partner's exposure of soft emotions and was provided with tentative feedback in this area.

19. Discuss Trait Differences (19)

A. The partners were guided in a discussion of central trait differences between them.

B. The partners were assisted in identifying the ways in which their central trait differences have been causing problems (e.g., one partner is solution oriented and one is expression oriented).

C. The partners were reinforced for showing more tolerance for their central trait differences.

20. Apply Trait Differences to Problem Areas (20)

A. The partners were directed to identify how behavioral and emotional problems resulting from their central trait differences will likely cause difficulty during an event that will be occurring in the near future.

B. The partners identified events occurring in the near future and realistically predicted how central trait differences might cause behavioral and emotional problems; they were provided with positive feedback in this area.

C. The partners were provided with specific examples of how central trait differences can be applied to problem areas.

21. Encourage Acceptance of Trait Differences (21)

A. The partners were encouraged to accept the inevitability of their trait differences.

B. The partners were led in a discussion of what they can do to reduce the level of conflict, given that trait differences are not going away.

C. The partners were reinforced for expressing acceptance of their trait differences.

D. The partners have not accepted the inevitability of trait differences and were provided with feedback and encouragement in this area.

22. Track Successful Adaptation (22)

A. The partners reported that they handled a conflict well at home and were asked to specifically elucidate what they thought or did differently that caused the situation to improve.

B. As the partners identified specific thoughts or behaviors that helped to handle a conflict at home, their patterns were identified.

23. Track Problematic Responses (23)

A. The partners reported that a conflict was handled poorly at home and were asked to identify specific respective thoughts, behaviors, and hard emotions that contributed to the difficulty.

B. The partners were provided with feedback about patterns of problem thoughts, behaviors, and hard emotions that contributed to the difficulties.

24. Externalize Problem (24)

A. The problematic interaction patterns were reframed as an external problem, rather that as the fault of either partner.

B. The partners were supported for their acceptance of the reframing of their problematic interaction patterns as an external problem.

C. The partners continued to place significant blame for the problem and were redirected to externalize the problem.

25. Describe Positive Features of Problematic Behaviors (25)

A. One partner was asked to describe the positive features of the other partner's problematic behavior, while the other partner listened.

B. One partner was able to identify the ways in which the other partner's problematic behavior actually serves a positive function in the relationship and positive feedback was provided in this area.

C. The listening partner was asked to, in turn, identify the positive feature of the other partner's problematic behavior.
D. The partners were provided with specific examples of how problematic behavior serves a positive function in the relationship.

26. Reframe Problematic Behavior as a Balance (26)

A. The partners' problematic behaviors were reframed in terms of how they balance the relationship.
B. The partners were provided with specific examples of how problematic behaviors can balance a relationship (e.g., a hyper-responsible man may get involved with a spontaneous woman).
C. The partners identified how each other's problematic behavior balances their own behavior and positive feedback was provided in this area.

27. Explain Benefits of Balancing Behaviors (27)

A. It was explained to the clients that they each are bringing only one part of the balancing act to the relationship.
B. The partners were asked whether there is anything that they can learn from the other partner's opposite, but balancing, behavior that formerly has caused consternation.
C. As the partners identified that they can learn from the each other's formerly upsetting behaviors, they were provided with feedback and encouragement.
D. The partners were unable to identify any positive learning from their partner's opposite, but balancing, behavior and were provided with specific examples based on the therapist's observations.

28. Predict Relapse (28)

A. It was explained to the partners that no matter how they try to improve, they would sometimes fall back into their well-practiced, old patterns.
B. The partners were advised to prepare for relapse into old patterns and not to be too surprised or disappointed when the inevitable occurs.
C. The partners indicated that they have sometimes fallen back into their well-practiced, old patterns, but were well-prepared for them and this was processed.
D. The partners were not prepared for relapses and were provided with additional feedback and direction in this area.

29. Practice Relapses (29)

A. The couple was directed to practice falling back into their old patterns in the session.
B. Each partner was asked to express thoughts and feelings about the problematic interactions.
C. The therapist emphasized the naturalness of each person's perspective and response.

30. Assign Relapses (30)

A. The partners were assigned to each enact or practice problematic behaviors several times during the week to get a sense of the pattern when not already upset.
B. The partners reported practicing relapsing through the week and what they have learned was processed.
C. The partners have not practiced relapses and were redirected to do so.

31. Stop Practicing from Becoming a Real Argument (31)

A. Each partner was assigned to let the other in on the problem practice sessions soon after the argument ensued to prevent further escalation.

B. The partners noted that when told that the other had been practicing the problematic behavior, they were able to easily discontinue the argument and were praised for this.

C. The partners reported that they continued to argue even after the partner had notified that they had been practicing, and they were directed to discontinue practice in this setting.

D. The partners reported a general decrease in arguments as they expected that the other partner was only practicing problematic behaviors and this beneficial outcome was reinforced.

32. Practice Problem Behaviors in Session (32)

A. The partners were asked to take turns practicing problematic behaviors in session.

B. Emotional reactions to the problem behaviors were reviewed and discussed.

33. Review Homework (33)

A. The homework practice of problematic behaviors was reviewed in session.

B. The partners' emotional reaction to the homework of problematic behaviors was reviewed within the session.

C. The partners have not completed the homework of problematic behaviors and were redirected to do so.

34. Identify Needs to Be Met Outside of the Relationship (34)

A. The clients were assisted in identifying acceptable ways of satisfying needs outside of the relationship.

B. It was noted that the use of outside relationships could reduce the pressure on the relationship to meet all of the couple's core needs.

C. The partners identified mutually acceptable ways of satisfying needs outside of the relationship, and these were reviewed and supported.

D. The partners were unable to identify any acceptable ways of satisfying needs outside of the relationship and were provided with additional feedback in this area.

35. List Ways to Satisfy Soft Emotions (35)

A. The clients were directed to list ways in which they could satisfy needs arising from soft emotions (e.g., relief from hurt or fear) within the relationship.

B. The partners identified ways in which they satisfy needs arising from soft emotions without resorting to destructive, hard emotion-laced escalation, and these were reviewed within the session.

C. The partners failed to identify helpful ways to satisfy soft emotions and were provided with additional feedback in this area.

36. Rehearse Alternative Means of Meeting Soft Emotions (36)

A. The clients were directed to rehearse, in session, alternative means of meeting needs arising from their soft emotions.

B. The clients rehearsed the alternative means of meeting needs arising from their soft emotions and were provided with positive feedback.

JEALOUSY

CLIENT PRESENTATION

1. Fear of Losing Partner to a Rival (1)[*]

A. The client identified concerns about losing his/her partner's affection, attention, and love to a rival.

B. One of the partners identified a fear of losing the other partner's affection, attention, and love to a rival.

C. One partner has identified specific concerns about the other partner's involvement with a rival.

D. As treatment has progressed, the partners described decreased concerns about loss of affection, attention, and love to a rival.

2. Obsessive Thoughts (2)

A. The jealous partner described obsessive thoughts about the other partner being with another person and being verbally and/or physically intimate with that person.

B. The jealous partner identified an inability to stop the obsessive thoughts about the other partner being verbally or physically intimate with another.

C. The jealous partner has greatly decreased the pattern of obsessive thoughts, and reports an ability to control and limit these types of thoughts.

D. The jealous partner described a discontinuation of the obsessive thoughts regarding the other partner being verbally and/or physically intimate with another person.

3. Frequent Accusations (2)

A. The jealous partner frequently makes accusations about the other partner being with another person and being verbally and/or physically intimate with that person.

B. The partners described frequent accusations and long arguments about issues related to fidelity.

C. As treatment has progressed, accusations about the partner being verbally and/or physically intimate with another person have been significantly decreased.

D. No accusations regarding partner infidelity have been made recently.

4. Monitoring Partner's Activities (3)

A. The jealous partner described a pattern of monitoring the other partner's activities (e.g., mileage, appointments, travel, money spent) based on suspicion of the partner having an affair.

B. The jealous partner often focuses on inconsistencies in the partner's activities as evidence of that partner having an affair.

C. The jealous partner has demonstrated an increase in trust regarding the other partner's activities.

[*]The numbers in parentheses on Client Presentation pages correlate to the number of the Behavioral Definition statement in the companion chapter with the same title in *The Couples Psychotherapy Treatment Planner* (Jongsma, O'Leary, and Heyman) by John Wiley & Sons, 1998. The numbers in parentheses on the Interventions Implemented page correspond to the number of the Therapeutic Intervention statement in the companion chapter in the same book.

5. Control over Partner's Activities (4)

A. The jealous partner often attempts to control the other partner's actions.

B. The jealous partner often demands that the partner stay at home, limits the amount of money available to the partner, or does other controlling actions to restrict the other partner's activity.

C. The controlling partner is fearful of losing the other partner's attention.

D. As the partners have made progress, the jealous partner has shown a decreased pattern of attempting to control the other partner's freedom.

6. Anger Regarding Disloyalty (5)

A. The jealous partner described feelings of anger regarding a perceived loss of face to friends and family because the other partner did not show enough loyalty or attention.

B. The partner without jealousy problems described a pattern of the jealous partner reacting negatively to a perceived loss of face to friends and family because the nonjealous partner did not show enough loyalty or attention.

C. The jealous partner has become more realistic regarding the level of loyalty or attention that the other partner displays.

7. Periodic Angry Outbursts (6)

A. The jealous partner often engages in angry outbursts directed at the partner.

B. The jealous partner has often shouted and derided the other partner.

C. As the level of jealousy has decreased, the angry outbursts have decreased in intensity and frequency.

D. The jealous partner has not engaged in angry outbursts recently.

8. Blames Partner (7)

A. The jealous partner often blames the other partner for not being trustworthy or honest.

B. The jealous partner often projects feelings of dishonesty or untrustworthiness onto the other partner.

C. The partners often argue about the level of trust and honesty within the relationship.

D. As the partners have worked through jealousy issues, the issues of blame, trustworthiness and honesty have decreased.

9. Depression (8)

A. The jealous partner described feelings of depression regarding a perceived loss of the partner's attention, affection, and love.

B. The jealous partner presents with a recurrent pattern of depression.

C. The jealous partner displays symptoms of depression including sleep and appetite changes; irritability; sadness; lack of energy; and feelings of worthlessness, hopelessness, and helplessness.

D. As treatment has progressed, the jealous partner's pattern of depression symptoms has significantly decreased.

E. The jealous partner reports experiencing no symptoms of depression.

10. Fear of Loneliness (9)

A. The jealous partner described fears of being left alone.
B. The jealous partner described worries about not being able to cope if the other partner leaves the relationship for another.
C. As the jealous partner has become more secure in the relationship, fears of being left alone and not being able to cope have decreased.
D. The jealous partner has come to feel more at ease with the possibility of being left alone.

11. General Anxiety (10)

A. The jealous partner described a pattern of general anxiety.
B. The jealous partner experiences periodic physiological symptoms of anxiety (e.g., sleep disturbance, rapid heart beat, tightness of chest, sweating, shortness of breath, dizziness, shakiness, and an empty feeling in the stomach).
C. As the couple has progressed in treatment, anxiety symptoms have decreased.

INTERVENTIONS IMPLEMENTED

1. Inquire about Jealousy (1)

A. The jealous partner was asked to describe feelings of jealousy.
B. The jealous partner was asked to identify feelings of jealousy that are irrational.
C. The jealous partner was not able to see jealous feelings as irrational and was provided with feedback on this issue.
D. The jealous partner was reinforced for identifying both rational and irrational feelings of jealousy.
E. The jealous partner denied any feelings of jealousy and was provided with tentative feedback in this area.

2. Ask Partner about Jealousy (2)

A. The nonjealous partner was asked to describe what seemed to be rational feelings of jealousy from the partner.
B. The nonjealous partner was asked to describe what seemed to be irrational feelings of jealousy from the partner.
C. The nonjealous partner was provided with feedback regarding identified rational and irrational feelings of jealousy that are displayed by the jealous partner.
D. The nonjealous partner was quite cautious about providing information about the rational and irrational feelings of jealousy from the jealous partner and was provided with support and encouragement.

3. Describe Jealous Behaviors (3)

A. The nonjealous partner was asked to describe the jealous behaviors displayed by the jealous partner.
B. The nonjealous partner was provided with feedback regarding identified patterns of jealous behavior.

4. Describe Controlling Behaviors (4)

A. The nonjealous partner was asked to describe the controlling behaviors displayed by the jealous partner.

B. The nonjealous partner was provided with feedback regarding identified patterns of controlling behavior.

5. Confirm Jealous/Controlling Behaviors (5)

A. The jealous partner was asked to confirm the jealous and controlling behaviors described by the nonjealous partner.

B. The jealous partner was encouraged to clarify or more clearly define the jealous and controlling behaviors described by the nonjealous partner.

C. The jealous partner was reinforced for acknowledging the jealous and controlling behaviors described by the nonjealous partner.

D. The jealous partner denied any pattern of jealous and controlling behaviors and was provided with additional feedback in this area.

6. Prioritize Jealousy-Provoking Behavior (6)

A. The jealous client was asked to prioritize the behaviors that the nonjealous partner can change to minimize jealous reactions.

B. Feedback was provided to the jealous client regarding realistic changes that the nonjealous partner can make to minimize feelings of jealousy.

7. Encourage Reconsideration of Inappropriate Demands (7)

A. The jealous partner was identified as making irrational or overly demanding requests for change from the partner.

B. The jealous partner was encouraged to reconsider inappropriate, irrational, or over-demanding requests for change from the partner.

C. Feedback was provided to the jealous partner as irrational or overly demanding requests were modified to more rational and appropriate expectations.

D. The jealous partner denied any requests as being irrational or overly demanding and was provided with additional feedback in this area.

8. Develop Agreement to Minimize Jealousy (8)

A. The partners were encouraged to jointly conclude which behaviors would be reasonable to change for reaching the goal of minimizing jealousy.

B. The partners were provided with feedback about the behaviors that they have jointly concluded to be reasonable to change for reaching the goal of minimizing jealousy.

C. The partners have developed unrealistic expectations of how to minimize jealousy and were given more realistic feedback in this area.

D. The partners were unable to jointly conclude which behaviors would be reasonable to change for reaching the goal of minimizing jealousy and were provided with assistance with arbitrating these differences.

9. Clarify Feelings/Reasons for Jealousy (9)

A. The jealous partner's reasons for jealous feelings were explored.
B. The client was encouraged and allowed to express anger toward the partner to the therapist as often as necessary.
C. An emphasis was placed on providing understanding about how the jealous partner feels.
D. Individual sessions were held to process the jealous partner's reasons for feeling jealous and having emotions related to the jealousy.
E. Time was taken during the conjoint sessions to allow the client to express anger to the partner.

10. Explore Precursors to Distrust (10)

A. The jealous partner's history of hurt and abandonment were explored.
B. The jealous partner was assisted in resolving feelings of hurt and abandonment that contribute to current feelings of distrust.
C. The jealous partner was supported for describing a sense of moving on from the past instances of hurt and abandonment.
D. The jealous partner denied any history of hurt and abandonment that might contribute to current unreasonable feelings of distrust, and this was interpreted as a defense mechanism.

11. Separate Past Hurts from Current Needs (11)

A. The jealous partner was assisted in separating feelings over past hurts from other people and the reaction of trying to protect self from hurt from the current partner.
B. The jealous partner was assisted in developing insight regarding how past hurts from other people prompt the desire to protect self from hurt with current partner.
C. The jealous partner was reinforced for acknowledging that jealousy is based on past hurts that are unrelated to the current partner.
D. The jealous partner seems to continue to have a difficult time separating past hurts from the current behavior of the partner and was provided with specific feedback in this area.

12. Identify Current Hurts (12)

A. The jealous partner was assisted in identifying hurts from the current partner that have fueled feelings of jealousy and distrust.
B. Specific experiences of hurt from the current relationship were identified as fueling the feelings of jealousy and distrust and these experiences were processed.

13. Begin Process of Forgiveness (13)

A. The jealous client was encouraged to begin a process of forgiveness from past hurts from the partner.
B. The jealous client was recommended to read material on forgiveness.
C. The jealous partner was recommended to read *Forgive and Forget* (Smedes) and *How Good Do We Have to Be*? (Kushner).
D. The jealous client was urged to renew feelings of trust.

14. Focus on Here and Now (14)

A. Both partners were encouraged to focus on the here and now so as to minimize emphasis on past hurts and problems.

B. It was pointed out that the partners do not have to forget past wrongs, but each should try to work toward the future.

C. Both partners were reinforced for acknowledging the need to focus on the here and now instead of past hurts and problems.

15. Encourage Acceptance for Satisfaction (15)

A. Each partner was encouraged to accept some responsibility for both satisfaction and dissatisfaction within the relationship.

B. Positive reinforcement was provided when each partner displayed acceptance of responsibility for satisfaction or dissatisfaction within the relationship.

16. Identify Contributions to Dissatisfaction (16)

A. The nonjealous client was asked to describe personal actions that may have led to the jealous partner's dissatisfaction.

B. The jealous client was asked to describe personal behaviors that have led to dissatisfaction.

C. The partners' description of behaviors that have led to the jealous partner's dissatisfaction were summarized and presented for validation.

D. The partners were supported as they validated the identification of specific patterns of actions that have led to the jealous partner's dissatisfaction.

17. Identify Relationship Improvements (17)

A. The nonjealous partner was asked to describe personal changes that could make the relationship better.

B. The jealous partner was asked to describe personal changes that could make the relationship better.

C. Patterns of changes that could make the relationship better were identified and presented to the clients.

18. Encourage Appreciated Behaviors (18)

A. The nonjealous client was encouraged to engage in some behaviors that would be appreciated by the other partner.

B. The nonjealous client was assisted in developing clear examples of ways to help the partner reduce jealousy.

C. The nonjealous client has declined to engage in behaviors that would be appreciated by the partner and was redirected in this area.

D. Although the nonjealous client has engaged in behaviors expected to be appreciated by the partner, the jealous partner continues to display significant jealousy, and this was reflected to them.

19. Remind about Minimizing Blame (19)

A. The partners were reminded about the desirability of minimizing blame toward each other.

B. The partners were specifically focused on decreasing the hostile expression of blame.

20. Develop Basic Rules of Freedom (20)

A. Each partner was asked to describe the basic rules of how committed partners should behave when around people of the opposite sex.

B. Each partner was asked to express the degree of individual freedom that each partner should have within the relationship.

C. The partners were supported for citing realistic descriptions of basic rules for committed partners and the level of freedom that should be experienced.

D. Each partner described very different expectations regarding how partners should behave with others, and the level of individual freedom each should have, and they were assisted in resolving some of these differences.

21. Teach about Relationship Rules Changing (21)

A. The partners were informed that the basic rules of the relationship may have to be altered if the life situations of one or both partners have changed markedly since the relationship began.

B. The partners were provided with specific examples of life stage changes that alter basic rules of a relationship (e.g., when a stay-at-home parent enters college or a workplace setting).

C. The partners were reinforced for their clear understanding of how the basic rules of a relationship may have to change, and this was supported.

D. The partners were assisted in identifying how their life situation has required a change in the basic rules of their relationship.

22. Stress Need for Emotional Intimacy Rules (22)

A. It was stressed to the partners that there is a need for general agreement about the rules regarding emotional intimacy with others.

B. It was pointed out that violations of emotional intimacy rules are a violation of trust.

C. The partners agreed about the level of emotional intimacy expected with others and were provided with positive feedback about their realistic expectations in this area.

23. Caution about Retaliation (23)

A. The nonjealous partner was cautioned about retaliating when targeted for intermittent outbursts of anger by the other partner.

B. The nonjealous partner was assisted in identifying when there is some rational basis for the jealousy, and encouraged to take this into account when the jealous partner displays anger.

C. The nonjealous partner endorsed the need to be cautious about retaliation and was encouraged for this helpful support of the jealous partner.

D. The nonjealous partner declined to withhold retaliation when the jealous partner becomes angry and was provided with additional feedback in this area.

24. Confront Flaunting (24)

A. The nonjealous partner was confronted about being insensitive to the jealous partner's insecurity by openly flaunting behaviors that are threatening to the relationship.

B. The nonjealous partner was reinforced for accepting the need to alter behavior that is reasonably viewed by the jealous partner as a potential threat to the relationship.

C. The nonjealous partner rejected the need to change flaunting behaviors and was provided with additional redirection in this area.

25. Encourage Positive Feedback (25)

A. The nonjealous partner was encouraged to provide reasonably frequent positive feedback to the other partner.

B. The nonjealous partner was requested to focus positive attention on issues that may lessen the partner's insecurity.

26. Educate about Process of Recovery (26)

A. The partners were informed that coping with problems of jealousy often takes an extended period of time.

B. The nonjealous partner was told to be prepared for coping with occasional setbacks.

C. The partners were reinforced for their clear understanding of the long time usually required for recovery from jealousy issues.

D. The partners continued to expect immediate changes in the jealousy problems and were provided with feedback about this unrealistic expectation.

JOB STRESS

CLIENT PRESENTATION

1. Lack of Respect and Support of Supervisor (1)*

A. The client described a pattern of rebellion against and conflict with authority figures within the employment situation.

B. The client often displays a lack of respect for authority figures within the employment situation.

C. The client often fails to support the supervisor.

D. The client's authority conflicts within the employment situation have resulted in dismissal.

E. The client's authority conflicts within the employment situation have resulted in failure to achieve promotions.

F. The client has developed a more accepting attitude toward authority and is willing to take direction within the employment arena.

2. Worry about Being Replaced (2)

A. The client reported severe feelings of anxiety related to perceived job jeopardy.

B. The client's employer indicated the likelihood of replacing higher salaried people with lower salaried individuals.

C. The client's negative perception regarding job stability has been reversed via consultation with the supervisor and reassurances of job security.

D. The client has begun to develop an alternative plan of action to prepare for possible job loss.

3. Frustration Regarding Competition (3)

A. The client reported a pattern of frustration and helplessness stemming from a competing company's product that could replace the mainstay product of the client's employer.

B. The client often complains about the concern that a competing company would put the client's company out of business.

C. The client feels less frustrated and helpless due to making a plan of action for the problems created by competition.

D. The client reports a decreased level of concern that a competing company could put the client's employer out of business.

4. Highly Critical Supervisor (4)

A. The client reported feelings of anxiety and depression secondary to experiencing a high level of criticism from the supervisor.

B. The client has become more withdrawn and isolated within the work environment due to supervisor conflict.

C. The client has begun to resolve conflicts with the supervisor, and this has resulted in an improved emotional state.

D. The client reported feeling comfortable with and enjoying interaction with the supervisor.

*The numbers in parentheses on Client Presentation pages correlate to the number of the Behavioral Definition statement in the companion chapter with the same title in *The Couples Psychotherapy Treatment Planner* (Jongsma, O'Leary, and Heyman) by John Wiley & Sons, 1998. The numbers in parentheses on the Interventions Implemented page correspond to the number of the Therapeutic Intervention statement in the companion chapter in the same book.

5. Decreased Salary (5)

A. The client reported a decrease in salary due to a decrease in profits.
B. The client reported anxiety due to decreased salary or wages.
C. The client has developed a specific plan for coping with reduction of income.
D. The client is more accepting of the current level of compensation.

6. Fear of Technology (6)

A. The client is anxious about being unable to master the employer's new computer software system.
B. The client tends to obsess about the struggles and unknowns related to the employer's technological advances.
C. The client is seeking appropriate help for gaining a better understanding of the employer's technology needs.
D. The client reports being confident about the challenge of new technology.

7. Office Move (7)

A. The client reported being concern about being moved to a less desirable office.
B. The client described anguish related to the loss of status associated with being moved to a less desirable office.
C. The client is more accepting of changes in office assignment, status, and so forth.

8. Depression Due to Job Loss (8)

A. The client has been fired.
B. The client has been laid off.
C. The client reported feelings of depression secondary to losing employment.
D. The client's feelings of depression related to loss of employment have diminished, and the client is developing a plan of seeking new employment.

9. Coworker Conflict (9)

A. The client reported feelings of anxiety and depression secondary to experiencing perceived harassment, shunning, and confrontation from coworkers.
B. The client has become more withdrawn and isolated within the work environment due to coworker conflict.
C. The client has begun to resolve conflicts with coworkers, and this has resulted in an improved emotional state.
D. The client reported feeling comfortable with and enjoying interaction with coworkers.

10. Lack of Recognition (10)

A. The client believes that occupational excellence and hard work is neither recognized nor rewarded by the employer.
B. The client sighted specific examples where excellence and hard work have not been recognized or rewarded.
C. The client experiences anxiety, frustration, and anger due to the lack of recognition or reward for hard work.

D. The client is taking steps toward gaining greater recognition and reward with the present employer.
E. The client is seeking other employment in search of greater recognition and reward.
F. The client feels more appropriately recognized and rewarded for excellence and hard work.
G. The client is more accepting of the lack of recognition and reward from outside sources and focuses on the internal, positive feelings resulting from good work.

11. Salary Discrimination (11)

A. The client described feelings of being discriminated against in terms of salary.
B. The client believes that the compensation provided by the employer is less than what is deserved for the level of work performed.
C. The client is taking assertive steps to obtain more appropriate compensation.
D. The client is more comfortable with the level of compensation provided by the employer.

12. Depression Symptoms (12)

A. The client reported intermittent feelings of depression related to the level of job stress, including low energy and other endogenous and exogenous symptoms of depression.
B. The client reports a pattern of sleep disturbance due to the level of job stress.
C. As the client's level of job stress has decreased, the pattern of depression symptoms has lifted.

13. Decreased Interest in Sex (13)

A. The partner experiencing job stress has reported a decreased interest in sexual interactions.
B. The partner experiencing job stress appears to be so preoccupied with these concerns so as to limit interest in sexual interactions.
C. As job stress has decreased, the partner's level of sexual interaction has increased.
D. Although job stress remains, the couple's level of sexual interaction has returned to a normal level, and the couple uses this as a way to communicate affection and support.

14. Anger Outbursts (14)

A. The partner with the job stress frequently has anger outbursts.
B. The partner with the job stress tends to take out anger and other negative emotions on the other partner, resulting in unkind comments and arguments.
C. As the level of job stress has decreased, anger expression has become controlled.

INTERVENTIONS IMPLEMENTED

1. List Work Stressors (1)

A. The client was asked to list all the work-related factors that prompt feelings of depression, anger, or discouragement.
B. The client was assisted in developing a list of work-related factors that prompt depression, anger, and discouragement.

C. The client was provided with support and empathy as the list of work-related stressors was reviewed and processed.

2. Rank Order Employment Stressors Creating Depression (2)

A. The client was directed to rank order the employment factors that are most significant in prompting depression.
B. The client was assisted in rank ordering the employment factors that are most significant in prompting depression.
C. The client has developed a taxonomy of employment factors that are most significant in prompting depression, and these were reviewed and processed.

3. Develop Coping Plan (3)

A. The client was directed to develop a plan to address coping with (versus solving) the most important work-related stressors.
B. The client was reinforced for developing a specific plan to address coping with the most important work related stressors; additional ideas were provided.
C. The client was provided with specific coping skills to help deal with the most important work-related stressors (e.g., increased recreational diversions, relaxation and deep-breathing techniques, physical exercise, assertiveness training, job transfer).

4. Request Partner Rank Causes of Depression (4)

A. The client's partner was asked to rank order the perceived causes and associated factors of depression in the job-stressed client.
B. The partner has rank ordered the perceived causes of depression in the job-stressed client, and these were reviewed and processed within the session.
C. The partner was reinforced for providing helpful insights into the job-stressed client's emotional functioning.

5. List Work Stressors Creating Anger (5)

A. The client was asked to list all the work-related factors that prompt feelings of anger.
B. The client was assisted in developing a list of work-related factors that create anger.
C. The client was provided with support and encouragement as the list of work-related stressors was reviewed and processed.

6. Rank Order Employment Stressors Prompting Anger (6)

A. The client was directed to rank order the employment factors that are most significant in prompting anger.
B. The client was assisted in rank ordering the employment factors that are most significant in prompting anger.
C. The client has developed a taxonomy of employment factors that are most significant in prompting anger, and these were reviewed and processed.

7. Develop Coping Plan for Anger Issues (7)

A. The client was directed to develop a plan to address coping with (versus solving) the most important work-related, anger-producing stressors.

B. The client was reinforced for developing a specific plan to address coping with the most important work-related, anger-producing stressors; additional ideas were provided.
C. The client was provided with specific coping skills to help deal with the work-related causes for anger (e.g., increased communication, assertiveness training, problem pinpointing/resolution training).

8. Request Partner Rank Causes of Anger (8)

A. The client's partner was asked to rank order the perceived causes and associated factors contributing to anger in the job-stressed client.
B. The partner has ranked the perceived causes for anger in the job-stressed client, and these were reviewed and processed within the session.
C. The partner was reinforced for providing helpful insights into the job-stressed client's emotional functioning.

9. Explore Other Emotional Causes (9)

A. The possibility of some cause other than work for the client's unhappiness was explored.
B. The couple identified other problems that may be the primary cause for unhappiness, and these were reviewed and processed.
C. After reviewing possible alternative causes for the client's unhappiness, the couple identified the job-stress as the primary cause for unhappiness.
D. The partners did not give very much importance to other causes for the client's unhappiness and were provided with tentative examples in this area.

10. Refer for Medication Evaluation (10)

A. A referral to a physician was made for the purpose of evaluating the client for a prescription of psychotropic medications.
B. The client has followed through on a referral to a physician and has been assessed for a prescription of psychotropic medications, but none were prescribed.
C. The client has been prescribed psychotropic medications.
D. The client declined evaluation by a physician for a prescription of psychotropic medication and was encouraged to reconsider this need.
E. The client was encouraged to take the medication on a regular basis.

11. Review Medical Leave (11)

A. The advantages and disadvantages of taking medical leave were explored with the client.
B. After careful review, the client has decided to take medical leave to work on stress and emotional struggles.
C. After careful review, the client has decided not to take a medical leave.

12. Review Medical Leave with Partner (12)

A. The use of a medical leave was explored with the client's partner.
B. The client's partner was assisted in reviewing the advantages and disadvantages of a medical leave.
C. The client's partner appeared to be supportive of a medical leave, and this was interpreted to the client.

D. The client's partner did not seem to be supportive of a medical leave, and this was interpreted to the client.

13. Assign Feedback (13)

A. The client was assigned to obtain feedback about job performance from supervisor and peers.
B. After a review of the client's current situation, it was determined that obtaining feedback about job performance from supervisors and peers is not practical.
C. The client has obtained feedback about job performance from supervisor and peers, and this was reviewed and processed.

14. Assess Technical Proficiency (14)

A. The client was asked to assess the technical aspects of the job.
B. After careful review, the client has assessed that he/she is able to perform the technical aspects of the job.
C. After careful review, the client has assessed that he/she is not able to perform the technical aspects of the job.

15. Develop Partner Support (15)

A. The client was directed to advise his/her partner on how the partner can best support him/her during the next few months to assist in coping with job stress.
B. Within the session, feedback was provided as the client practiced advising the partner on how the partner can best support him/her during the next few months to assist in coping with job stress.
C. The partner's understanding of how to best support the client during the next few months was reviewed and processed.
D. The client identified that the partner has been much more helpful in coping with job stress, and the positive aspects of this were reviewed.

16. Explore Increased Partner Financial Support (16)

A. The possibility of increased financial support from the nonjob-stressed partner was explored.
B. The job-stressed partner reacted negatively to requesting more financial support from the nonjob-stressed partner, and this was reviewed.
C. The couple identified that the nonjob-stressed partner could provide increased financial support, and it was agreed to pursue this option.
D. It was noted that the nonjob-stressed partner is unable to provide more financial support, and this was accepted.

17. Review for Job Skills (17)

A. The client was referred to an agency that can provide assessment regarding job skills.
B. The client was referred to an agency that can provide job-skill training.
C. The client has been assessed and will begin job-skill training.
D. The client has not followed up on a job-skill assessment and training and was redirected to do so.

18. Refer for Education (18)

A. The client was referred to an educational institution with a curriculum that could enhance job skills.

B. The client was referred to an educational institution with a curriculum that could enable the client to obtain a new degree or certification.

C. The client has sought out additional educational opportunities and reports a decreased sense of stress due to these positive steps.

D. The client has begun classes, but reports an increased pattern of stress due to this new responsibility and was encouraged to stick with this time-limited stressor.

E. The client has not sought out educational opportunities and was redirected toward these.

19. Obtain Commitment for Further Training/Education (19)

A. The client's plan for further training or education was reviewed and processed.

B. The client was supported and encouraged for taking responsibility for obtaining further training or education.

C. The client was reinforced for implementation of a proactive plan to obtain further training or education.

D. The client has not verbally committed to further training or education and was directly asked to do so.

20. Support Education Plan (20)

A. The client was supported and encouraged as he/she pursued an education to resolve the employment conflicts.

B. The client was encouraged to share his/her emotions as he/she entered the educational system.

C. The client was confronted on not being consistent regarding pursuing further training and was redirected to pursue this more diligently.

21. Explore Alternative Jobs (21)

A. The alternative jobs that would be available upon completion of a course of study were explored with the client.

B. The client was assisted in reviewing the variety of employment situations that may be of interest upon completion of the course of study.

C. The client was reinforced for verbalizing and understanding the options available upon completion of studies.

22. Assign Positive Statements (22)

A. The client was asked to make one positive statement to someone at work each day about the work and/or work environment.

B. Support and encouragement were provided to the client for following through on making positive statements about the work and work environment on a daily basis and recording them.

C. The client has developed a pattern of describing the work and work setting in a more positive manner, and the benefits of this were processed.

D. The client has not followed through on making one positive statement about work or the work setting and was encouraged to do so.

23. Assign Positive Comments Told to Partner (23)

A. The client was asked to make one positive statement to the partner each day about the work and/or work environment.
B. Support and encouragement were provided to the client for following through on making positive statements about the work and work environment on a daily basis and recording them.
C. The client has developed a pattern of describing the work and work setting to the partner in a more positive manner, and the benefits of this were processed.
D. The client has not followed through on making one positive statement about work or the work setting to the other partner and was encouraged to do so.

24. Assign Partner Support (24)

A. The client's partner was assigned to support the client's affirmations of the positive aspects of work.
B. The client's partner was asked to provide additional positive perspectives on the client's work.
C. The couple reported increased affirmation of positive aspects of work by both the client and the partner; the benefits of this approach were reviewed.
D. The partners have not affirmed positive aspects of work and were redirected to focus on this area.

25. Counsel about Negative Comments (25)

A. The client and partner were advised to avoid making negative comments about work to colleagues.
B. The client and partner were supported for endorsing the wisdom of not making negative comments about work to colleagues.
C. The client reported a more positive outlook and better relationships at work due to discontinuing making negative comments about work to colleagues.
D. The client continues to make negative comments about work to colleagues and was redirected in this area.

26. Assign Partner to Reinforce Decreased Negative Comments (26)

A. The client's partner was assigned to support the client when he/she refrains from making negative comments about work.
B. The couple reported a decrease in negative comments about work by both the client and the partner; the benefits of this approach were reviewed.
C. The partners have not decreased their negative comments about work and were redirected to focus on this area.

27. List Advantages of Reducing Complaints (27)

A. The client was asked to list advantages of reducing complaining and critical comments about the work situation.

B. The client identified several advantages of reducing complaining about the work situation, and these were processed within the session.
C. The client's partner was asked to identify the advantages of reducing complaining and critical comments about the work situation.
D. The client's partner identified several advantages of reducing complaining and critical comments about the work situation, and these were processed.
E. The client and partner did not fully comprehend the advantages of discontinuing the negative comments about the work situation and were provided with additional feedback in this area.

28. Explore Improvements in Workspace (28)

A. The client was asked to explore possible acceptable ways of making the workspace or office more pleasant or attractive.
B. The client's ideas regarding how to make the workspace more pleasant and attractive were reviewed and elaborated on.
C. The client has implemented workspace changes, and the advantages of these changes were reviewed.
D. The client has not made changes in his/her workspace or office and was redirected to do so.

29. Encourage Decorating (29)

A. The client was directed and encouraged to take something attractive to work to decorate the office.
B. The client has decorated the office and was provided with positive feedback for making this change.
C. The client has not decorated the office and was redirected to do so.

30. Encourage Straightening of Office (30)

A. The client was directed and encouraged to straighten up around the office.
B. The client was reinforced for straightening up the office.
C. The client has not straightened up the office and was redirected to do so.

LIFE-CHANGING EVENTS

CLIENT PRESENTATION

1. Individual Distress (1)*

A. One partner identified feelings of anxiety following an environmental event that required adaptation.

B. Anxiety has been experienced by one partner due to the depth of changes that have occurred following a stressful environmental change.

C. Both partners identify a pattern of individual distress following environmental changes.

D. As treatment has progressed, the partners identified better coping skills for environmental changes, and a decrease in feelings of distress.

2. Relationship Distress Regarding Emotional Support (2)

A. The partners described increased relationship distress during the period of transition.

B. The partners identified the inability to support each other emotionally during the transition period.

C. A repeating cycle was identified, including each partner decreasing support due to a perception of decreased support from the other partner.

D. As treatment has progressed, both partners have shown the ability to support each other during the transition period.

3. Arguments Resulting from Transition (3)

A. The partners report persistent arguments over the adaptations that life changes have forced both partners to make.

B. The partners have frequently been at odds with each other and blamed each other for conflict related to life changes.

C. As the couple has adjusted to life changes, the arguments between the partners have decreased.

4. Employment Changes (4)

A. The partners described that the relationship distress has been caused by a change in employment.

B. One partner has had a major change in employment status.

C. As the partner's employment changes have become more stable, relationship distress has decreased.

D. The partners have developed coping skills for the problems within the employment situation.

5. New Child (5)

A. The couple has recently given birth to a child, resulting in significant changes in their lifestyle.

B. The couple has recently adopted a child, resulting in significant changes to their lifestyle.

*The numbers in parentheses on Client Presentation pages correlate to the number of the Behavioral Definition statement in the companion chapter with the same title in *The Couples Psychotherapy Treatment Planner* (Jongsma, O'Leary, and Heyman) by John Wiley & Sons, 1998. The numbers in parentheses on the Interventions Implemented page correspond to the number of the Therapeutic Intervention statement in the companion chapter in the same book.

C. The partners described frequent arguments and other relationship stress caused by the lifestyle changes subsequent to a new child.
D. The partners have adapted to the new child, and no longer are stressed by the changes required.

6. Move to a New Community (6)

A. The partners have recently moved to a new community resulting in severance of existing social support networks.
B. The partners described relationship problems subsequent to a move to a new community.
C. The partners have struggled to establish a new social support network subsequent to severing the existing support network with a move to a new community.
D. Relationship distress has decreased as the couple has adjusted to the new community and developed a social support network.

7. Deteriorating Health (7)

A. The partners described relationship distress related to a debilitating medical condition.
B. The partners have experienced significant lifestyle changes due to a debilitating medical condition, which has resulted in ongoing relationship distress.
C. The partners have adjusted to the medical condition, which has decreased the level of stress on the relationship.

INTERVENTIONS IMPLEMENTED

1. Identify Life-Changing Events (1)

A. Each partner was asked to define the life-changing event that has caused them so much stress.
B. Each partner was asked to identify the meaning of the life-changing event, individually and to the relationship.
C. The partners were provided with emotional support, feedback, and a summarization of the life-changing events and the effect on them individually and to the relationship.

2. Explore Predictability of the Event (2)

A. The partners were asked to identify whether the life-changing event was expected or unexpected.
B. The partners were supported as they identified the life-changing event as one that they expected, which has assisted them in preparing for the event.
C. The partners identified the life-changing event as unexpected, and this was noted to have caused greater consternation for them.

3. Normalize Changes in Life (3)

A. The partners were reminded about the process of change in everyone's life, and that this was a normal expectation.
B. Common changes that occur in the various developmental stages of life were identified and reviewed.

C. The partners were reinforced as they identified their life-changing event as a normal pattern of change within their life stage.

D. It was accepted at face value when the partners denied this life-changing event as within the normal developmental stage of life.

4. Administer Relationship Dissatisfaction Questionnaire (4)

A. The couple was administered a questionnaire/survey to identify each partner's adaptation stage in reaction to the current change stressor.

B. The partners were administered the Stages of Change Questionnaire (Prochaska et al.).

C. The couple was identified as being in one of the four stages of change (e.g., precontemplation, contemplation, action, or maintenance).

D. The results of the questionnaire/survey regarding the stage of adaptation were reviewed in a conjoint session.

5. Review Success Coping Techniques (5)

A. Each partner was asked about ways in which stress has been managed or de-escalated appropriately in the past.

B. The partners were encouraged to implement the techniques previously used to manage or de-escalate stress.

6. Review Counterproductive Coping Techniques (6)

A. Each partner was asked about the counterproductive ways in which stress has been managed in the past.

B. The partners identified negative experiences regarding managing stress in the past, and these were processed.

7. Discuss Positive and Negative Aspects (7)

A. The partners were asked to discuss the positive aspects of the life-changing event.

B. The partners were asked to discuss the negative aspects of the life-changing event.

C. As the partners described the positive and negative aspects of the life-changing event, they were provided with support and encouragement.

D. The partners tended to see the life-changing event in "black-and-white" terms, with all negative connotations and were urged to look for positive portions of the event.

8. Teach about Normal Responses to Life-Changing Events (8)

A. The partners were taught that anxiety and strain are normal responses when coping with life-changing events, regardless of the positive or negative connotations.

B. The partners were taught how anxiety and strain help to develop healthy coping mechanisms for life-changing events.

C. The partners were reinforced for reporting a greater understanding and acceptance of the anxiety and strain that they experience when coping with the life-changing events.

9. Practice Supportive Listening Skills (9)

A. One partner was directed to describe how the life-changing event might have personal positive effects.

B. The other partner was directed to respond to the description of the positive effects with active listening skills (i.e., paraphrasing, reflecting).
C. The partners were provided with feedback about their communication style.

10. Practice Supportive Listening Skills Regarding Negatives (10)

A. One partner was directed to describe how the life-changing event might have personal negative effects.
B. The other partner was directed to respond to the description of the negative effects with active listening skills (i.e., paraphrasing, reflecting).
C. The partners were provided with feedback about their communication style.

11. Identify Positive Effects on Relationship (11)

A. Each partner was asked to describe how the life-changing events might have a positive effect on the relationship.
B. The partners were provided with support and feedback as they identified the positive effects of the life-changing events on the relationship.
C. The partners denied any positive effects and were provided with some tentative examples of the positive effects the life-changing events might have on the relationship.

12. Identify Negative Effects on Relationship (12)

A. Each partner was asked to describe how the life-changing event might have a negative effect on the relationship.
B. The negative effects of the life-changing event on the relationship were processed.
C. The partners denied any negative effects and were provided with some tentative examples of the negative effects the life-changing event might have on the relationship.

13. Identify Day-to-Day Changes (13)

A. The partners were asked to identify the concrete, day-to-day changes that the life-changing event will require.
B. The partners were provided with feedback as they identified the day-to-day effects of the life-changing event.
C. The partners denied any day-to-day effects and were provided with some tentative examples of possible day-to-day effects the life-changing event might have.

14. Identify Short-Term Changes (14)

A. The partners were asked to identify short-term changes that each will need to make to accommodate the life-changing event.
B. The partners were provided with feedback about their identified short-term changes.
C. The partners were provided with feedback about significant areas in which they had not identified the need for life changes.

15. Identify Long-Term Changes (15)

A. The partners were asked to identify long-term changes that each will need to make to accommodate the life-changing event.
B. The partners were provided with feedback about their identified long-term changes.

C. The partners were provided with feedback about significant areas in which they had not identified the need for life changes.

16. **Identify Supportive Behaviors (16)**

A. Each partner was asked to identify supportive behaviors that could be used to develop a smoother transition to the life-changing event.

B. As each partner described supportive behaviors, the other partner was directed to respond using active listening skills.

C. The partners were provided with feedback about supportive behaviors and active listening skills.

17. **Identify Negative Behaviors to Decrease (17)**

A. Each partner was asked to identify negative behaviors that should be discontinued to develop a smoother transition to the life-changing event.

B. As each partner described negative behaviors that should be discontinued, the other partner was directed to respond using active listening skills.

C. The partners were provided with feedback about the negative behaviors to decrease, and the active listening skills they used.

18. **Discuss Support Systems Already in Place (18)**

A. The support systems outside of the relationship that are already in place were identified and discussed.

B. Emphasis was placed on how the present support systems can help the partners cope with the life-changing events (e.g., friends, self-help and support groups, the religious community).

C. The partners reported limited support systems available to them and were redirected to find more.

19. **Discuss Support Systems to Be Added (19)**

A. The partners were directed to identify support systems outside of the relationship that can be added to help them cope with the life-changing events.

B. The partners identified a variety of support systems that can help them cope with the life-changing events, and these were reviewed and processed.

C. The partners struggled to identify support systems that can be added to help them cope with the life-changing events, and they were provided with examples, such as friends, self-help, support groups, and religious community.

20. **Teach Relaxation Skills (20)**

A. The partners were taught the use of relaxation skills, such as diaphragmatic breathing and progressive relaxation, to facilitate reduced anxiety symptoms.

B. The partners reported implementation of relaxation skills in daily life to reduce levels of muscle tension and the experience of anxiety; the benefits of the relaxation techniques were reviewed.

C. The couple has not followed through on implementation of relaxation skills to reduce anxiety symptoms and was redirected to do so.

D. The partners reported that their level of anxiety has decreased since relaxation techniques have been taught to them.

21. Encourage Stress-Reducing Activities (21)

A. Both partners were asked to commit to regularly engaging in individual stress-reducing activities (e.g., diaphragmatic breathing, deep muscle relaxation techniques, exercise, music, or hobbies).

B. The partners were asked to specifically schedule regular individual stress-reducing activities.

C. The partners have regularly scheduled stress-reducing activities, and the benefits of these were reviewed.

D. The partners have not used stress-reducing activities on a scheduled basis, and the barriers to this practice were identified and resolved.

22. Identify Ways to Support (22)

A. Each partner was asked to identify actions that the couple could take to be a source of support and anxiety-reduction to each other.

B. The partners have identified ways to be a source of support for each other and were asked to regularly schedule these anxiety-reducing activities.

C. The partners were provided with examples of how to help each other reduce stress and anxiety (e.g., foot rubs, back rubs, social engagements, walks, sex, or shared hobbies).

D. The partners were reinforced for regularly using stress-reducing activities.

23. Identify Problems within Control (23)

A. The partners were asked to identify those problems that are within their control.

B. The partners were provided with feedback as they identified the problems that are within their control.

C. The partners were asked to identify those problems that are not in their control.

D. The partners were provided with feedback as they described the problems that are not within their control.

24. Identify Adaptations (24)

A. The partners were asked to pinpoint adaptations that have been required related to personal, relational, and social domains.

B. The partners were assisted in developing very specific information related to the adaptations that they have made to problems within their control.

25. Practice Brainstorming (25)

A. The partners were taught about brainstorming, including the need to identify at least two solutions for each problem before trying to solve them.

B. The partners were asked to practice brainstorming within the session.

C. The partners were provided with positive feedback as they used helpful brainstorming techniques to solve the problem.

D. The partners needed additional feedback and redirection to identify helpful techniques to resolve problem areas.

26. Evaluate Brainstormed Solutions (26)

A. The partners were taught to evaluate the pros and cons of each of the brainstormed solutions.
B. The partners were directed to practice the evaluation of brainstormed solutions within the session.
C. Feedback was provided regarding the use of brainstorming techniques within the session.

27. Develop a Specific Plan (27)

A. The partners were directed to develop a specific, pinpointed plan for resolving the events within their control.
B. The partners were directed to include a time in the future to re-evaluate the progress on the solution.
C. During the session, the partners were directed to practice making a specific, pinpointed plan for resolving problems within their control.
D. Specific feedback was provided to the partners regarding their planning, execution, and evaluation of specific plans for resolving situations within their control.

28. Role-Play Support and Acceptance (28)

A. The partners were directed to provide support and acceptance to each other related to problems outside of their control.
B. The partners were directed to role-play within the session, having one person vent about difficult aspects of coping with the transition.
C. The listener was directed to practice validation skills (i.e., conveying understanding empathy with the speaker's feelings regardless of the level of agreement).
D. The partners were reinforced for displaying helpful skills related to venting and listening.
E. The partners struggled to vent and support/validate in a helpful manner and were provided with additional training and redirection in this area.

29. Focus on Support (29)

A. The partners were instructed to avoid trying to solve the external problem that is outside of their control.
B. The partners were assisted in focusing themselves on supporting each other.
C. The partners were directed to focus on how they can accept the unchangeable problems.
D. The partners were redirected when they focused away from acceptance and support and onto trying to solve the unchangeable problem.

30. Switch Perspectives (30)

A. The partners problem-solving skills were at an impasse, so they were directed to switch places and discuss the issue from the other's perspective.
B. The partners were reinforced for their increased understanding of each other through discussing the issue from the other's perspective and ability to provide additional support to each other.
C. The partners struggled to maintain their focus when trying to discuss the issue from the other partner's perspective and were provided with redirection in this area.

31. Envision Functional Adaptation (31)

A. The partners were asked to envision themselves six months from now and to describe their functional adaptation to the transition.

B. The partners were reinforced as they provided an optimistic description of adaptation to the transition to the life-changing event.

C. The partners were consistently pessimistic about their ability to functionally adapt to the transition and were encouraged to develop a more positive outlook.

32. Assign Positive Activities (32)

A. The partners were directed to schedule regular, positive activities with each other during the stressful transition.

B. Follow-up was done regarding the partners' assignment to schedule regular, positive activities with each other, and they were supported for doing this on a regular basis.

C. The partners have not regularly participated in positive activities with each other, and the reasons for this were problem-solved and resolved.

LOSS OF LOVE/AFFECTION

CLIENT PRESENTATION

1. Infrequent Words of Caring (1)*

A. The partners rarely verbalize any caring for each other.
B. The partners respond to questions about caring for each other with noncommittal or unenthusiastic responses.
C. The partners do not use typical rituals to verbalize caring for each other, such as Valentine's Day, Wedding Anniversary, and so forth.
D. The partners have begun to regularly express caring for each other.

2. Limited Verbalizations of Love (2)

A. The partners did not express love for each other.
B. One partner does not return the expressions of love to the other.
C. When asked about love for the other partner, the partners do not commit to expressing this to each other.
D. Both partners have verbalized their love for each other.

3. Questioning Love of Partner (3)

A. One partner identified significant personal questioning about love for the other partner.
B. One partner often makes statements about feeling uncertain regarding love for the other partner.
C. Both partners identified significant personal questioning about love for the other partner.
D. Both partners often make statements about uncertainty about love for the other partner.
E. Both partners have affirmed their love for the other partner.

4. Lack of Kindness/Thoughtfulness (4)

A. The partners do not participate in acts of kindness or thoughtfulness for each other.
B. The partners often act in a thoughtless manner toward each other.
C. The partners have begun to act more kindly and thoughtful toward each other.

5. Little Affection (5)

A. The partners describe very little affectionate touching or kissing.
B. The partners described the absence of any affectionate touching or kissing.
C. As the partners have improved their relationship, affectionate touching and kissing has increased.

6. Infrequent Sexual Interaction (6)

A. The partners report no sexual interaction within the relationship.
B. The partners report less frequent sexual interaction than is desired.
C. The partners' sexual interaction is characterized by a lack of fulfillment by both partners.

*The numbers in parentheses on Client Presentation pages correlate to the number of the Behavioral Definition statement in the companion chapter with the same title in *The Couples Psychotherapy Treatment Planner* (Jongsma, O'Leary, and Heyman) by John Wiley & Sons, 1998. The numbers in parentheses on the Interventions Implemented page correspond to the number of the Therapeutic Intervention statement in the companion chapter in the same book.

D. As the partners have increased their emotional connection and their level of affection, their sexual interaction has become more frequent and fulfilling.

7. Limited Involvement in Social/Recreational Activities (7)

A. The partners report limited time spent with each other on social or recreational activities.
B. The partners are involved in social and recreational activity with others, rather than with each other.
C. As the partners have grown closer, their pattern of social and recreational activities with each other has increased.

8. Infrequent Communication Regarding Intimate Matters (8)

A. The partners rarely talk about intimate concerns.
B. The partners generally keep their conversation focused on less intimate matters.
C. The partners have begun to talk about close personal issues.
D. The partners often engage in intimate discussions.

9. Little Planning for Future (9)

A. The partners report difficulties in planning for their future because of arguments or distance in the relationship.
B. The partners are uncertain about how to plan for the future because of arguments or distance in the relationship.
C. Both partners talk in a tentative manner about the future of the relationship.
D. As counseling has progressed and the couple has grown closer, they look forward to the future with mutual anticipation.

10. Avoidance (10)

A. The partners often seem to be avoiding each other.
B. One partner seems to prefer to spend time at work or with coworkers to spending time with the other partner.
C. The partners often engage in other activities to avoid each other.
D. As treatment has progressed, the partners have begun to spend more time with each other.
E. The partners regularly spend time with each other and prefer each other's company to other available social options.

INTERVENTIONS IMPLEMENTED

1. List Reasons for Erosion of Caring (1)

A. Each partner was asked to list the reasons that caring has eroded in the relationship.
B. Support and feedback were provided as each partner described the reasons why the partners do not care for each other as much as in the past.
C. The partners failed to identify reasons for why caring has eroded in the relationship and were provided with tentative reasons in this area.

2. Review Reasons for Erosion of Caring (2)

A. In a conjoint session, the reasons for the erosion of caring between partners were reviewed with the partners.

B. The partners were assisted in discussing and processing the reasons for the erosion of caring between partners within the relationship.

C. The partners were confronted when they minimized the reasons for the erosion of caring between partners.

D. The partners were hesitant or unable to identify reasons for the erosion of caring within the relationship and were provided with tentative examples in this area.

3. Assess for Individual Therapy (3)

A. The partners were assessed for the need for individual therapy to help cope with individual problems that interfere with the development of caring in the relationship.

B. Individual therapy was recommended to the partners because they were identified as experiencing significant problems that interfere with the development of caring in the relationship,

C. After assessment, the partners do not display the need for individual therapy, and this was reflected to them.

4. Obtain Commitment for Restitution (4)

A. Each partner was asked to commit to making restitution for respective wrongs and transgressions in the relationship.

B. The partners were asked to request forgiveness and perform actions to make up for the problems and transgressions in the relationship.

C. The partners were reinforced for agreeing to make restitution for respective wrongs and transgressions in the relationship.

D. The partners questioned the need to make restitution for respective wrongs and transgressions in the relationship and were encouraged to reconsider this need.

5. Focus on Commitment to Relationship (5)

A. One partner's actions were identified as having caused the other to experience jealousy.

B. The partner whose actions prompt jealous feelings was asked to work especially hard at reassuring the other of the commitment to the relationship.

C. The partner whose behavior prompts jealous emotions was reinforced for agreeing with the need to reassure the other partner about the commitment to the relationship.

6. Build Mutual Trust (6)

A. The partners were asked to provide feedback to each other about specific actions that will help build mutual trust.

B. The partners identified specific actions that will help build mutual trust, and these were discussed within the session.

7. Emphasize Positive Role of Forgiveness (7)

A. The positive role that forgiveness plays in intimate relationships was emphasized to the partners.

B. It was acknowledged that negative actions might not be easily forgotten, but still can be forgiven.
C. The partners were supported as they embraced the usefulness of forgiveness for the hurts of the past.
D. The partners denied the role of forgiveness in their relationship and were provided with additional feedback and encouragement in this area.

8. Assist with Forgiveness (8)

A. The partners were assisted with forgiving and/or trying to forgive past wrongs and hurts.
B. The partners were assisted in discussing and expressing forgiveness related to past wrongs and hurts.
C. Positive feedback was provided to the partners for their willingness to forgive and forget past wrongs and hurts.

9. Educate about Negative Effects of Remaining Angry (9)

A. The partners were taught the negative effects of harboring anger and resentment over past wrongs and hurts.
B. The partners were informed about both negative physical and emotional effects of harboring anger and resentment over past wrongs and hurts.
C. The partners were supported as they identified how harboring resentment over past wrongs and hurts has affected their relationship and individual functioning.

10. Recommend Readings on Forgiveness (10)

A. The partners were encouraged to read a book related to forgiveness.
B. The partners were encouraged to read *Forgive and Forget* (Smedes).
C. The partners have read the assigned book on forgiveness, and the key points were reviewed.
D. The partners have not read the book on forgiveness and were redirected to do so.

11. Commit to Moving Forward (11)

A. A verbal commitment was requested between the partners to attempt to move forward and put past painful issues behind them, at least for a specified period.
B. The partners were reinforced for agreeing to move forward and put past painful issues behind them for a specified period.
C. The partners have been able to focus on the future, and this was reflected to them.
D. The partners still tend to be focused on past painful issues and were reminded of their commitment to move forward.

12. Teach about Eye Contact (12)

A. The partners were taught to maintain eye contact with each other while speaking and listening.
B. The partners were supported as they role-played maintaining eye contact with each other while speaking and listening within the session.

13. Provide Feedback about Eye Contact (13)

A. The partners displayed persistent eye contact with each other while speaking and listening, and this was reflected to them as a helpful communication skill.

B. When the partners began to revert back to poor eye contact, they were redirected to maintain more appropriate eye contact.

14. Educate about the Negative Impact of Hostile Statements (14)

A. The partners were taught about the very negative impact of making critical and hostile comments to each other in therapy sessions or at home.

B. The partners were assisted in identifying the negative impact of past critical and hostile comments between them.

C. The partners were reinforced for acknowledging the very negative impact that critical and hostile comments toward each other can cause.

15. Obtain Commitment to Minimize Critical Comments (15)

A. A verbal commitment was requested between the partners to minimize critical and hostile comments.

B. The partners were reinforced for agreeing to minimize critical and hostile comments to each other.

C. The partners have minimized critical and hostile comments to each other, and this was reflected to them.

D. The partners still make critical and hostile comments toward each other and were reminded of their commitment to minimize this practice.

16. Consider Individual Therapy (16)

A. The partners were advised that individual therapy might be needed as an adjunct or precursor to conjoint therapy.

B. Expressions of anger by one or both partners have not been contained within the conjoint session, and individual therapy was recommended.

C. Individual therapy has been used to help decrease the expressions of anger and enabling conjoint therapy to continue.

D. The partner referred for individual therapy has not followed through on this referral and was redirected to do so.

17. Identify Pleasing Feedback for Partners (17)

A. Each partner was assisted in identifying the types of positive feedback that are pleasing to the other partner.

B. Each partner identified the types of positive feedback that they believe are pleasing to the other partner, and these were checked for accuracy.

C. The couple's pattern of verbal communication has become more positive, and the benefits of this were reviewed.

D. The partners were noted to be continuing in a pattern of limited positive communication and were redirected to increase this pattern.

18. Rehearse Positive Comments (18)

A. Behavioral rehearsal techniques were used to have the partners make positive comments about each other.
B. The partners were asked to rehearse making positive comments about each other's behaviors.
C. Feedback was provided on the behavioral rehearsal of making positive comments about each other.
D. The partners reported an increase in positive comments about each other, and the benefits of this were reviewed within the session.
E. The partners continue to make very limited positive comments about each other and were provided with additional rehearsal of these techniques.

19. Reinforce Verbal Support (19)

A. Whenever the partners provided verbal support to each other, they were reinforced.
B. The partners were praised for a general increase in verbal support of each other.
C. Although many comments between the couple were negative, the few verbally supportive comments made were immediately reinforced.

20. Identify Helpful Behavior for Partners (20)

A. Each partner was assisted in identifying the type of helpful behavior that is pleasing to the other partner.
B. Each partner identified the types of helpful behavior that each believes are pleasing to the other partner, and these were checked for accuracy.
C. The couple's pattern of interaction has been more helpful, and the benefits of this were reviewed.
D. The partners were noted to be continuing in a pattern of very limited helpful behavior and were redirected to increase this pattern.

21. Obtain Specific Agreement for Helpful Gestures (21)

A. The partners were asked to agree to specific, helpful, thoughtful gestures that each will perform during the week.
B. The partners outlined specific, helpful, thoughtful gestures to be performed during the week and were provided with feedback about how realistic these expectations were.
C. The partners were assessed for their participation in acts of kindness and helpfulness toward each other.

22. Reinforce Nonverbal and Nonphysical Affectionate Gestures (22)

A. Whenever the partners provided nonverbal and nonphysical affectionate gestures, they were reinforced.
B. The partners were praised for a general increase in nonverbal and nonphysical affectionate gestures for each other.

23. Prompt Expressing and Logging of Positive Comments (23)

A. The partners were prompted to express praise, compliments, recognition, and gratitude during the therapy session.

B. The partners were prompted to perform mutual expressions of praise, compliments, recognition, and gratitude between therapy sessions.
C. The partners were assigned to log giving and receiving of praise, compliments, recognition, and gratitude between sessions as a means of reinforcing the process.

24. Monitor Mutual Reinforcement (24)

A. The partners' progress in mutually reinforcing each other was monitored within the session and by reviewing their log of such comments.
B. The partners were reinforced for increasing the number of mutually reinforcing comments to each other.
C. The partners have not displayed an increase in mutual reinforcement of each other and were redirected to increase this effort.

25. Describe Social and Recreational Activities (25)

A. The partners were asked to describe the social and recreational activities that they might like to do together.
B. The partners were supported as they described a variety of social and recreational activities that they enjoy.
C. The partners described very few social and recreational activities that they might like to do together and were provided with additional examples, as well as directives to increase this list.

26. Facilitate Agreement on Social or Recreational Activities (26)

A. The partners were asked to agree to a specific plan for some social or recreational activities together.
B. The partners were reluctant to commit to a specific plan for social or recreational activities together and were provided with direct prompts to help facilitate this agreement.
C. The partners were reinforced for agreeing to specific social and recreational activities.
D. The couple was asked to bring in a planning calendar (i.e., the place where they record important dates such as dental appointments), and plan out a number of "date nights."

27. Review Mutual Activity (27)

A. The partners have participated in a mutual activity and were praised for following through in this area.
B. The partners were assisted in reviewing and clarifying how each partner felt during the mutual activity.
C. The partners were challenged and assisted in expanding mutually involved activities wherever possible.
D. The partners have not participated in a mutual activity and were redirected to do so.

28. Educate about Change (28)

A. The partners were informed about the usual course of change, with an emphasis on how initial changes in behavior generally lead to subsequent changes in feelings and attitudes.
B. The partners were provided with specific examples of the process of change.

C. The partners were prompted to provide their own examples of how initial changes in behavior have led to subsequent changes in feelings and attitudes.

D. The partners were reinforced for displaying adequate understanding of the process of change.

E. The partners struggled to understand the concepts related to the process of change and were provided with remedial feedback.

29. Educate about Patience (29)

A. The partners were taught the need for patience when seeking changes in positive relationship feelings.

B. The couple was provided with examples of the need for patience when seeking changes in positive relationship feelings.

C. The partners were supported as they endorsed an understanding of the need for patience when seeking changes in positive relationship feelings.

D. The partners do not clearly understand the need for patience when seeking changes in positive relationship feelings and were provided with additional feedback and direction in this area.

30. Set Realistic Goals (30)

A. The partners were assisted in setting realistic goals about changes in caring and love.

B. The partners identified their own expectations for goals about changes in caring and love for each other, and these were reviewed and processed.

C. Positive feedback was provided for the realistic expectations that the partners stated regarding the changes in love, affection, and caring.

D. The partners were provided with a more realistic set of goals about the process of changes in caring and love for each other.

31. Advise about Coercive Sexual Activities (31)

A. Examples of forced sexual activities and coercive sexual activities were provided to the couple.

B. The partners were advised about how forced or coerced sexual activities often backfire, leading to resentment and withdrawal.

C. The partners were supported as they displayed a healthy understanding about the negative impact of forced or coerced sexual activities.

D. One partner continues to hold to antiquated, possessive notions about forcing or coercing the other partner into sexual activity and was provided with additional feedback and information in this area.

32. Obtain Commitment Regarding Sexual Activity (32)

A. The partners were requested to commit to only initiate and engage in sexual actions that are mutually agreed on.

B. A special emphasis was placed on the partner who has been the most frequent initiator of sexual activity to only initiate and engage in sexual actions that are mutually agreed on.

C. The partners were reinforced for committing to only initiate and engage in sexual actions that are mutually agreed on.

D. The partners were reminded to talk openly about what type of sexual activity is mutually desired.
E. The partners reported a pattern of initiating and engaging in sexual actions that are mutually agreed on and were provided with positive feedback about how helpful this is for the relationship.
F. The partners reported continued forced or coercive sexual activity and were redirected in this area.

33. Explain Sexual Satisfaction as a Mirror to the Relationship (33)

A. It was explained to the partners that sexual satisfaction in marital and long-term relationships often increases naturally when other aspects of the relationship improve (i.e., communication and nonsexual expressions of caring).
B. The partners were urged to see the sexual relationship as a mirror of the rest of the relationship, improving as communication and nonsexual expressions of caring improve.
C. The partners were reinforced for endorsing the expectation that sexual satisfaction depends on nonsexual expressions of caring and communication.
D. The partners were provided with additional feedback because they failed to understand the relationship between sexual satisfaction and the rest of the communication within the relationship.

34. Teach Sensate Focus (34)

A. The partners were taught about the use of sensate focus techniques.
B. The partners were reinforced for their clear understanding of the use of sensate focus.
C. The partners have used the sensate focus techniques to improve the giving and receiving of sensual pleasure, and the benefits of this were reviewed.

35. Assign Readings about Sex (35)

A. Independent reading related to sexuality issues was assigned.
B. The partners were assigned to read information related to sexuality issues together.
C. The partners were assigned to read *Sexual Awareness* (McCarthy and McCarthy) or *The Gift of Sex* (Penner and Penner).
D. The partners have read the information about sexuality, and the important points were reviewed in the session.
E. The partners have not read the information related to sexuality and were redirected to do so.

36. Process Emotions Related to Physically Intimate Contact (36)

A. The partners were assessed for their emotions related to the increase in physically intimate contact.
B. The partners' emotions related to an increase in physically intimate contact were reviewed and discussed.
C. The partners were noted to have primarily positive feelings related to increasing physical intimacy.
D. The partners' emotions related to increasing physically intimacy were reviewed and processed.

MIDLIFE CRISIS

CLIENT PRESENTATION

1. Depressed Mood (1)*

A. The client reported feeling deeply sad and has periods of tearfulness on an almost daily basis.

B. The client's depressed affect was clearly evident within the session as tears were shed on more than one occasion.

C. The client has begun to feel less sad and can experience periods of joy.

D. The client appeared to be happier within the session and there is no evidence of tearfulness.

E. The client reported no feelings of depression.

2. Periodic Crying Spells (2)

A. The client reported a pattern of recurrent feelings of sadness and crying spells.

B. The client cried often within the session.

C. The client reported an inability to improve his/her mood or keep himself/herself from crying.

D. As the client has progressed in treatment, he/she displays a decreased pattern of sadness.

E. The client reported that his/her crying has greatly diminished to appropriate levels, and he/she feels more upbeat.

3. Sleeplessness/Hypersomnia (3)

A. The client reported periods of inability to sleep and other periods of sleeping for many hours without the desire to get out of bed.

B. The client's problem with sleep disturbance has diminished as the depression has lifted.

C. Medication has improved the client's problems with sleep disturbance.

D. The client reported a normal sleep routine resulting in feeling rested.

4. Fidelity Conflicts (4)

A. The client identified conflict between commitment to his/her current partner versus a desire to be with another partner.

B. The client described a preoccupation of thoughts with another partner, despite his/her current commitment to his/her present partner.

C. As the couple has progressed in treatment, the client's conflict between commitment to his/her current partner, and the desire to be with another partner has decreased.

D. The client has rediscovered an appreciation for and commitment to his/her existing intimate relationship.

5. Job Stability Conflict (5)

A. The client described a conflict between staying in his/her current job versus attempting to get another job.

*The numbers in parentheses on Client Presentation pages correlate to the number of the Behavioral Definition statement in the companion chapter with the same title in *The Couples Psychotherapy Treatment Planner* (Jongsma, O'Leary, and Heyman) by John Wiley & Sons, 1998. The numbers in parentheses on the Interventions Implemented page correspond to the number of the Therapeutic Intervention statement in the companion chapter in the same book.

B. The client described a pattern of dissatisfaction in his/her current job, which he/she believes will be resolved by a new job.
C. The client has been applying himself/herself to resolving the core issues related to his/her current job.
D. The client has found new employment and feels more at ease regarding this conflict.

6. Changing Careers (6)

A. The client described conflicts regarding a possible change in careers.
B. The client has initiated a change in careers and described a variety of problems that have occurred, including financial changes, time commitment, and changes within the relationship.
C. The client's career change appears to have stabilized his/her relationship and is more in accord with his/her overall values.
D. The client has resolved the conflict regarding changing careers and feels more at ease with these decisions.

7. Conflict over Goals (7)

A. The client reported internal conflict over his/her goals and use of time (e.g., time spent with family members versus time on job versus time with friends).
B. The client reported conflict with his/her partner regarding goals and use of time.
C. The client described changing values regarding his/her goals and time and has modified his/her behavior and relationships to be more consistent with these values.

8. Religious Conflict (8)

A. The client has seriously questioned his/her religious values and practices.
B. Changing and maturing religious values and practices have created conflict within the couple's relationship.
C. The client has resolved his/her conflict over religious values and practices.

9. Concern about Sexual Opportunities (9)

A. The client described a concern about his/her declining opportunity to have another sexual partner.
B. The client described his/her fantasy regarding opportunities to have another sexual partner.
C. The client has been actively seeking opportunities to have another sexual partner.
D. The client has rediscovered an appreciation for his/her current intimate relationship.

10. Attractiveness Concerns (10)

A. The client described his/her concern about a perceived decline in physical attractiveness.
B. As the client has matured, his/her body has also matured.
C. The client has become more at ease with his/her current physical attractiveness.

INTERVENTIONS IMPLEMENTED

1. Probe Cognitive Distortions (1)

A. The client's description of anxiety and uneasiness was probed for causes related to cognitive distortion.

B. The client was asked to identify specific thoughts that lead to anxiety and uneasiness.
C. The client was provided with feedback about the cognitive distortions that he/she displays that lead to anxiety and uneasiness.

2. Assign Diary (2)

A. The client was assigned to keep a daily diary of thoughts that precipitate anxious and depressed feelings.
B. The client has kept a daily diary of thoughts that precipitate anxious and depressed feelings, and this was reviewed and processed within the session.
C. The client has not kept a daily diary of thoughts that precipitate anxious and depressed feelings and was redirected to do so.

3. Assist in Positive Cognition Development (3)

A. The client was asked to develop a list of positive cognitive messages that are reality based and reinforce the client's feeling of confidence about self and the future.
B. The client's partner was enlisted to help develop a list of positive cognitive messages that are reality based and reinforce the client's feelings of confidence about self and the future.
C. The client was provided with assistance in developing a list of positive cognitive messages that are reality based and reinforce feelings of confidence about self and the future.

4. Identify Value Foundation (4)

A. The partners were asked to identify what values are most important to them.
B. The partners were assisted in developing the values that are most important to each of them.
C. It was reflected to the partners that they have identified a variety of common values, enough to form a foundational basis for their relationship.
D. It was reflected to the partners that they have identified very few common values, and they questioned whether there is a foundational basis of mutual values for the relationship.

5. Review Congruency Between Values and Lifestyle (5)

A. The client's history was reviewed to determine the degree of congruency between his/her values and lifestyle.
B. The client's current functioning was reviewed to determine the degree of congruency between his/her values and lifestyle.
C. It was noted that the client has a high degree of congruity between his/her values and lifestyle.
D. It was noted that the client's lifestyle does not reflect his/her stated values.

6. Review Incongruity with Values (6)

A. The client's history was reviewed to determine how life decisions have been in conflict with his/her stated values.
B. The client's current functioning was reviewed to determine how life decisions have been in conflict with his/her stated values.
C. The client was assisted in identifying several ways in which his/her current and past life have been in conflict with his/her stated values.

D. The client failed to identify significant ways in which his/her life decisions have been in conflict with his/her stated values and was provided with tentative examples of these types of decisions.

7. Identify Lifestyle Changes (7)

A. The partners were asked to identify how various areas of life could be changed to achieve greater harmony with values.
B. The partners were assisted in identifying a variety of areas of life that could be changed to achieve greater harmony with values.
C. The partners failed to identify areas in their life that could be changed to achieve greater harmony with values and were provided with tentative examples in this area.

8. Explore Spiritual Satisfaction (8)

A. Each partner's spiritual life was explored.
B. Each partner was asked about the degree of satisfaction felt about their spiritual life.
C. Both the partners were noted to describe a high degree of satisfaction regarding their spiritual life.
D. The partners were noted to display variable levels of satisfaction with their spiritual lives.
E. It was reflected to the partners that they both described a low level of satisfaction with their spiritual lives.

9. Encourage Discussions about Spiritual Beliefs/Plans (9)

A. The partners were encouraged to discuss their spiritual beliefs with each other.
B. The partners were directed to formulate a plan for increasing their closeness to a higher power and a community of believers.
C. The partners have regularly discussed their spiritual beliefs with each other, and the benefits of this communication were processed.
D. The partners have developed a plan for increasing their closeness to a higher power and a community of believers, and this was processed.
E. The partners have not regularly discussed their spiritual beliefs with each other or developed a plan for increasing their closeness to a higher power and a community of believers and were redirected to do so.

10. Describe Expectations from Youth (10)

A. The client was asked to describe his/her goals and wishes as a late teen and young adult.
B. The client was asked to describe how his/her goals and wishes have changed over the years.
C. The client was focused on the developmental changes in his/her goals and perceived expectations of others and self.

11. Describe Parent's Goals and Wishes (11)

A. The client was asked to describe the goals and wishes that his/her parents had held for him/her.
B. The client was assisted in describing the goals and wishes that his/her parents had held for him/her.

C. The client described his/her parents' goals and wishes for him/her in some detail, and this material was summarized and processed.
D. The client had little concept of what his parents expected for him/her and was urged to research this from family, friends, and other sources.

12. Describe Partner's Goals and Wishes (12)

A. The client was asked to describe the goals and wishes that his/her partner has held for him/her.
B. The client was assisted in describing the goals and wishes that his/her partner has held for him/her.
C. The client described his/her partner's goals and wishes for him/her in some detail, and this material was summarized and processed.
D. The client had little concept of what his/her partner expected for him/her and was urged to seek this information out from the other partner.

13. Verify Partner's Goals and Wishes (13)

A. The client's partner was asked to provide feedback regarding the goals and wishes that he/she has for the client.
B. The client's partner was asked to verify the client's perception of the goals and wishes that the partner has for the client.
C. It was noted that the client's understanding of and the actual goals and wishes that his/her partner has for him/her were quite congruent.
D. It was noted that there was significant discrepancy between the client's understanding of his/her partner's goals and wishes and the partner's actual goals and wishes held for the client.

14. Describe Unfulfilled Goals (14)

A. The client was asked to describe his/her unfulfilled goals.
B. The client was assisted in identifying the goals that he/she has not yet fulfilled in his/her life.
C. The client was assisted in identifying the emotions associated with the lack of fulfillment of goals.

15. Identify Unrealistic Goals (15)

A. The client was assisted in identifying goals that probably are not realistically attainable.
B. The client was urged to accept that some of his/her goals are unrealistic and not likely to be attained.
C. The client's emotions related to accepting some personal goals as unattainable were reviewed and discussed.

16. Identify Attainable Goals and Plans (16)

A. The client was asked to list the goals that he/she has set for himself/herself that are still realistically attainable.
B. The client was asked to identify the specific plan that he/she has to reach his/her realistically attainable goals.
C. Reinforcement was provided for the client's realistic plans.

D. The client does not have any specific plans related to his/her realistically attainable goals and was asked to develop such plans.

17. Assign Value to Alternative Goals (17)

A. The client was asked to identify alternative goals.
B. The client was assisted in assigning values to alternative goals.
C. The client was given feedback for the value he/she has assigned to alternative goals.
D. The client has not assigned values to alternative goals and was redirected to do so.

18. Consult Others about Alternative Goals (18)

A. The client was assigned to consult with other individuals whom he/she respects regarding possible alternative goals for himself/herself and their value.
B. The client has consulted with other individuals whom he/she respects regarding possible alternative goals for self and their value, and the results of this consultation were reviewed.
C. The client was given positive feedback as he/she displayed a greater understanding of alternative goals based on consultation with other individuals.
D. The client has not consulted with other individuals regarding alternative goals and was redirected to do so.

19. Determine Goal Plausibility (19)

A. The client was asked about the likelihood of the attainment of alternative goals.
B. The client was assisted in determining the likelihood of attaining alternative goals.
C. The client sees his/her alternative goals as quite attainable and was provided with feedback in this area.
D. The client sees his/her alternative goals as difficult to attain and was provided with feedback.

20. Obtain Alternative Goal Feedback (20)

A. Each partner was asked to provide feedback about the perceived value of alternative goals for self and relationship.
B. Feedback from each partner about the perceived value of alternative goals for themselves and the relationship was reviewed and synthesized.
C. Feedback from both partners indicated agreement about the value of alternative goals.
D. The partners have disparate views about the value of the alternative goals, and this was reflected to them and processed.

21. Describe Respected Older Individual (21)

A. The client was asked to identify an older individual whom he/she respects.
B. The client was asked to describe the attributes of an older individual whom he/she respects.
C. As the client described the attributes of an older person that he/she respects, he/she was directed to notice the advantages that come with maturity.

22. Identify Advantages of Maturity (22)

A. The client was asked to identify the advantages that usually come with maturity (e.g., less impulsive judgments, greater experiential wisdom, broader views of values in life, knowledge of more lifestyle alternatives, more concern about others).

B. The client was reinforced for identifying the advantages that usually come with maturity (e.g., less impulsive judgments, greater experiential wisdom, broader views of values in life, knowledge of more lifestyle alternatives, more concern about others).

C. The client was unable to identify maturity as providing advantages and was given tentative examples in this area (e.g., less impulsive judgments, greater experiential wisdom, broader views of values in life, knowledge of more lifestyle alternatives, more concern about others).

23. Explore/Resolve Emotional Response to Aging (23)

A. The client's possible feelings of anxiety and depression related to aging were explored.

B. The client identified feelings of anxiety related to aging, including the fear of physical deterioration and/or declining health, and these emotions were accepted.

C. The client identified feelings of sadness and depression related to aging, physical deterioration and/or declining health, and these emotions were accepted.

D. The client was helped to resolve his/her emotional responses to aging.

E. As the client was helped to identify and process his/her emotions related to aging, he/she verbalized acceptance and peace regarding these issues.

F. The client continues to feel anxious and depressed about his/her aging, physical deterioration and declining health and was provided with additional support and feedback.

24. Replace Focus on Self with Altruism (24)

A. The client was asked to identify things that he/she might do for others, therefore, reducing the focus on himself/herself.

B. Positive feedback was provided as the client identified ways in which he/she can help others, and a reduced focus on himself/herself was noted.

C. The client failed to identify things that he/she might do for others and was provided with tentative examples.

25. Educate about Benefits of Altruism (25)

A. The client was taught about the value of acts done for the benefit of others.

B. The client was reinforced for his/her understanding about how doing actions for others has value.

C. The client was provided with specific examples of how acts done for the benefit of others can be of value to one's self.

26. Assign Altruistic Acts (26)

A. The client was assigned to do something for others each week, even if the act of kindness is a small one.

B. The client has been regularly doing something for someone else, and the benefits of this were reviewed.

C. The client has not been doing altruistic acts, and the barriers to completing this assignment were problem-solved.

27. Clarify Benefits of Family Time (27)

A. The client was asked about what he/she perceives the benefits are of giving time to immediate and extended family members.
B. The client endorsed the benefits and need for increased time with family members; this was processed and positive feedback provided.
C. The client was provided with additional examples of the benefits of increased contact with immediate and extended family members (i.e., better relationships, a sense of belonging, a feeling of having roots).

28. Encourage Increased Contact with the Family (28)

A. The client was encouraged to write, call, or visit immediate or extended family members.
B. The client endorsed a plan for writing, calling, or visiting immediate or extended family members.
C. The client has increased contact with immediate or extended family members, and the benefits of this involvement were reviewed.
D. The client has not increased contact with immediate or extended family members and was provided with additional review and feedback in this area.

29. Educate about Positive Impact of Family Contact (29)

A. The client was asked about his/her sense of value and satisfaction regarding giving of self to family members.
B. The client endorsed a sense of value and satisfaction with giving of self to family members, and this was processed.
C. The client did not see the benefit of increasing contact with family members and was provided with feedback on how this can be rewarding.

30. Teach Value of Touching (30)

A. The client was taught about the value of touching in intimate relationships.
B. The client was reinforced as he/she identified ways in which touching can increase partners' feelings of importance and enhance mutual feelings of closeness, warmth, caring, and security.
C. The client has increased his/her touching within the intimate relationship and was provided with positive feedback about this.
D. The client and his/her partner report that touching in the intimate relationship has not increased, and the barriers to this were problem-solved.

31. Encourage Physical Affection (31)

A. The client was encouraged to be more physically affectionate with his/her intimate partner.
B. The client has become more physically affectionate with his/her partner, and the benefits of this were reviewed.
C. The client has not become more physically intimate with others and was assisted in resolving the barriers to this useful practice.

32. Assign Physical Affection Acts (32)

A. The client was assigned to engage in some act of physical affection at least every few days.

B. The client has engaged in acts of physical affection and recorded them in a journal; the helpfulness of this was reviewed.

C. The client reports very little physical affection with intimates, and barriers to this were problem-solved.

D. The client was supported as he/she described his/her disappointment when physical affection was not returned in the manner in which he/she sought.

33. Rediscover Benefits of Partner Relationship (33)

A. The client was asked to focus on the positive aspects of maintaining the current intimate relationship between self and partner.

B. As the client has used different techniques to increase closeness with the current partner, the effects of these changes on maintaining the current intimate relationship were identified and reviewed.

C. The client expressed a renewed commitment to maintaining the current relationship between self and partner.

D. The client has reviewed the current intimate relationship between self and partner and was noted to be disillusioned with this relationship.

34. Explore Emotions Related to Employment (34)

A. The partners were asked to express their feelings regarding the client's current employment and what impact it has on each partner and the family.

B. It was reflected back to the partners that they have generally positive feelings related to the client's current employment.

C. It was reflected to the partners that they have very little positive feelings about the client's current employment and its impact on each partner and family.

35. Assist with Career Directions (35)

A. The client was assisted in identifying possible alternative career directions.

B. The advantages and disadvantages of each possible alternative career direction were reviewed, both for the client and for the relationship.

C. The client was given feedback as he/she has developed a clearer understanding of the alternative career directions.

D. The client was provided with tentative feedback relating to the alternative career directions.

36. Accept Present Employment (36)

A. The client was assisted in accepting his/her present employment.

B. The client was urged to commit himself/herself to his/her present employment.

C. The client was noted to express a sense of satisfaction with accepting and committing to his/her present employment situation.

D. The client has been reluctant to commit to and accept his/her present employment situation and was provided with feedback and further review of these concerns.

37. Develop Responsible Career Exploration (37)

A. The client was assisted in developing a plan for responsibly exploring alternative career directions.

B. The client was warned about impulsive actions that could have devastating long-term consequences.

C. The client's plan for developing alternative career directions was reviewed, and feedback about the long-term consequences was provided.

ONE PARTNER UNWILLING TO ATTEND THERAPY

CLIENT PRESENTATION

1. Emotional Distress over Relationship (1)*

A. One partner has identified emotional distress regarding the current state of the relationship.
B. Both partners have identified emotional distress regarding the current state of the relationship.
C. The emotional distress is displayed through a pattern of anger and tension within the relationship.
D. As treatment has progressed, the level of emotional distress has decreased.

2. Cognitive Distress over the Relationship (1)

A. One partner has identified cognitive distress regarding the current state of the relationship.
B. Both partners have identified cognitive distress regarding the current state of the relationship.
C. The cognitive distress is displayed through a pattern of blaming and a lack of concentration.
D. As treatment has progressed, the level of cognitive distress has decreased.

3. Behavioral Problems within the Relationship (1)

A. One partner has identified behavioral difficulties regarding the current state of the relationship.
B. Both partners have identified behavioral difficulties regarding the current state of the relationship.
C. The distress within the relationship is displayed through arguments and withdrawal between the two partners.
D. As treatment has progressed, the level of arguing, withdrawal, or other behavioral problems has decreased.

4. Refusal to Attend Counseling (2)

A. The client indicated that the other partner is refusing to attend counseling sessions.
B. After initial attendance, one partner has refused to continue to attend counseling sessions.
C. Despite repeated attempts to engage the other partner, refusal to attend counseling sessions has continued.
D. As the client has begun to make changes, the other partner has displayed interest in attending counseling sessions.
E. The partner previously refusing to attend counseling sessions has begun attending and has found this to be beneficial.

5. Inability to Attend Counseling Sessions (3)

A. The client has indicated that the other partner is unable to attend counseling sessions due to other responsibilities.

*The numbers in parentheses on Client Presentation pages correlate to the number of the Behavioral Definition statement in the companion chapter with the same title in *The Couples Psychotherapy Treatment Planner* (Jongsma, O'Leary, and Heyman) by John Wiley & Sons, 1998. The numbers in parentheses on the Interventions Implemented page correspond to the number of the Therapeutic Intervention statement in the companion chapter in the same book.

B. The partner unable to attend counseling sessions has nonetheless indicated a desire for involvement in treatment.
C. The partner previously unable to attend counseling sessions has prioritized the relationship and has worked around schedule conflicts in order to attend counseling sessions.

INTERVENTIONS IMPLEMENTED

1. **Investigate Invitations to Partner (1)**

A. The client was asked about whether the other partner has been requested to attend therapy.
B. The client reported on how the partner has been asked to attend therapy, and this was processed in the session.
C. The client has not actually asked the other partner to attend therapy, due to an expectation that the other partner would decline involvement; this decision was processed.

2. **Review Invitation (2)**

A. The client was asked to provide detailed information about how his/her partner was invited to attend counseling sessions.
B. The client provided specific details about how the invitation was extended to the other partner, and this was assessed for both encouraging and discouraging elements.
C. The client gave rather vague information about how the invitation was extended to his/her partner and was asked to provide more specific information (e.g., when the invitation occurred, how the invitation occurred, and in what context it occurred).
D. The client was given feedback about how the invitation was destined for failure due to the context in which it occurred.
E. Positive feedback was provided to the client regarding the positive, proactive context and manner in which the invitation was provided.

3. **Assess Potential Dangers (3)**

A. An assessment was made of the potential dangers (such as fear of assault) of attempts to engage the other partner in treatment.
B. Due to the potential dangers with attempting to engage the other partner in therapy, any direct invitations were discouraged for the time being.
C. Attempts to engage the other partner in therapy have been discouraged, pending the resolution of potential dangers; the client has been referred for additional domestic violence services.
D. The potential dangers of attempting to engage the other partner in therapy were reviewed and judged to be unsubstantiated.

4. **Role-Play Invitation to Therapy (4)**

A. Role-play techniques were used to help the client appropriately ask his/her partner to attend counseling sessions.
B. The client was provided with the following example of an invitation to treatment: "I care about you, and I am concerned that our relationship is at risk. I'm going to attend therapy to

work on improving our relationship, and I'd appreciate your being willing to come with me."

C. The client was able to display a clear understanding about how to invite the other partner and was provided with feedback about how this was displayed during the role-play.
D. The client performed poorly during the role-play and was provided with additional feedback and direction.

5. Contact Partner to Provide Information about Client (5)

A. Permission was obtained from the client to call the partner with an invitation to attend sessions to provide information that might be useful to the presenting client's treatment.
B. With the client's permission, the other partner was contacted and invited to attend sessions to provide information that might be useful to the presenting client's treatment.
C. The other partner has made a commitment to attend therapy to provide information that might be useful to the presenting client's treatment and was positively reinforced for this commitment.
D. The partner not attending treatment has declined to attend sessions to provide information that might be useful to the presenting client's treatment and was encouraged to do so in the future.

6. Assess Developmental Stage of Relationship (6)

A. The relationship was identified as currently being in the *early marriage* stage.
B. The relationship was identified as currently being in the *parents of young children* stage.
C. The relationship was identified as being currently in the *long-term marriage* stage.

7. Assess Satisfaction with the Relationship (7)

A. The client's history of satisfaction with the relationship was assessed.
B. Assessment of the client's history of satisfaction with the relationship focused on recent changes, including those within the relationship.
C. Discussion was focused on the client's level of unhappiness and thoughts about divorce.
D. The client was engaged in a discussion about expectations about marriage and divorce.
E. The client's general history of satisfaction with the relationship was identified and reflected to the client.

8. Assess Current Relationship Satisfaction (8)

A. The client was asked to complete a standardized assessment of relationship satisfaction.
B. The client was requested to complete the Locke Wallace Marital Adjustment Test.
C. The client was asked to complete the Relationship Satisfaction Questionnaire (Burns).
D. The client was asked to complete the Dyadic Adjustment Scale (Spanier).
E. The client has completed a standardized assessment scale of relationship satisfaction, and the results were reviewed within the session.
F. The client has not completed the standardized assessment scale of relationship satisfaction and was redirected to do so.

9. Assess for Presence/Suspicion of Affairs (9)

A. The client was asked specifically about suspicions regarding affairs.
B. A history of affairs was identified, and the impact of this on the course of treatment was reviewed.
C. No history or suspicion of affairs has been identified within the relationship.

10. Assess Violence/Intimidation (10)

A. The history of the relationship was reviewed to assess for incidence of violence or intimidation.
B. Specific testing was provided to assess for relationship violence or intimidation.
C. The Revised Conflict Tactics Scale (Straus et al.) was administered.
D. A history of violence and intimidation was identified, and the goal of treatment was reassessed.
E. No history of violence or intimidation was identified.

11. Assess Regarding Divorce (11)

A. The steps each partner has taken toward divorce were assessed.
B. The client was interviewed about his/her sense of hope and vision of the future.
C. A standardized questionnaire was used to assess the steps toward divorce.
D. The Marital Status Inventory (Weiss and Cerreto) was administered.
E. The partners' test results indicated the partners have taken significant steps toward divorce.
F. The couple was assessed as not having moved toward divorce, and this was reflected to the client.

12. State Pros and Cons (12)

A. The client was directed to state his/her point of view on preserving the relationship.
B. The client was directed to identify the pros and cons of separation or divorce.
C. Feedback was provided to the client regarding preserving the relationship versus separation or divorce.

13. Identify Problem Areas (13)

A. The client was directed to list the current problem areas in the relationship.
B. The client was assisted in identifying and prioritizing the current problem areas within the relationship.
C. The client was provided with additional, tentative examples of possible problem areas within the relationship.

14. Educate about Individual Therapy Benefits (14)

A. The client was taught that individual therapy could be a form of relationship therapy.
B. Emphasis was placed on how changes on the part of one partner can cause changes in the nature of the relationship.
C. The client was able to identify how the changes that he/she makes in individual therapy can make a change in the relationship.

D. The client was provided with specific examples of how changes made in individual therapy can make changes in the nature of the relationship.

15. Identify Problems within Sphere of Influence (15)

A. The client was directed to identify and list which current problems he/she has at least some influence over.
B. Active listening was used as the client identified specific relationship problems over which he/she has at least some influence (e.g., communication problems, anger problems).
C. The client identified several relationship problem areas within his/her sphere of influence, and feedback was provided regarding the level of influence the client may have over this area.
D. The client struggled to identify relationship areas within his/her sphere of influence and was provided with additional, tentative examples in this area.

16. Generate List of Improvements (16)

A. The client was asked to generate a list of changes that he/she could make to improve their relationship.
B. The "It would please my partner if I . . ." section of Areas of Change Questionnaire (Weiss and Birchler) were used to identify changes that the client could make to improve the relationship.
C. The list of changes to improve the relationship was reviewed and processed with the client.
D. The client was provided with additional examples of ways to improve the relationship.

17. Rate Sacrificial Behavior (17)

A. The client was asked to prioritize the behaviors that he/she could perform to benefit the relationship.
B. The client was asked to provide estimates of the perceived sacrifice entailed in performing each behavior.
C. Cost-Benefit Analysis (Weiss) was used to help the client prioritize behaviors and the level of sacrifice to benefit the relationship.
D. The client was provided with feedback regarding the many behaviors that he/she could do to benefit the relationship.

18. Prioritize Beneficial Behaviors (18)

A. The client was asked to list the beneficial behaviors from the least to greatest in terms of the amount of sacrifice that an act would require.
B. The client was provided with assistance to help prioritize the beneficial behaviors in terms of the amount of sacrifice that each would require.
C. The client was assigned to perform three to five beneficial behaviors per week.
D. The client has regularly performed beneficial behaviors, and the improvement in the relationship was reviewed.
E. The client has not regularly performed beneficial behaviors and was redirected to do so.

19. List Variety of Desired Activities (19)

A. The client was asked to generate a list of desired activities by using the *Inventory of Rewarding Activities* (Weiss).

B. The client was assisted in generating a list of desired activities to be done alone.

C. The client was assisted in identifying a list of desired activities to be done with the other partner.

D. The client was assisted in identifying desired activities to be done with the partner and other family members.

E. The client was assisted in developing a list of desired activities to be done with the partner and nonfamily members.

F. The client was assisted in developing a list of desired activities to be done with nonfamily members.

20. Role-Play Request for Positive Activities (20)

A. Role-playing techniques were used to rehearse how the client could ask the partner to engage in positive activities together.

B. The therapist modeled how the client would ask the other partner to engage in positive activities together.

C. The client was supported as he/she rehearsed how to ask the partner to engage in positive activities together, and feels confident to use this with the partner.

21. Assign Invitation (21)

A. The client was assigned to ask the partner to engage in positive activities together.

B. The client was asked to report on the other partner's response to the invitation to engage in positive activities.

C. The partner has accepted the invitation to engage in positive activities together, and the benefits of this were reviewed.

D. The partner declined to engage in positive activities together with the client, and the emotional effects of this were reviewed.

22. Assign Alternative Activities (22)

A. The client was assigned to increase the amount of positive activities that he/she does alone or with nonfamily members.

B. The client has increased his/her involvement in activities that do not require participation by the other partner, and his/her experience and enjoyment of these activities was reviewed.

C. The client has not increased the number of rewarding activities that do not include the partner and was redirected to do so.

23. Describe Goal of Situational Analysis (23)

A. Situational analysis was described as working toward large payoffs by making small, observable changes that have a beginning, middle, and end.

B. The client was asked to repeat the rationale for situational analysis in his/her own words.

C. The client displayed a complete understanding of the concepts related to situational analysis.

D. The client was provided with remedial information to assist in his/her understanding of the goal and rationale for situational analysis.

24. Assign Situational Analysis Homework (24)

A. The client was assigned to complete a situational analysis regarding a problematic situation.
B. The client was directed to include the following elements in his/her situational analysis: a description of the beginning, middle, and the end of an observable situation; the cognitions; the behavior; the actual outcome; and the desired outcome.
C. The client has completed a situational analysis, and this was reviewed and critiqued.
D. The client has not completed a situational analysis and was redirected to do so.
E. The client was provided with an example of a situational analysis to assist him/her in completing this task.

25. Review Situational Analysis (25)

A. The client was asked to read aloud from the situational analysis homework sheet.
B. The client's statements were paraphrased to check the therapist's complete understanding of the key elements of the situational analysis.
C. The client endorsed the therapist's paraphrasing and understanding of the key elements of the situational analysis.
D. The client's situational analysis was difficult to understand, and he/she was asked more specific questions to help elucidate this information.

26. Review Each Thought in Situational Analysis (26)

A. The client was asked to critique each thought within the situational analysis to identify whether that thought was helpful in reaching the desired outcome.
B. The client was asked to critique each thought within the situational analysis to identify whether that thought was anchored to the specific situation described (i.e., situationally specific, not global).
C. The client was asked to critique each thought within the situational analysis to identify whether that thought was accurate (i.e., overt evidence can be marshaled to support it).

27. Rework Thoughts (27)

A. Specific thoughts within the situational analysis were identified as not being helpful, anchored to the specific situation, or accurate.
B. The client was assisted in reworking the thought, until it does meet all three criteria: helpful, anchored to the specific situation, and accurate.
C. The client was provided with specific examples of reworking thoughts (i.e., "She's always on my back," can become "There's something happening here that she thinks is important").
D. The client was provided with feedback as he/she reworked the thoughts so that they meet all three criteria.
E. The client had difficulty understanding how to rework his/her thoughts to meet all three criteria and was provided with assistance and guidance in this area.

28. Review Desired Outcome (28)

A. The client was asked to state whether the desired outcome was achievable (i.e., under his/her control).
B. The client indicated that the outcome was achievable, and this was accepted.
C. The client identified that the desired outcome was not actually achievable and was assisted in reworking the desired outcome so that it is achievable.
D. The client was provided with an example of how to rework a desired outcome (i.e., "I want him to listen to me when I'm upset," can become "I want to ask him to schedule a time for us to talk about problems that we're having").
E. The client was able to modify his/her desired outcome to be achievable.
F. The client was provided with remedial assistance in modifying his/her desired outcome to become achievable.

29. Summarize Situational Analysis (29)

A. The client was asked to summarize the situation and derive a lesson to be learned from the situational analysis.
B. The client was able to abstract a general lesson to be learned from the situational analysis, and feedback was provided.
C. The client struggled to summarize the situation and was assisted in identifying a global lesson to be learned from the situational analysis.

30. Apply Lessons Learned (30)

A. The client was asked to identify how the lesson learned within the situational analysis could be applied to other situations.
B. The client was provided with feedback as he/she applied the lesson of the situational analysis to new situations.
C. The client was provided with tentative examples of how to apply the lesson learned within the situational analysis to a new situation.

31. Teach about Hard and Soft Emotions (31)

A. Hard emotions were defined as protective emotions such as anger, retribution, and resentment.
B. Soft emotions were defined as vulnerable emotions such as hurt, insecurity, and fear.
C. The client was taught the different consequences of expressing hard versus soft emotions.
D. Positive feedback was provided as the client displayed a clearer understanding of the difference between hard and soft emotions.
E. The client struggled to identify the difference between hard and soft emotions and was redirected in this area.

32. Replace Hard Emotions with Soft Emotions (32)

A. When the client expressed a hard emotion, redirection was provided identify the soft emotion that underlies the hard emotion.
B. Positive feedback was provided to the partner for identifying the soft emotions that underlie the hard emotions.

C. The partner struggled to identify the soft emotions that underlie the hard emotions and was provided with tentative feedback in this area.

33. Externalize Problem (33)

A. The problematic interaction patterns were reframed as an external problem, rather that as the fault of either partner.

B. The client was supported for the acceptance of the reframe of the problematic interaction patterns as an external problem.

C. The partner continued to place significant blame for the problem and was redirected to externalize the problem.

34. Describe Positive Features of Problematic Behaviors (34)

A. The client was asked to describe the positive features of the other partner's problematic behavior.

B. The client was able to identify the ways in which the other partner's problematic behavior actually serves a positive function in the relationship, and positive feedback was provided in this area.

C. The client was provided with specific examples of how problematic behavior serves a positive function in the relationship.

35. Reframe Problematic Behavior as a Balance (35)

A. The partner's problematic behaviors were reframed in terms of how they balance the relationship.

B. The client was provided with specific examples of how problematic behaviors can balance a relationship (e.g., a hyper-responsible man may get involved with a spontaneous woman).

C. The client identified how his/her partner's problematic behaviors balance the client's own behavior, and positive feedback was provided in this area.

36. Explain Benefits of Balancing Behaviors (36)

A. It was explained to the client that each partner brings only one part of the balancing act to the relationship.

B. The partner was asked whether there is anything that can be learned from the other partner's opposite, but balancing, behavior that formerly has caused consternation.

C. As the client identified what can be learned from the each partner's formerly upsetting behaviors; feedback and encouragement were provided.

D. The client was unable to identify any positive learning from the partner's opposite, but balancing, behavior and was provided with specific examples based on the therapist's observations.

37. Identify Needs to Be Met Outside of the Relationship (37)

A. The client was assisted in identifying acceptable ways of satisfying needs outside of the relationship.

B. It was noted that the use of outside relationships could reduce the pressure on the relationship to meet all of the couple's core needs.

C. The partner identified ways of satisfying needs outside of the relationship, and these were reviewed and supported.
D. The partner was unable to identify any acceptable ways of satisfying needs outside of the relationship and was provided with additional feedback in this area.

38. List Ways to Satisfy Soft Emotions (38)

A. The client was directed to list ways in which needs arising from soft emotions (e.g., relief from hurt or fear) could be satisfied within the relationship.
B. The client has identified ways in which needs arising from soft emotions can be satisfied without resorting to destructive, hard emotion-laced escalation, and these were reviewed within the session.
C. The client failed to identify helpful ways to satisfy soft emotions and was provided with additional feedback in this area.

39. Rehearse Alternative Means of Meeting Soft Emotions (39)

A. The client was directed to rehearse, in session, alternative means of meeting needs arising from soft emotions.
B. The client rehearsed the alternative means of meeting needs arising from soft emotions and was provided with positive feedback.

PARENTING CONFLICTS—ADOLESCENTS

CLIENT PRESENTATION

1. Frequent Arguments (1)*

A. The partners described a pattern of frequent arguments with one another regarding parenting.
B. The arguments between the partners interfere with effective parenting of the adolescent child.
C. The partners have become more of a team for parenting the adolescent.
D. As treatment has progressed, arguments between the partners have decreased and communication for effective parenting has been increased.

2. Disagreements Regarding Parenting Strategies (2)

A. The partners described a lack of agreement regarding strategies for dealing with various types of negative adolescent behaviors.
B. One partner seems to advocate for stricter control, while the other partner endorses a more permissive approach.
C. The adolescent's behavior seems to be unaffected by the parents' variable pattern of disciplinary response.
D. As communication has increased, the partners have gained an agreement regarding strategies for dealing with various types of negative adolescent behaviors.

3. Ineffective Parental Responses (3)

A. The partners described that their responses to the adolescent's negative behaviors have been ineffective (e.g., efforts do not result in the desired outcomes).
B. As treatment has progressed, more effective responses to negative adolescent behavior were developed and implemented.
C. The partners described increased efficacy of their responses to negative adolescent behavior.

4. Lack of Mutual Support (4)

A. The partners describe that they rarely discuss each other's parenting efforts.
B. Each partner identified that the other partner often does not support the parenting efforts.
C. The adolescent has displayed an ability to "split" the parents to the adolescent's own advantage.
D. The partners have increased their discussion and support of each other's parenting efforts, which has achieved a commensurate increase in positive adolescent behavior.

INTERVENTIONS IMPLEMENTED

1. Describe Problem Behavior (1)

A. The parents were asked to describe their main concerns about the adolescent's problem behavior and its history.

*The numbers in parentheses on Client Presentation pages correlate to the number of the Behavioral Definition statement in the companion chapter with the same title in *The Couples Psychotherapy Treatment Planner* (Jongsma, O'Leary, and Heyman) by John Wiley & Sons, 1998. The numbers in parentheses on the Interventions Implemented page correspond to the number of the Therapeutic Intervention statement in the companion chapter in the same book.

B. The partners disagreements regarding their child's behavior became evident as they attempted to describe their concerns.
C. The partners described the behaviors about which they are concerned and the history of these behaviors; this was summarized and reflected back to them to check for accuracy.
D. The partners were uncertain about the context of the adolescent's problem behavior and were provided with more specific inquiries and tentative examples to elicit this history.

2. Identify Extent of Problem Behavior (2)

A. The parents were asked to specifically detail the extent of the adolescent's problem behavior.
B. The partners were asked about how frequently and intensely the problem occurs, how long it lasts, and in which situations it occurs.
C. The partners' details about the adolescent's problem behavior was summarized and reflected to them for accuracy.

3. Assign Questionnaire Assessments (3)

A. The partners were asked to complete a questionnaire assessment to help identify specific areas of conflict and problem behaviors.
B. The partners were directed to complete the Issues Checklist (Robin and Foster).
C. The partners were asked to complete the Conflict Behavior Questionnaire (Friends, Foster, Kent, and O'Leary).
D. The results of the questionnaires/checklists were reviewed with the partners.
E. The partners have not completed the questionnaires/checklists and were redirected to do so.

4. Identify Philosophies/Expectations (4)

A. Each partner's parenting philosophy and strategies were probed and identified.
B. Each partner's expectations for the adolescent's behavior were questioned and identified.
C. Questionnaires were used to help identify each partner's parenting philosophy, strategy, and expectations for the adolescent.
D. The parents were administered the Family Beliefs Inventory (Roehing and Robin).
E. The parents were administered the Parent-Adolescent Relationship Questionnaire (Robin, Koepke, and Moye).
F. The identified parenting philosophies and strategies, as well as each partner's expectations for the adolescent's behavior, were summarized and reflected to the partners.

5. Identify Problem Maintainers (5)

A. The parent-adolescent behavioral patterns were reviewed to assist in identifying the behavioral patterns that may be maintaining the problem.
B. Specific behavioral patterns that may be maintaining the behavioral problem were identified and reflected to the partners (e.g., unintentionally reinforcing problem behavior through nagging or emotional parenting).
C. The parents endorsed an understanding of ways in which the parent-adolescent behavioral patterns may be maintaining the problem and were supported for this insight.

D. No obvious parent-adolescent behavioral patterns were identified to explain the behavioral problems, but the partners were advised to monitor this pattern.

6. Identify Social Context (6)

A. The couple was asked to identify the social context that may be maintaining the problem (e.g., family transitions, inconsistent rules, school, or social difficulties).
B. Feedback was provided to the partners as they identified a variety of social context factors that may be maintaining the problem.
C. The partners were provided with tentative examples of social context factors that may be maintaining the problem.
D. No social context factors were identified as maintaining the problem; the couple was provided with examples of these types of factors (e.g., family transitions, inconsistent rules, school, or social difficulties) and asked to monitor for them.

7. Identify Parents' Stressors (7)

A. The parents were asked to identify stressors that may be maintaining the adolescent's negative behavior.
B. The parents were provided with examples of possible stressors that may be maintaining the adolescent's negative behavior (e.g., unemployment, substance use, and depression).
C. The parents identified several stressors that may be maintaining the adolescent's negative behavior and were provided with support and feedback.
D. The parents denied any stressors that they may be experiencing that are contributing to the maintenance of the adolescent's negative behavior and were urged to monitor for these.

8. Identify Parental Relationship Impact (8)

A. The parents were directed to identify ways in which their relationship conflict has had a negative impact on their adolescent's behavior.
B. The couple was provided with positive feedback for their ability to openly identify ways in which their relationship conflict has had a negative impact on their adolescent's behavior.
C. The parents tended to deny any effect of their relationship conflict on their adolescent's behavior and were confronted for this denial.

9. Describe Adolescent's Behavior Impact (9)

A. The couple was asked to describe how their adolescent's behavior problems impact on their relationship conflict.
B. The partners were supported as they identified ways in which the adolescent's behavior has tended to create arguments between the partners.
C. The parents interpreted the adolescent as being purposefully attempting to divide them and were provided with feedback about this pattern.
D. The parents indicated no impact of their adolescent's behavior problems on their relationship conflict and were provided with feedback about this pattern of denial.

10. Observe Problem-Solving Attempt (10)

A. The partners were directed to use behavioral rehearsal of their problem solving focused on the adolescent's behavior.

B. The partners were allowed to continue their attempt at solving a major parenting problem without significant interruption, although skills and deficiencies were quietly observed and noted.

11. Review Problem-Solving Interaction (11)

A. The partners were asked to discuss their problem-solving interaction.
B. The partners were asked to note their strengths and weaknesses as a parenting team.
C. The partners were provided with feedback about their strengths and weaknesses as a parenting team.

12. Assign Reading on Parenting (12)

A. The parents were assigned appropriate reading material regarding parenting adolescents.
B. The couple was assigned to read *Parents and Adolescents: Living Together. Vol. I: The Basics* and *Vol. II: Family Problem Solving* (Patterson and Forgatch).
C. The parents have read the material on parenting adolescents, and the important topics were reviewed and processed.
D. The parents have not read the assigned material and were redirected to do so.

13. Assign Monitoring of Adolescent's Activities (13)

A. The parents were assigned to coordinate monitoring of their adolescent's activities, keeping track of where the adolescent is, who the adolescent is with, what the adolescent is doing, and when the adolescent will be home.
B. The parents have coordinated monitoring of their adolescent's activities on a regular basis.
C. The parents have not monitored their adolescent's activities, and deficiencies in this area were reviewed.

14. Record Monitoring Efforts (14)

A. The parents were assigned to record their joint monitoring efforts.
B. The parents have regularly recorded joint monitoring efforts of the adolescent, and this record was reviewed.
C. The parents have not regularly recorded their monitoring activities of the adolescent and were redirected to do so.

15. Review Monitoring Success and Areas for Improvement (15)

A. The parents were asked to discuss the successes that they have had at monitoring the adolescent's whereabouts.
B. The partners were asked to identify times and situations where their monitoring of the adolescent's whereabouts needs to be improved.
C. The parents were unable to identify any ways in which their monitoring of the adolescent needs to be improved, and their thorough record of monitoring the adolescent was noted to be consistent with this assessment.
D. The parents were unable to identify any areas in which they needed to improve their monitoring of the adolescent, but were confronted with examples of where they have not been able to successfully monitor the adolescent, as indicated in the record that they have kept.

16. Investigate Behavior Pattern to Be Reinforced (16)

A. The parents were asked to identify one of their adolescent's behavior patterns that they would like to reinforce.

B. The parents were assigned to record the occurrence of the adolescent's positive behavior pattern every day for a week.

C. The couple was asked to note the situations that precede the identified positive behavior (i.e., antecedents) and follow the behavior (i.e., consequences).

D. The parents have regularly identified the occurrence of the adolescent's positive behavior, antecedents, and consequences and were encouraged to continue this.

E. The parents have not regularly recorded the occurrence, antecedents, and consequences of the identified positive behavior pattern and were redirected to do so.

17. Identify and Practice Rewards (17)

A. The parents were directed to identify an appropriate reward (e.g., praise, use of the car, increase of allowance) to reinforce the adolescent's positive behavior.

B. The parents were provided with assistance in identifying an appropriate reward to reinforce the adolescent's positive behavior.

C. The parents were asked to rehearse praising a positive behavior pattern in the session.

D. The couple was provided with feedback about their practice of praising positive behavior.

18. Increase Recreational Activity (18)

A. The parents were assigned to increase their amount of focused, adolescent-centered activity.

B. The couple was provided with feedback regarding their changes in recreational activity with the adolescent experiencing difficulty.

C. The parents were refocused onto using recreational activities that are more adolescent-centered.

19. Increase Conversation with Adolescent (19)

A. Each parent was assigned to increase the number of parent-initiated, casual, positive conversations with the adolescent experiencing difficulty.

B. The partners were asked to report on their use of casual, positive conversations with the adolescent.

C. The partners were asked to provide feedback about each other's use of casual, positive conversations with the adolescent.

D. The parents reported significant struggles in increasing the number of parent-initiated, casual, positive conversations with the adolescent, and this pattern was analyzed and problem-solved.

20. Investigate Behavior Pattern to Decrease (20)

A. The parents were asked to identify one of their adolescent's negative behavior patterns that they would like to decrease.

B. The parents were assigned to record the occurrence of the adolescent's negative behavior pattern every day for a week.

C. The couple was asked to note the situations that precede the identified negative behavior (i.e., antecedents) and follow the behavior (i.e., consequences).

D. The parents have regularly identified the occurrence of the adolescent's negative behavior, antecedents, and consequences and were encouraged to continue this.

E. The parents have not regularly recorded the occurrence, antecedents, and consequences of the identified negative behavior pattern and were redirected to do so.

21. Identify and Practice Negative Consequences (21)

A. The parents were directed to identify an appropriate negative consequence (e.g., loss of privilege, five-minute work chore) to discourage the adolescent's negative behavior.

B. The parents were provided with assistance in identifying an appropriate consequence to discourage the adolescent's negative behavior.

C. The parents were asked to rehearse implementation of the negative consequence in the session.

D. The couple was provided with feedback about their use of negative consequences.

22. Teach Logical and Natural Consequences (22)

A. The parents were taught about establishing logical and natural consequences to adolescent misbehavior.

B. The parents were provided with specific examples about logical and natural consequences (e.g., break curfew and lose privilege to go out, make a mess and have to clean up the mess).

C. The couple was reinforced as they displayed a clear understanding of natural and logical consequences.

D. The partners had difficulty identifying natural and logical consequences and were provided with additional feedback in this area.

23. Contract Change in Own Behavior (23)

A. The parents' modeling of the behavior that they would like to extinguish was reviewed.

B. The parents admitted their own modeling of the behaviors that they are trying to extinguish with the adolescent (yelling, being sarcastic, smoking) and were urged to change their own behavior.

C. The partners were reinforced for contracting to change their own behavior before trying to change the same behavior in the adolescent.

24. Assign Daily Communication (24)

A. The parents were assigned to confer with each other at least once a day regarding the adolescent's behavior.

B. The partners were asked to log their review of their adolescent's behavior each day.

C. The parents have regularly conferred with each other at least once a day regarding the adolescent's behavior, and the benefits of this were reviewed.

D. The parents have not regularly checked in with each other about the adolescent's behavior and were redirected to do so.

25. Identify Specific Time to Confer (25)

A. The parents were encouraged to plan a mutually acceptable time to confer about their adolescent's behavior.

B. The partners were directed to confer during times when arguments are less likely to erupt (e.g., not immediately upon arriving home in the evening).
C. The partners have used a specific time to confer with each other about the adolescent's behavior, and the benefits of this were reviewed.
D. The partners have not regularly used specific times to confer with each other and were redirected to do so.

26. Track Satisfaction with Check-Ins (26)

A. The partners were instructed to track their satisfaction with the daily conferring about the adolescent's behavior.
B. The partners were directed to bring the tracking sheet to treatment sessions.
C. The partners were reinforced for regularly tracking their satisfaction with the daily conferring.
D. The partners have not been satisfied with the daily check-ins, and the reasons for this were problem-solved.
E. The partners have not been tracking their daily conferring and were redirected to do so.

27. Practice Argument Control (27)

A. Modeling and behavioral rehearsal techniques were used to assist the partners in argument control (e.g., calling for time out, using "I" messages in place of "you" messages).
B. The partners practiced the argument control techniques within the session and were provided with feedback about their ability to use these techniques.
C. The partners were assigned to employ techniques to cool off during parenting discussions if either believes that the conversation is becoming unsupportive.
D. The partners were reinforced for regularly using argument control techniques.
E. The partners reported that they have not used argument control techniques and were redirected to do so.

28. Role-Play Discussions about Positive Adolescent Behavior (28)

A. The partners were directed to role-play discussions that they will have when the adolescent is well behaved.
B. The supportive partner was prompted to ask the other partner what the adolescent has been doing and was urged to support the other partner's parenting behaviors.
C. Feedback was provided to the partners' role-play of discussions when the adolescent is well-behaved.

29. Role-Play Discussions for Adolescent's Negative Behavior (29)

A. The partners were directed to role-play discussions that they will have when the adolescent displays negative behavior.
B. The supportive partner was prompted to ask in a supportive, nonthreatening manner about the specifics about the misbehavior.
C. Feedback was provided to the partners about the role-play of discussions that they would have when the adolescent displays negative behavior.

30. Role-Play Support When Dealing with Adolescent Misbehavior (30)

A. The partners were directed to role-play exercises for dealing with adolescent misbehavior.

B. The supportive partner was prompted to ask, in a supportive, nonthreatening manner, how the other partner dealt with the misbehavior.

C. The supportive partner was prompted to ask about ways to help the other partner in the future.

D. The benefits of providing nonthreatening support regarding dealing with adolescent misbehavior were reviewed.

31. Contract about Not Interfering (31)

A. The partners were asked to contract to support each other's parenting by not interfering during the other's parent-adolescent interactions and by not interfering with the other's decisions (i.e., avoiding splitting up parents' unity).

B. The partners agreed to support each other by not interfering during parent-adolescent interactions or with each other's decisions and were urged to maintain this contract.

C. The partners were provided with examples of how not interfering with the other's parent-adolescent interactions can be supportive and helpful.

D. The couple was provided with examples of how interfering with parent-adolescent interactions and decisions can be disruptive and split the parents' unity.

32. Identify Help in Challenging Situations (32)

A. The partners discussed what each could do to help the other in challenging situations (e.g., when the adolescent is disrespectful).

B. The partners were reinforced for identifying general guidelines for what each can do in challenging situations.

C. The partners failed to identify helpful guidelines for how to help each other in challenging situations and were provided with specific examples.

33. Contract on When to Discuss Disagreements (33)

A. The partners were asked to contract to put disagreements over parenting strategy on hold until a situation has ended and they can meet privately.

B. The partners were asked to contract about discussing disagreements over parenting strategies when they are calm and able to problem-solve without accusations or defensiveness.

C. The partners have contracted to put disagreements over parenting strategy on hold until an appropriate time, and the benefits of doing so were reviewed and processed.

D. The partners have not put discussions of disagreements off until a more appropriate time and were redirected to do so.

34. Schedule Problem-Solving Discussions (34)

A. The partners were assigned to schedule discussions for problem-solving parenting issues two or three times per week.

B. The partners were provided with positive feedback for the use of scheduling parenting problem-solving discussions.

C. The partners reported that they have not scheduled parenting problem-solving discussion times and were redirected to do so.

35. Practice Pinpointing (35)

A. The partners were directed to take turns pinpointing problems.

B. The partners were directed to make requests for change that are specific, observable, and ask for increases in positive behaviors rather than decreases in the other partner's negative behavior.

C. The partners were taught how pinpointing leads to an understandable, positive pattern of communication.

D. The partners have failed to master the skill of pinpointing and were provided with remedial assistance in this area.

36. Teach Paraphrasing (36)

A. While one partner was serving as the speaker, the other partner was directed to paraphrase, by rephrasing the speaker's major point.

B. The speaking partner was asked to acknowledge whether the paraphrasing partner had accurately described the intended message.

C. The partners were provided with positive feedback as they displayed several examples of appropriately paraphrasing each other's comments.

37. Limit Problem Focus (37)

A. The partners were advised to limit themselves to solving one problem at a time.

B. The partners were reinforced for limiting themselves to solving one problem at a time.

C. The partners have not limited themselves to solving one problem at a time and were provided with additional discussion in this area.

38. Brainstorm Solutions (38)

A. Each partner was encouraged to brainstorm at least two possible solutions to each of the adolescent's problem behaviors.

B. The partners were encouraged to share the brainstormed ideas of possible solutions to the adolescent's problem behaviors without critiquing them.

C. Positive feedback was provided to the partners for creativity in brainstorming solutions to the adolescent's problem behaviors.

39. Role-Play Choosing a Solution (39)

A. The partners were directed to role-play choosing a solution together by judging the advantages and disadvantages of each possible solution.

B. The partners were provided with positive feedback about the ability to judge the advantages and disadvantages of each possible solution.

40. Plan to Implement Solution (40)

A. The partners were assisted in jointly developing a specific plan for implementing solutions.

B. As the partners developed a specific plan for implementing solutions, they were provided with feedback.

C. The partners have failed to identify a positive plan for implementing solutions and were provided with additional feedback.

41. Evaluate Effectiveness (41)

A. The partners were asked to establish a time to review the progress of the implemented solution.

B. The partners have reviewed the progress of the implemented solution, and this was summarized within the session.

C. The partners were assisted in troubleshooting the implemented solution as necessary.

D. The partners have not reviewed the effectiveness of the implemented solution and were redirected to do so.

42. Invite Adolescent to Family Session (42)

A. It was arranged for the adolescent to attend the family session.

B. The parents were directed to employ communication skills and problem-solving techniques with the adolescent as well as with each other (i.e., defining the problem, brainstorming, evaluating alternatives, implementing a solution, and evaluating a solution).

C. The parents and the adolescent were reinforced for using problem-solving techniques.

D. When the adolescent was unwilling to engage in problem-solving techniques with the parents, the parents were directed to use these skills in the session.

43. Identify Thoughts and Emotions during Problematic Situations (43)

A. The couple was asked to track their thoughts and emotional reactions during problematic situations with their adolescent.

B. The couple expressed their thoughts and emotional reactions during problematic situations with their adolescent, and these were reviewed and accepted.

C. The parents have not tracked their thoughts and emotional reactions during problematic situations with their adolescent and were redirected to do so.

44. Identify/Challenge Unreasonable Assumptions (44)

A. The partners were assisted in identifying unreasonable assumptions about their adolescent through a request to provide evidence for the assumption and persuasively illuminating the illogical premise involved.

B. The partners were provided with a specific example of an unreasonable assumption (i.e., "If my daughter stays out late, she will become pregnant or a drug addict," can be replaced by "I can make my opinions and house rules known, but ultimately her behavior is up to her").

C. The partners were provided with positive feedback for their identification and challenge of unreasonable assumptions.

D. The partners have not regularly identified and challenged unreasonable assumptions and were provided with additional feedback in this area.

45. Assign Family Meeting (45)

A. The parents were assigned to initiate regular family meetings for constructive problem solving and evaluation of earlier contracts.

B. The family was urged to make the family meetings time-limited and to establish ground rules to be observed.

C. The couple was directed to page 117 of *Parents and Adolescents: Living Together. Vol. II: Family Problem-Solving* (Patterson and Forgatch) for detailed information about running family meetings.
D. The couple has initiated regular family meetings, and the benefits of these were reviewed.
E. The couple has struggled with the use of regular family meetings, and the barriers in this area were problem-solved.
F. The partners have not scheduled family meetings and were redirected to do so.

46. Set Respectful Expectations for Family Meetings (46)

A. The couple was urged to use and expect respectful communication skills during family meetings.
B. Examples of respectful communication were provided, including taking turns talking, treating each other with respect, and not lecturing
C. The parents were directed to page 118 of *Parents and Adolescents: Living Together. Vol. II: Family Problem-Solving* (Patterson and Forgatch) to identify respectful expectations during family meetings.
D. The family reported respectful communication during family meetings and the benefits of this were reviewed.
E. The partners reported disrespectful communication during the meetings, and this was problem-solved.

47. Establish House Rules for Family Meetings (47)

A. The parents were encouraged to establish consistent house rules for family meetings.
B. The family was asked to identify the consequences for rule violations and for compliance.
C. The family was directed to modify and negotiate rules within the family meeting, if necessary.
D. The partners was supported for developing clear expectations regarding house rules for family meetings.
E. The parents have not established and maintained house rules for family meetings and this was problem-solved.

48. Discuss Family Dinners (48)

A. The partners were assisted in discussing the feasibility of the family eating together, the frequency that dinners can occur, and the expectations for attendance by the adolescent.
B. The partners were supported for agreeing on the frequency and feasibility of family dinners and expectations for attendance by the adolescent.

49. Meet with Adolescent to Implement Family Dinner Plan (49)

A. The parents were directed to meet with the adolescent (as a homework assignment) to discuss the implementation of the family dinner plan at least once or twice a week.
B. The adolescent was invited to the session, and the parents discussed the implementation of the family dinner plan.
C. The partners have not met with the adolescent to discuss the implementation of the family dinner plan, and the reasons for this were brainstormed and problem-solved.

PARENTING CONFLICTS—CHILDREN

CLIENT PRESENTATION

1. Frequent Arguments (1)*

A. The partners described a pattern of frequent arguments with each other regarding parenting.

B. The arguments between the partners interfere with effective parenting of the child.

C. The partners have become more of a team for parenting the child.

D. As treatment has progressed, arguments between the partners have decreased, and communication for effective parenting has been increased.

2. Disagreements Regarding Parenting Strategies (2)

A. The partners described a lack of agreement regarding strategies for dealing with various types of negative child behaviors.

B. One partner seems to advocate for stricter control, while the other partner endorses a more permissive approach.

C. The child's behavior seems to be unaffected by the parents' variable pattern of disciplinary response.

D. As communication has increased, the partners have gained an agreement regarding strategies for dealing with various types of negative child behaviors.

3. Ineffective Parental Responses (3)

A. The partners described that their responses to the child's negative behaviors have been ineffective (e.g., efforts do not result in the desired outcomes).

B. As treatment has progressed, more effective responses to negative child behavior were developed and implemented.

C. The partners described increased efficacy of their responses to negative child behavior.

4. Lack of Mutual Support (4)

A. The partners describe that they rarely discuss each other's parenting efforts.

B. Each partner identified that the other partner often does not support the parenting efforts.

C. The child has displayed an ability to "split" the parents to the child's own advantage.

D. The partners have increased their discussion and support of each other's parenting efforts, which has achieved a commensurate increase in positive child behavior.

INTERVENTIONS IMPLEMENTED

1. Describe Problem Behavior (1)

A. The parents were asked to describe their main concerns about the child's problem behavior and its history.

*The numbers in parentheses on Client Presentation pages correlate to the number of the Behavioral Definition statement in the companion chapter with the same title in *The Couples Psychotherapy Treatment Planner* (Jongsma, O'Leary, and Heyman) by John Wiley & Sons, 1998. The numbers in parentheses on the Interventions Implemented page correspond to the number of the Therapeutic Intervention statement in the companion chapter in the same book.

B. The partners' disagreements regarding their child's behavior became evident as they attempted to describe their concerns.
C. The partners described the behaviors about which they are concerned and the history of these behaviors; this was summarized and reflected back to them to check for accuracy.
D. The partners were uncertain about the context about the child's problem behavior and were provided with more specific inquiries and tentative examples to elicit this history.

2. Identify Extent of Problem Behavior (2)

A. The parents were asked to specifically detail the extent of the child's problem behavior.
B. The partners were asked about how frequently and intensely the problem occurs, how long it lasts, and in which situations it occurs.
C. The partners' details about the child's problem behavior were summarized and reflected to them for accuracy.

3. Assign Questionnaire Assessments (3)

A. The partners were asked to complete a questionnaire assessment to help identify specific areas of conflict and problem behaviors.
B. The partners were directed to complete the Child Behavior Checklist (Achenbach).
C. The partners were asked to complete the Parenting Scale (Arnold, O'Leary, Wolff, and Acker).
D. The results of the questionnaires/checklists were reviewed with the partners.
E. The partners have not completed the questionnaires/checklists and were redirected to do so.

4. Identify Philosophies/Expectations (4)

A. Each partner's parenting philosophy and strategies were probed and identified.
B. Each partner's expectations for the child's behavior were questioned and identified.
C. Questionnaires were used to help identify each partner's parenting philosophy, strategy, and expectations for the child.
D. The identified parenting philosophies and strategies, as well as each partner's expectations for the child's behavior, were summarized and reflected to the partners.

5. Identify Problem Maintainers (5)

A. The parent-child behavioral patterns were reviewed to assist in identifying the behavioral patterns that may be maintaining the problem.
B. Specific behavioral patterns that may be maintaining the behavioral problem were identified and reflected to the partners (e.g., unintentionally reinforcing problem behavior through nattering or emotional parenting).
C. The parents endorsed an understanding of ways in which the parent-child behavioral patterns may be maintaining the problem and were supported for this insight.
D. No obvious parent-child behavioral patterns were identified to explain the behavioral problems, but the partners were advised to monitor this pattern.

6. Identify Social Context (6)

A. The couple was asked to identify the social context that may be maintaining the problem (e.g., family transitions, inconsistent rules, school, or social difficulties).

B. Feedback was provided to the partners as they identified a variety of social context factors that may be maintaining the problem.
C. The partners were provided with tentative examples of social context factors that may be maintaining the problem.
D. No social context factors were identified as maintaining the problem; the couple was provided with examples of these types of factors (e.g., family transitions, inconsistent rules, school, or social difficulties) and asked to monitor for them.

7. Identify Parents' Stressors (7)

A. The parents were asked to identify stressors that may be maintaining the child's negative behavior.
B. The parents were provided with examples of possible stressors that may be maintaining the child's negative behavior (e.g., unemployment, substance use, and depression).
C. The parents identified several stressors that may be maintaining the child's negative behavior and were provided with support and feedback.
D. The parents denied any stressors that they may be experiencing that are contributing to the maintenance of the child's negative behavior and were urged to monitor for these.

8. Identify Parental Relationship Impact (8)

A. Parents were directed to identify ways in which their relationship conflict has had a negative impact on their child's behavior.
B. The couple was provided with positive feedback for their ability to openly identify ways in which their relationship conflict has had a negative impact on their child's behavior.
C. The parents tended to deny any effect of their relationship conflict on their child's behavior and were confronted for this denial.

9. Describe Child's Behavior Impact (9)

A. The couple was asked to describe how their child's behavior problems impact on their relationship conflict.
B. The partners were supported as they identified ways in which the child's behavior has tended to create arguments between the partners.
C. The parents interpreted the child as being purposefully attempting to divide them and were provided with feedback about this pattern.
D. The parents indicated no impact of their child's behavior problems on their relationship conflict and were provided with feedback about this pattern of denial.

10. Observe Problem-Solving Attempt (10)

A. The partners were directed to discuss a problem with their child's behavior in an attempt to find a mutually agreeable solution.
B. The partners were allowed to continue their attempt at solving a major parenting problem without significant interruption, although skills and deficiencies were quietly observed and noted.

11. Educate about Motives for Misbehavior (11)

A. The parents were informed regarding the three main motives for a child's misbehavior: attention-seeking, escape from demand, and fun-seeking.

B. The parents were reinforced for their understanding of the main motives for a child's behavior.

C. The parents did not understand the main motives for a child's misbehavior and were provided with specific examples in this area.

12. Identify Attention-Seeking Misbehavior (12)

A. The parents were assisted in identifying examples of a child's attention-seeking misbehavior.

B. The parents were given specific examples of a child's attention-seeking misbehavior (e.g., misbehavior that only occurs when someone is around, and for which the child secures attention prior to performing it).

C. The parents identified their child's examples of attention-seeking misbehavior; feedback and review were provided.

13. Identify Demand- and Escape-Motivated Misbehavior (13)

A. The parents were assisted in identifying examples of a child's demand-motivated misbehavior.

B. The parents were provided with examples of a child's demand-motivated misbehavior (i.e., misbehavior that promotes the child getting something that the child wants).

C. The parents were assisted in identifying examples of a child's escape-motivated misbehavior.

D. The parents were provided with specific examples of a child's escape-motivated misbehavior (i.e., misbehavior that promotes the child getting out or delaying something the child does not want to do).

E. The parents were provided with positive feedback for displaying understanding of demand- and escape-motivated misbehavior.

14. Identify Fun-Seeking Misbehavior (14)

A. The parents were assisted in identifying examples of fun-seeking misbehavior.

B. The parents were given specific examples of fun-seeking misbehavior (e.g., misbehavior that does not require someone to see it and that the child attempts to hide).

C. The parents identified their child's examples of fun-seeking misbehavior; feedback and review were provided.

15. Investigate Behavior Pattern to Reinforce (15)

A. The parents were asked to identify one of their child's behavior patterns that they would like to reinforce.

B. The parents were assigned to record the occurrence of the child's positive behavior pattern every day for a week.

C. The couple was asked to note the situations that precede the identified positive behavior (i.e., antecedents) and follow the behavior (i.e., consequences).

D. The parents have regularly identified the occurrence of the child's positive behavior, antecedents, and consequences and were encouraged to continue this.
E. The parents have not regularly recorded the occurrence, antecedents, and consequences of the identified positive behavior pattern and were redirected to do so.

16. Investigate Behavior Pattern to Decrease (16)

A. The parents were asked to identify one of their child's negative behavior patterns that they would like to decrease.
B. The parents were assigned to record the occurrence of the child's negative behavior pattern every day for a week.
C. The couple was asked to note the situations that precede the identified negative behavior (i.e., antecedents) and follow the behavior (i.e., consequences).
D. The parents have regularly identified the occurrence of the child's negative behavior, antecedents, and consequences and were encouraged to continue this.
E. The parents have not regularly recorded the occurrence, antecedents, and consequences of the identified negative behavior pattern and were redirected to do so.

17. Review Motives for Observed Misbehaviors (17)

A. The parents' tracking sheets of their child's misbehavior were reviewed.
B. The parents were asked to identify the child's motives for each misbehavior observed (i.e., attention-seeking, demand or escape, fun-seeking).
C. Feedback was provided to the parents as they identified the motives for each child misbehavior observed.
D. The parents were provided with tentative interpretations of the motives of each child misbehavior.

18. Teach Purposeful Ignoring (18)

A. The parents were taught about the use of purposeful ignoring a child's misbehavior through role-plays.
B. The parents were encouraged to use the purposeful ignoring technique to discourage the child's attention-seeking misbehavior.
C. The parents were warned that inconsistent use of the purposeful ignoring technique (e.g., ignoring misbehaviors sometimes but attending at other times) will only strengthen misbehavior.

19. Practice Firm Responses (19)

A. The parents were taught about the use of firm, purposeful responses to a child's demand/escape misbehavior.
B. The parents were assisted in practicing the use of firm, purposeful responses to the child's demanding/escape misbehavior.
C. The couple was provided with feedback to help troubleshoot the use of firm, purposeful responses to their child's demanding/escape misbehavior.

20. Teach Commands and Reprimands (20)

A. The parents were taught to use commands and reprimands for a child's fun-motivated misbehavior.

B. The parents were taught to keep commands and reprimands firm, immediate, and brief, with a clear statement of what behavior is expected from a child.

C. The partners were assisted in role-playing implementation of the commands and reprimands to their child.

D. The partners were assisted in trouble-shooting the use of commands and reprimands to their child.

21. Teach Logical and Natural Consequences (21)

A. The parents were taught about establishing logical and natural consequences to child misbehavior.

B. The parents were provided with specific examples about logical and natural consequences (e.g., refused to eat and therefore went hungry).

C. The couple was reinforced as they displayed a clear understanding of natural and logical consequences.

D. The partners had difficulty identifying natural and logical consequences and were provided with additional feedback in this area.

22. Develop Function-Based Responses (22)

A. The parents were assisted in developing a plan for appropriate, function-based responses to child misbehavior.

B. The parents were reinforced for formulating plans to ignore attention misbehaviors, refrain from giving in to demand/escape behaviors, and making fun misbehavior less fun.

C. Feedback was provided to the parents regarding their appropriate, function-based responses to their child's misbehavior.

23. Identify and Brainstorm Interventions for Chronic Misbehavior (23)

A. The parents were asked to list the child's misbehavior situations that are consistently problematic.

B. The parents were assisted in identifying the motivators for the child's misbehavior, and brainstorming ways of preventing the misbehaviors (e.g., shorten duration of shopping trips, pack snacks for child).

C. The parents were provided with feedback about their plans for preventing chronic misbehavior by their child.

24. Teach the Time-Out Technique (24)

A. The parents were taught the time-out technique as consisting of a child sitting in the chair with no attention for one to two minutes per year of age.

B. The parents were assisted in responding to a child's serious misbehavior with the time-out technique.

C. The parents were assisted in troubleshooting the use of the time-out technique in disciplining their child.

D. The benefits of the use of the time-out technique were reviewed.

25. Teach Reinforcing Positive Behaviors (25)

A. The parents were taught to notice and reinforce the child's positive behaviors.
B. The parents were asked to practice child behavior reinforcement in the session.
C. The partners were provided with feedback about their use of the behavior reinforcement.

26. Teach about Good Behavior Charts (26)

A. The parents were instructed about the use of "good behavior charts" for their child.
B. Good behavior charts were provided to the parents through the use of which children earn points/tokens for appropriate behavior and trade their points/tokens for things that they want.
C. The parents were provided with positive feedback for their use of good behavior charts for their child.
D. The parents have not regularly used good behavior charts and were redirected in this area.

27. Increase Recreational Activity (27)

A. The parents were assigned to increase their amount of focused, child-centered activity.
B. The couple was provided with feedback regarding their changes in recreational activity with the child experiencing difficulty.
C. The parents were refocused onto using recreational activities that are more child-centered.

28. Increase Conversation with Child (28)

A. Each parent was assigned to increase the number of parent-initiated, casual, positive conversations with the child experiencing difficulty.
B. The partners were asked to report on their use of casual, positive conversations with the child.
C. The partners were asked to provide feedback about each other's use of casual, positive conversations with the child.
D. The parents reported significant struggles in increasing the number of parent-initiated, casual, positive conversations with the child, and this pattern was analyzed and problem-solved.

29. Contract Change in Own Behavior (29)

A. The parents' modeling of the behavior that they would like to extinguish was reviewed with the parents.
B. The parents admitted their own modeling of the behaviors that they are trying to extinguish with the child (yelling, being sarcastic, smoking) and were urged to change their own behavior.
C. The partners were reinforced for contracting to change their own behavior before trying to change the same behavior in the child.

30. Assign Daily Communication (30)

A. The parents were assigned to confer with each other at least once a day regarding the child's behavior.
B. The partners were asked to log their review of their child's behavior each day.

C. The parents have regularly conferred with each other at least once a day regarding the child's behavior, and the benefits of this were reviewed.
D. The parents have not regularly checked in with each other about the child's behavior and were redirected to do so.

31. Identify Specific Time to Confer (31)

A. The parents were encouraged to plan a mutually acceptable time to confer about their child's behavior.
B. The partners were directed to confer during times when arguments are less likely to erupt (e.g., not immediately upon arriving home in the evening).
C. The partners have used a specific time to confer with each other about the child's behavior, and the benefits of this were reviewed.
D. The partners have not regularly used specific times to confer with each other and were redirected to do so.

32. Track Satisfaction with Check-Ins (32)

A. The partners were instructed to track their satisfaction with the daily conferring about the child's behavior.
B. The partners were directed to bring the tracking sheet to treatment sessions.
C. The partners were reinforced for regularly tracking their satisfaction with the daily conferring.
D. The partners have not been satisfied with the daily check-ins, and the reasons for this were problem-solved.
E. The partners have not been tracking their daily conferring and were redirected to do so.

33. Practice Argument-Control Techniques (33)

A. Modeling and behavioral rehearsal techniques were used to assist the partners in argument control (e.g., calling time-out, using "I" messages in place of "you" messages).
B. The partners practiced the argument control techniques within the session and were provided with feedback about their ability to use these techniques.
C. The partners were assigned to employ techniques to cool off during parenting discussions if either believes that the conversation is becoming unsupportive.
D. The partners were reinforced for regularly using argument-control techniques.
E. The partners reported that they have not used argument-control techniques and were redirected to do so.

34. Role-Play Discussions about Positive Child Behavior (34)

A. The partners were directed to role-play discussions that they will have when the child is well-behaved.
B. The supportive partner was prompted to ask the other partner what the child has been doing and was urged to support the other partner's parenting behaviors.
C. Feedback was provided to the partners' role-play of discussions when the child is well-behaved.

35. Role-Play Discussions for Child's Negative Behavior (35)

A. The partners were directed to role-play discussions that they will have when the child displays negative behavior.

B. The supportive partner was prompted to ask in a supportive, nonthreatening manner about the specifics of the misbehavior.

C. Feedback was provided to the partners about the role-play of discussions that they would have when the child displays negative behavior.

36. Role-Play Support When Dealing with Child Misbehavior (36)

A. The partners were directed to role-play exercises for dealing with child misbehavior.

B. The supportive partner was prompted to ask, in a supportive, nonthreatening manner, how the other partner dealt with the misbehavior.

C. The supportive partner was prompted to ask about ways to help the other partner in the future.

D. The benefits of providing nonthreatening support regarding dealing with child misbehavior were reviewed.

37. Contract about Not Interfering (37)

A. The partners were asked to contract to support each other's parenting by not interfering during the other's parent-child interactions, and by not interfering with the other's decisions (i.e., avoiding splitting up parents' unity).

B. The partners agreed to support each other by not interfering during parent-child interactions or with each other's decisions and were urged to maintain this contract.

C. The partners were provided with examples of how not interfering with the other's parent-child interactions can be supportive and helpful.

D. The couple was provided with examples of how interfering with parent-child interactions and decisions can be disruptive and split the parents' unity.

38. Identify Help in Challenging Situations (38)

A. The partners discussed what each could do to help the other in challenging situations (e.g., play with or supervise the children while the other partner is on the phone).

B. The partners were reinforced for identifying general guidelines for what each can do in challenging situations.

C. The partners failed to identify helpful guidelines for how to help each other in challenging situations and were provided with specific examples.

39. Contract on When to Discuss Disagreements (39)

A. The partners were asked to contract to put disagreements over parenting strategy on hold until a situation has ended and they can meet privately.

B. The partners were asked to contract about discussing disagreements over parenting strategies when they are calm and able to problem-solve without accusations or defensiveness.

C. The partners have contracted to put disagreements over parenting strategy on hold until an appropriate time, and the benefits of doing so were reviewed and processed.

D. The partners have not put discussions of disagreements off until a more appropriate time and were redirected to do so.

40. Schedule Problem-Solving Discussions (40)

A. The partners were assigned to schedule discussions for problem-solving parenting issues two or three times per week.
B. The partners were provided with positive feedback for the use of scheduled parenting problem-solving discussions.
C. The partners reported that they have not scheduled parenting problem-solving discussion times and were redirected to do so.

41. Practice Pinpointing (41)

A. The partners were directed to take turns pinpointing problems.
B. The partners were directed to make requests for change that are specific, observable, and ask for increases in positive behaviors rather than decreases in the other partner's negative behavior.
C. The partners were taught how pinpointing leads to an understandable, positive pattern of communication.
D. The partners have failed to master the skill of pinpointing and were provided with remedial assistance in this area.

42. Teach Paraphrasing (42)

A. While one partner was serving as the speaker, the other partner was directed to paraphrase by rephrasing the speaker's major point.
B. The speaking partner was asked to acknowledge whether the paraphrasing partner had accurately described the intended message.
C. The partners were provided with positive feedback as they displayed several examples of appropriately paraphrasing each other's comments.

43. Limit Problem Focus (43)

A. The partners were advised to limit themselves to solving one problem at a time.
B. The partners were reinforced for limiting themselves to solving one problem at a time.
C. The partners have not limited themselves to solving one problem at a time and were provided with additional discussion in this area.

44. Brainstorm Solutions (44)

A. Each partner was encouraged to brainstorm at least two possible solutions to each of the child's problem behaviors.
B. The partners were encouraged to share the brainstormed ideas of possible solutions to the child's problem behaviors without critiquing them.
C. Positive feedback was provided to the partners for creativity in brainstorming solutions to the child's problem behaviors.

45. Role-Play Choosing a Solution (45)

A. The partners were directed to role-play choosing a solution together by judging the advantages and disadvantages of each possible solution.

B. The partners were provided with positive feedback about the ability to judge the advantages and disadvantages of each possible solution.

46. Plan to Implement Solution (46)

A. The partners were assisted in jointly developing a specific plan about how to implement solutions.

B. As the partners developed a specific plan for implementing solutions, they were provided with feedback.

C. The partners have failed to identify a positive plan for implementing solutions and were provided with additional feedback.

47. Evaluate Effectiveness (47)

A. The partners were asked to establish a time to review the progress of the implemented solution.

B. The partners have reviewed the progress of the implemented solution, and this was summarized within the session.

C. The partners were assisted in troubleshooting the implemented solution as necessary.

D. The partners have not reviewed the effectiveness of the implemented solution and were redirected to do so.

48. Establish House Rules (48)

A. The parents were directed to discuss and establish consistent house rules.

B. Positive feedback was provided to the partners for their discussion and establishment of consistent house rules.

C. The partners have not discussed and established consistent house rules and were redirected to do so.

PERSONALITY DIFFERENCES

CLIENT PRESENTATION

1. Introversion versus Extroversion (1)*

A. The couple described one partner as introverted and the other partner as more extroverted.

B. The couple presented within the session with one partner as introverted and the other partner as more extroverted.

C. One partner described enjoying quiet, solitary, mellow activities, whereas the other partner described enjoying lively, active, socially focused activities.

D. The partners often clash regarding their introverted versus extroverted styles.

E. As treatment has progressed, the partners have been able to value the social characteristics of the other partner.

F. The partners have become more similar regarding their level of inward versus outward focus.

2. Assertion versus Passivity (2)

A. One partner is described as very passive, whereas the other partner presents as quite assertive.

B. One partner displays a very direct, forceful, and bold manner, whereas the other partner tends to be more accepting and avoids confrontations.

C. The partners often argue about the manner in which each relates to others.

D. As treatment has progressed, the partners have begun to value each other's different interactional style.

E. The partners have become more similar in interactional style.

3. Gregarious versus Solitary (3)

A. One partner is described as gregarious, whereas the other partner is described as being more solitary.

B. One partner prefers to either be alone or only with the other partner, whereas the other partner greatly enjoys meeting, talking, and socializing with others.

C. The partners often conflict with each other regarding their different socialization needs.

D. As treatment has progressed, the partners have begun to value each other's socialization style.

E. The partners have become more similar in their socialization style.

4. Religious Differences (4)

A. One partner is involved in religious activities, whereas the other is not.

B. The religious partner describes the couple as "unevenly yoked."

C. The partners often criticize and argue with each other regarding religious issues.

D. The partners have developed an alternative religious outlet, acceptable to both parties.

*The numbers in parentheses on Client Presentation pages correlate to the number of the Behavioral Definition statement in the companion chapter with the same title in *The Couples Psychotherapy Treatment Planner* (Jongsma, O'Leary, and Heyman) by John Wiley & Sons, 1998. The numbers in parentheses on the Interventions Implemented page correspond to the number of the Therapeutic Intervention statement in the companion chapter in the same book.

5. Different Activity Levels (5)

A. One partner is physically active, whereas the other partner prefers sedentary activities.
B. Physical concerns force one partner to be less physically active than the other.
C. The partners often become aggravated with each other due to differences in levels of their physical activity.
D. The partners have become more understanding of each other's preferences and capabilities related to physical activity.
E. The partners have developed lifestyle choices that maximize both partners' preferences regarding the level of activity.

6. Differences Regarding Music (6)

A. One partner enjoys listening to music, whereas the other does not.
B. The partners often clash about the enjoyment of music, radio, or other entertainment.
C. The partners have developed an acceptance of each other's tastes regarding music and other entertainment.
D. The partners have developed a level of compromise regarding music and other entertainment acceptable to both parties.

7. Differences about Sports (7)

A. One partner enjoys watching sports, whereas the other does not.
B. The partners often argue about the amount of time spent watching sports and other related activities.
C. The partners have become more understanding of each other's preferences related to watching sports and developed a compromise acceptable to both partners.

8. Independent versus Dependent (8)

A. One partner is described as independent, whereas the other is described as more dependent.
B. One partner is comfortable in making decisions, doing activities, and solving problems on a solitary basis, whereas the other partner seems to need more reassurance, feedback, and involvement from others.
C. The partners often argue about the level of independence necessary for activities, decisions, and solving problems.
D. The partners have begun to value each other's level of dependence and independence.
E. The partners have become more similar in their level of dependence on each other.

9. Recreational Activities Arguments (9)

A. The partners often argue about the choice of recreational activities.
B. The partners tend to ridicule, avoid, or grudgingly attend each other's recreational activity interests.
C. The partners have gained a greater understanding of each other's choices regarding recreational activities.
D. The partners willingly attend and enjoy each other's choices of recreational activities.

10. Moral Differences (10)

A. One partner is much more moralistic than the other partner.

B. One partner tends to be very rule oriented and more legalistic than the other partner.

C. One partner tends to engage in immoral or unethical practices, much to the consternation of the other partner.

D. The partners have developed a pattern of more moderate decisions regarding moral and ethical concerns.

11. Arguments and Avoidance (11)

A. The partners described a communication style that is argumentative and/or avoidant.

B. The partners presented for treatment due to the arguments and avoidance occurring related to their personality differences.

C. As treatment has progressed, the partners have developed a more healthy style of communication.

12. Decreased Expressions of Caring/Love (12)

A. The partners reported that the level of caring and love within the relationship has waned.

B. The partners rarely show each other physical, emotional, or verbal affection.

C. As the partners have begun to value each other and the different facets of each partner's personality, expressions of caring and love have increased.

INTERVENTIONS IMPLEMENTED

1. Identify Similarities in Personality Styles (1)

A. Each partner was asked to develop a list of his or her own personality traits that are similar to those of the partner.

B. Personality style similarities were identified and reviewed.

C. The partners could not identify similarities within their personality styles, but were provided with some examples of these similarities.

2. Differentiate Habits versus Personality Styles (2)

A. Habits were defined as changeable behaviors.

B. Personality styles were defined as long-standing ways of approaching the world.

C. The difference between habits and personality styles was highlighted.

D. Positive feedback was provided for the partners' clear understanding of the differences between habits and personality styles.

E. The partners failed to understand the difference between habits and personality styles and were given specific examples in this area.

3. Identify Differing Personality Styles (3)

A. Each partner was asked to develop a list of his or her own personality traits that differ significantly from those of the partner.

B. Personality style differences were identified and reviewed.

C. The partners could not identify differences within their personality styles, but were provided with some examples of these differences.

4. Identify Partner's Habits (4)

A. Each partner was asked to develop a list of the other partner's important habits.
B. The partners were assisted in developing lists of the other partner's important habits.
C. Each partner's list of the other partner's important habits was reviewed and summarized.

5. Identify Own Habits (5)

A. Each partner was asked to develop a list of his or her own important personal habits.
B. The partners were assisted in developing lists of his or her own important personal habits.
C. Each partner's list of his or her own important habits was reviewed and summarized

6. Highlight How Differences Enrich the Relationship (6)

A. It was noted to the partners that differences between the partners could often enrich the relationship.
B. The partners were asked to describe how their differences have sometimes enriched the relationship.
C. Feedback was provided as the couple identified specific ways in which the partners have each enriched the relationship with their different personality types.
D. The partners failed to identify how their differences enrich the relationship and were provided with specific examples that have already been observed in therapy.

7. Identify Social Benefit of Differences (7)

A. Each client was asked to identify how differences between self and the partner are valuable and help in social functioning.
B. The partners' examples of the social benefits of differences were reviewed and processed.
C. The partners failed to identify the social benefit of interpersonal differences and were provided with additional feedback and examples in this area.

8. Identify Benefit of Differences to the Intimate Relationship (8)

A. Each client was asked to identify how differences between self and the partner are valuable and help in the intimate relationship between them.
B. The partners' examples of the relationship benefits of differences were reviewed and processed.
C. The partners failed to identify the benefit of interpersonal differences on the intimate relationship and were provided with additional feedback and examples in this area.

9. Describe Negative Impact of Personality Differences (9)

A. Each partner was asked to describe how differences between self and the partner are detrimental to the relationship.
B. Each partner gave specific examples of how personality differences have caused problems within the relationship, and these were reviewed and processed.
C. The partners were asked to identify how the negative impact of personality differences has caused conflict within the relationship.

10. Elaborate on Negative Social Impact (10)

A. Each client was asked to describe how differences in self and the partner are detrimental to social functioning.

B. Each partner identified several examples of how personality differences have caused problems in social functioning, and these were reviewed and processed.

C. The partners were asked to identify how the negative social impact of personality differences has caused conflict within the relationship.

11. Elicit Commitment to Change Habits (11)

A. Each partner was asked to identify habitual patterns that are offensive to the other partner.

B. The partners identified personal habits that are offensive to the other partner and were asked to make a verbal commitment to change these habits.

C. The partners failed to identify habitual patterns that they are willing to change and were reminded about previously identified habits and other examples.

D. The partners were reinforced for making a commitment to change habitual patterns that are offensive to the other partner.

12. Elicit Commitment to Change Long-Standing Personality Patterns (12)

A. Each partner was asked to identify longstanding personality patterns that are offensive to the other partner.

B. The partners identified longstanding personality patterns that are offensive to the other partner and were asked to make a verbal commitment to change these patterns.

C. The partners failed to identify longstanding personality patterns that they are willing to change and were reminded about previously identified personality patterns and other examples.

D. The partners were reinforced for making a commitment to change longstanding personality patterns that are offensive to the other partner.

13. Teach Value of Differences for Parenting (13)

A. A discussion was held regarding the value of personality differences as they relate to rearing children.

B. As emphasis was placed on how personality differences in parents model very different behaviors for children.

C. The partners described increased understanding of how each other's personality differences are helpful for child rearing.

D. The partners tended to focus on the problems that occur due to differences in rearing children and were redirected to the more positive aspects in this area.

14. Identify Hard-to-Change Behaviors (14)

A. The partners were taught about the types of behaviors that are very difficult to change.

B. The partners were asked to identify both general and specific types of behavior that are very difficult to change.

C. The partners were supported as they identified a variety of specific and general types of behavior that are very difficult to change.

D. The partners struggled to understand how some types of behavior are very difficult to change and were provided with additional feedback in this area.

15. Identify Hard-to-Change Personality Styles (15)

A. The partners were taught about the difficulty inherent in changing personality styles.

B. The partners were asked to identify how it is difficult to change personality styles.

C. The partners were supported as they identified a variety of personality styles that are difficult to change.

D. The partners struggled to understand how personality style is very difficult to change and were provided with additional feedback in this area.

16. Characterize Differences as Nonthreatening (16)

A. The clients were presented with the concept that differences can exist between them without it being a detriment to each other.

B. The partners accepted the idea that differences can occur without harming each other.

C. The partners were reinforced for their acceptance of differences between them.

D. The partners continued to focus on the divisive nature of differences between them and were provided with additional feedback in this area.

17. Educate about Value of Personality Differences (17)

A. The clients were presented with the idea that personality differences may be of great value to the relationship.

B. The couple was provided with specific examples of how differences in their personality may be of value to the relationship.

C. The partners were reinforced for endorsing the idea that personality differences may be of great value to the relationship.

D. The partners were asked to provide specific examples of how differences in their personality have been of value to the relationship.

E. The partners denied the value of their differences and were provided with additional feedback.

18. Direct Discussion about Differences (18)

A. The partners were asked to make comments to each other within the therapy session about the value of their differences.

B. The partners' review of differences was coordinated, summarized, and reflected back to them.

C. The partners' description of the value of each other's differences was summarized.

19. Assign Comments to Others (19)

A. The partners were directed to make comments to family and friends about the value of each other's differences.

B. The partners' pattern of comments to family and friends about the value of their differences was reviewed and feedback provided.

PHYSICAL ABUSE

CLIENT PRESENTATION

1. Intentional Pain or Injury (1)*

A. One partner has intentionally inflicted physical pain or injury on the other partner.

B. One partner's actions were perceived by the other partner as having the intent of inflicting physical pain or injury.

C. One partner has been throwing objects at the other partner, pushing, hitting, grabbing, choking, using extreme verbal sexual coercion, or forcing sex on the other partner.

D. As treatment has progressed, the abusing partner has discontinued the pattern of abuse.

2. Intentional Psychological Pain (2)

A. One partner has intentionally inflicted psychological pain on the other partner.

B. One partner's actions were perceived by the other partner as having the intent of inflicting psychological pain.

C. One partner has purposely attempted to cause psychological pain to the other partner by damaging the partner's prized possessions, injuring pets, belittling the partner, telling the partner that he/she can't survive alone, monitoring the partner's whereabouts, or restricting the partner's access to friends.

D. The psychologically abusive partner has terminated the abusive behavior.

3. Fear of Abuse (3)

A. One partner has a fear of physical injury from the other partner

B. One partner has a fear of emotional abuse resulting from threats, intimidation, or berating by the abusive partner.

C. As treatment has progressed, the fearful partner reports less feelings of fear.

INTERVENTIONS IMPLEMENTED

1. Determine Individual versus Conjoint Treatment (1)

A. Individual sessions were used to assess the appropriateness of conjoint versus individual treatment.

B. A variety of factors were considered in selecting the appropriate modality of treatment, including antecedents, impact, function, fear, safety issues, extent of psychological coercion or abuse, openness to discuss issues directly, and resistance to disclose or discuss violence.

C. Conjoint treatment was recommended for the couple.

D. Individual therapy was recommended for the partners.

*The numbers in parentheses on Client Presentation pages correlate to the number of the Behavioral Definition statement in the companion chapter with the same title in *The Couples Psychotherapy Treatment Planner* (Jongsma, O'Leary, and Heyman) by John Wiley & Sons, 1998. The numbers in parentheses on the Interventions Implemented page correspond to the number of the Therapeutic Intervention statement in the companion chapter in the same book.

2. Contract for Prohibition of Abuse (2)

A. Both partners were asked to sign a contract stipulating that no abusive behavior will occur, even when feeling angry.

B. Both partners were reinforced for contracting for a prohibition of abusive behavior.

C. The partners have refused to sign a contract for a prohibition of abusive behavior, and conjoint treatment was terminated.

3. Establish Contingency Plan (3)

A. The couple was directed to establish a contingency plan for what a partner will do if the nonviolence contract is violated (e.g., call police, leave the situation, arrange for separation).

B. Feedback was provided for the partners' contingency plan for what to do if their nonviolence contract is violated.

4. Educate about Illegal and Maladaptive Nature of Abuse (4)

A. Both partners were educated on how partner abuse is illegal.

B. Both partners were educated about how partner abuse is maladaptive.

C. Both partners displayed an understanding of the maladaptive and illegal nature of partner abuse.

D. The partners struggled to understand the illegal and maladaptive aspects of partner abuse and were provided with more specific information in this area.

5. Define Abuse (5)

A. Both partners were assisted in defining physical and emotional abuse in concrete, behavioral terms.

B. Both partners were reinforced for their accurate understanding of the definition of emotional and physical abuse.

C. The partners displayed a poor understanding of the definitions of physical and emotional abuse and were provided with additional feedback in this area.

6. Refer for Additional Abuse-Related Services (6)

A. Due to the victim's level of fearfulness, a referral was made to services designed to support the victims of abuse.

B. Due to the severe abuse that has occurred, the aggressive partner was referred to a domestic violence treatment group.

C. The partners have followed through on referrals to additional services.

D. The partners have not followed through on referrals to additional services and were directed to do so.

7. Establish a Safety Plan (7)

A. The victim was directed to establish a safety plan in case further abuse appears imminent or occurs.

B. The victim was assisted in developing a comprehensive safety plan, including identification of violence cues and resources for assistance, prearrangement of items necessary for escape, and a plan of where to go and what to do if violence erupts.

C. The partner who was a victim of abuse was encouraged to take the appropriate initial steps for the implementation of the safety plan.

D. The partner who has been victimized has not developed and prepared for a comprehensive safety plan and was redirected to do so.

8. Teach about Gradations of Anger (8)

A. The partners were taught about the different gradations of anger.

B. The partners were taught to recognize the behaviors and cognitions associated with the different levels of anger.

C. The partners were reinforced for their accurate understanding of the gradations, behaviors, and cognitions associated with anger.

D. The partners did not display an adequate understanding of the gradations of anger and the behaviors and cognitions associated with each level of anger and were provided with remedial information in this area.

9. Train in Emotion Recognition (9)

A. The partners were trained to recognize and label emotions other than anger.

B. The partners were asked to identify the emotions that often precede anger.

C. The partners were reinforced for displaying a comprehensive understanding of the emotions that trigger anger and how to recognize them.

D. The partners have not mastered the recognition and labeling of emotions related to anger and were provided with remedial feedback in this area.

10. Assign Anger-Tracking Homework (10)

A. The partners were assigned to track anger experiences, listing the situations that trigger anger, as well as the thoughts and behaviors that occur during anger-eliciting situations.

B. The partners have completed the anger-tracking homework, and this material was reviewed and processed.

C. The partners have not completed the anger-tracking homework and were redirected to do so.

11. Teach Time-Out Techniques (11)

A. The partners were taught about the six components of time-out techniques (i.e., *self-monitoring* for escalating feelings of anger and hurt, *signaling* to the partner that verbal engagement should end, *acknowledging* the need of the partner to disengage, *separating* to disengage, *cooling down* to regain control of anger, and *returning* to controlled verbal engagement).

B. Positive feedback was provided as the partners displayed mastery of time-out techniques.

C. The partners were advised about the potential for misuse and manipulation of time-out techniques if used to avoid arguments or manipulate the other partner.

D. The partners have misused time-out techniques and were provided with additional feedback in this area.

E. The partners were reinforced for using time-out techniques appropriately to avoid escalation of conflict.

12. Educate Partners about Therapy Boundary (12)

A. The partners were educated regarding the negative impact that can occur to the therapy process if one of the partners is critical or angry about what the other partner says in a session.

B. Positive reinforcement was provided to the partners for their acceptance of the need to refrain from being critical or angry with each other for what is said in the session.

C. The partners are often critical or angry with each other for what is said in the session, and further intervention was delayed until this issue could be resolved.

13. Educate about Respect in Sessions (13)

A. The partners were educated regarding the need for each to respect the other in sessions, especially when feelings become strong.

B. Emphasis was placed on the therapist's responsibility for maintaining control of the session and for interrupting the partner's destructive patterns of interaction.

C. Encouragement was provided as the partners agreed to abide by the therapist's directions if the session process becomes destructive.

D. The partners have accepted the therapist's guidance within the session when feelings became strong and disrespect occurred.

E. The partners have failed to accept the therapist's direction when strong feelings led to disrespectful behaviors, and further interventions were postponed until this issue could be resolved.

14. Assess for Chemical Dependence (14)

A. The partners were assessed for the presence of chemical dependence.

B. The physically abusive partner was identified as having a chemical dependence problem.

C. The partner who has been abused was identified as having a chemical dependence problem.

D. The partners were provided with feedback about the ways in which chemical dependence has contributed to the abusive behavior.

E. No pattern of chemical dependence was identified.

15. Renegotiate Relationship Contract (15)

A. The partners were noted to have an unhealthy, dysfunctional, implicit relationship contract (i.e., who has the right to do what).

B. The partners' dysfunctional relationship contract was renegotiated with an emphasis on mutual respect for individual opinions, beliefs, and feelings.

C. The partners were reinforced for establishing a healthier, more functional relationship contract with the emphasis on respect for individual opinions, feelings, and beliefs.

D. The partners denied any pattern of dysfunctional, implicit relationship contract and were provided with feedback in this area.

16. Challenge Gender-Based Beliefs (16)

A. The partners were assisted in identifying gender-based beliefs that promote abuse (e.g., women are inferior, men have ultimate authority, women deserve abuse when they do not comply with men's wishes).

B. The couple's gender-based beliefs that promote abuse were challenged.
C. Positive feedback was provided to the partners for acknowledging that their gender-based beliefs are unreasonable and unfair.

17. Describe History of Victimization (17)

A. Each partner was asked to describe any history of psychological and/or physical victimization in childhood.
B. The physically abusive partner was supported while describing a history of psychological and/or physical victimization in childhood.
C. The abused partner was supported while describing a history of psychological and/or physical victimization in childhood.
D. Neither partner identified or acknowledged any history of psychological and/or physical victimization in childhood.

18. Educate about Destructive Consequences of Abuse (18)

A. The partners were educated regarding the destructive consequences that partner abuse has on each partner.
B. The harmful effects of the partner abuse on the children was emphasized.
C. The partners were reinforced for their understanding of how each family member can be negatively affected by the partner abuse.
D. The partners were provided with remedial information regarding the effects partner abuse has on all family members.

19. Confront Blaming of the Victim (19)

A. The aggressive partner was confronted regarding a tendency to excuse own abusive behavior by blaming the partner for provoking it.
B. The aggressive partner was provided with support for acknowledging that the victim is never to blame for the abuse.
C. The abusive partner persists in blaming the victim for the abuse and was provided with additional confrontation in this area.

20. Model and Reinforce Responsibility for Behavior (20)

A. Within the session, the taking of responsibility for one's own behavior was modeled.
B. Whenever either partner displayed acceptance of full responsibility for behavior, positive feedback was provided.

21. Educate about Assertive Communication (21)

A. The partners were educated about the differences between nonassertive, assertive, and aggressive communication.
B. The partners were provided with specific examples of nonassertive, assertive, and aggressive communication.
C. The partners identified their own examples of nonassertive, assertive, and aggressive communication and were provided with feedback about these examples.

22. Identify Function of Abuse (22)

A. The partners were assisted in understanding the function of partner abuse.

B. The partners endorsed specific functions of partner abuse, although it was acknowledged that this was an inappropriate way to meet this need.

C. The partners were assisted in developing nonabusive means to accomplish the goals previously achieved through partner abuse.

23. Process Recent Aggression (23)

A. An analysis of recent examples of the aggressive partner's angry feelings or anger outbursts was conducted.

B. Alternative behaviors that were available for the aggressive partner's angry feelings were identified.

24. List Alternative Behaviors (24)

A. The aggressive partner was assigned to list several positive alternative behaviors to be engaged in when anger is felt.

B. The aggressive partner identified several positive alternative behaviors (e.g., taking time out, calling a friend, taking a walk, writing out feelings, reviewing a list of negative consequences), and these were reviewed within the session.

C. The aggressive partner has not developed a list of positive alternative behaviors to use when anger is felt and was redirected to do so.

25. Assign Books on Anger (25)

A. The partners were directed to read material to help increase their understanding of anger.

B. The partners were referred to *Of Course You're Angry* (Rosellini and Worden) or *The Angry Book* (Rubin).

C. The partners have followed through on reading material on anger, and key ideas from this material were processed within the session.

D. The client has not followed through on reading assigned material and was encouraged to do so.

E. The partners were reinforced for reporting that they learned much from the material that was assigned, and for describing greater awareness of the causes for and targets of anger.

26. Confront Failure to Take Responsibility (26)

A. The aggressive partner was confronted regarding the need to take responsibility for the abuse.

B. The aggressive partner was directed to find specific ways to express remorse.

C. Positive feedback was provided to the aggressive partner for taking responsibility for the abuse and expressing remorse.

D. The aggressive partner required additional prompts and confrontation to take responsibility for the abuse and express remorse.

27. Confront Victim Taking Responsibility (27)

A. The victim's pattern of taking responsibility for the aggressive partner's behavior decisions was confronted.

B. The victim was reinforced for holding the aggressive partner responsible for the abusive behavior.

28. Reinforce Assertiveness (28)

A. The partners were reinforced for assertive behaviors during the session.
B. When the partners described assertive behaviors engaged in between sessions, positive feedback was provided.
C. The partners have not used assertiveness in situations between the sessions and were redirected to do so.

29. Review Life Experiences (29)

A. The aggressive partner's life experiences were reviewed, focusing on experiences that taught the aggressive partner that violence and verbal abuse are acceptable behaviors for expressing anger.
B. The aggressive partner was supported for insights about how past life experiences have taught the use of inappropriate, violent or verbally abusive responses.
C. The abusive partner denied any previous life experiences that have taught that violence and verbal abuse are acceptable behaviors for expressing anger and was redirected to review these areas more closely.

30. Review Victim's Life Experiences (30)

A. The victim's life experiences were reviewed, focusing on experiences that taught the victim that violence and verbal abuse are behaviors that are to be expected, excused, and tolerated.
B. Positive feedback was provided as the victim displayed insight into how previous life experiences have caused violence and verbal abuse to be expected, excused, and tolerated.
C. The victim displayed denial regarding the influence of previous life experiences and was given further feedback in this area.

31. Identify Self-Blame (31)

A. The victim was assisted in identifying a pattern of blaming self for the partner's abusive behavior.
B. The victim was provided with positive feedback for insight into a pattern of blaming self for the partner's abusive behaviors.
C. The victim was assisted in developing a clear understanding of the principle of personal responsibility for behavioral decisions.

32. Reinforce Focus on Responsibility (32)

A. The victim was reinforced for holding the aggressive partner responsible for the aggressive behavior.
B. During sessions, the victim was immediately supported and encouraged for holding the aggressive partner responsible for aggressive behavior.
C. The victim failed to hold the aggressive partner responsible for aggressive behavior and was provided with feedback and direction in this area.

33. List Hurtful Life Experiences (33)

A. The aggressive partner was assigned to list hurtful life experiences that have led to anger.
B. The aggressive partner was assisted in developing a list of hurtful life experiences that have led to anger.
C. The aggressive partner has not developed a list of hurtful life experiences that have led to anger and was redirected to do so.

34. Emphasize Emotions Related to Trauma (34)

A. The aggressive partner's feelings of hurt and anger related to past traumas were judged to be appropriate.
B. Positive feedback was provided to the aggressive partner for the identification of emotions related to past traumas.
C. The aggressive partner was assisted in clarifying the emotions of hurt and anger tied to the traumas of the past.
D. The aggressive partner denied feelings of hurt and anger tied to traumas of the past and was provided with confrontation of this denial and tentative reframes in this area.

35. Discuss Forgiveness (35)

A. The victim's forgiveness of the aggressive partner was described as a process of letting go of anger.
B. The victim endorsed the need to provide forgiveness to the aggressive partner as a way to let go.
C. The victim denied the need for forgiveness and was provided feedback in this area.

36. Assign Forgiveness Reading (36)

A. The aggressive partner was directed to read books related to forgiveness.
B. The aggressive partner was assigned to read the book *Forgive and Forget* (Smedes) to increase sensitivity to the process of forgiveness.
C. The client has read the assigned material on forgiveness, and key concepts were processed within the session.
D. The client has not followed through with completing the reading assignment related to forgiveness and was encouraged to do so.
E. The client acknowledged that holding on to angry feelings has distinct disadvantages over beginning the process of forgiveness.

37. Identify Negative Communication Patterns (37)

A. The partners were assisted in identifying negative communication patterns in the relationship that accompany and/or increase the likelihood of physical aggression.
B. The partners were reinforced for identifying and acknowledging their negative communication patterns (e.g., vocally blaming the partner for problems, fast reciprocation of a partner's anger, lack of empathy, contempt for or lack of respect for the partner, defensiveness, refusal to change, resistance, withdrawal, coercive control/entitlement).
C. The partners denied any pattern of negative communication in the relationship and were provided with specific examples of this from insession contacts.

38. Teach Positive Communication Skills (38)

A. Role-play and behavioral rehearsal were used to teach the partners positive communication skills (e.g., problem identification, "I" statements, listening skills, problem-solving skills, behavioral contracting).

B. The couple was reinforced for their display of mastery of positive communication skills (e.g., problem identification, "I" statements, listening skills, problem-solving skills, behavioral contracting).

C. The partners were assigned to practice positive communication skills as homework.

D. The partners have been regularly using positive communication skills, and the benefits of this were reviewed.

E. The partners have not completed homework assignments related to positive communication skills and were redirected to do so.

PSYCHOLOGICAL ABUSE

CLIENT PRESENTATION

1. Insults Partner (1)*

A. The abusive partner insults the other partner when alone.
B. The abusive partner insults the other partner in front of others.
C. The abusive partner makes veiled insults to the other partner.
D. As treatment has progressed, the frequency and intensity of the insulting behavior has decreased.
E. There have been no reports of insults given to either partner recently.

2. Swears at Partner (2)

A. The abusive partner often swears at the other partner.
B. The abusive partner often uses crass, foul language in reference to the other partner.
C. As the abusive partner has gained insight into the psychological abuse, the frequency and intensity of swearing has decreased.
D. The abusive cursing has stopped.

3. Demeaning Names (3)

A. The abusive partner often refers to the other partner in demeaning, degrading ways.
B. The abusive partner calls the other partner demeaning, degrading names (e.g., lazy, sloppy).
C. As treatment has progressed, the abusive partner has become more positive and uplifting in references to the other partner.
D. The demeaning, degrading references have stopped.

4. Critical of Physical Appearance (4)

A. The psychologically abusive partner often makes critical, demeaning comments about the other partner's body (e.g., fat, bald, ugly, skinny).
B. The abusive partner often focuses on physical traits to demean the other partner.
C. The abusive partner's comments now reflect a positive attitude toward the other partner's body.

5. Criticizes Job Performance (5)

A. The psychologically abusive partner often makes critical and demeaning comments about the other partner's work performance.
B. The abusive partner often brings up the other partner's previous employment defects or failures.
C. The abusive partner has decreased the critical and demeaning comments about the other partner's work performance.
D. Critical comments about work performance have ceased.

*The numbers in parentheses on Client Presentation pages correlate to the number of the Behavioral Definition statement in the companion chapter with the same title in *The Couples Psychotherapy Treatment Planner* (Jongsma, O'Leary, and Heyman) by John Wiley & Sons, 1998. The numbers in parentheses on the Interventions Implemented page correspond to the number of the Therapeutic Intervention statement in the companion chapter in the same book.

6. Critical of Home Role Performance (6)

A. The critical partner often makes disparaging comments about how tasks are completed around the home (e.g., cooking, fixing things, cleaning, taking care of yard).

B. The psychologically abusive partner often makes critical comments about the other partner's ability to perform roles in the home (e.g., "You are a lousy cook," or "It takes you a year to fix little things").

C. As treatment has progressed, the critical partner has become more evidence-based in the review of the other partner's home role performance.

D. The critical partner has begun to verbalize valuing the other partner's positive home role performance.

7. Unfounded Accusations of Promiscuity and Infidelity (7)

A. The psychologically abusive partner has, without cause, accused the other partner of sexual promiscuity and infidelity.

B. The psychologically abusive partner often responds to unrelated insecurities with accusations about the other partner's fidelity.

C. The psychologically abusive partner often uses information from the other partner's sexual history prior to the relationship to support accusations of promiscuity and infidelity.

D. As the psychologically abusive partner has gained greater stability, accusations of sexual promiscuity and infidelity have decreased in intensity and frequency.

8. Criticism about Sexuality (8)

A. The psychologically abusive partner often makes critical comments about the other partner's sexuality and sexual performance.

B. The abusive partner often attempts to humiliate the other partner regarding sexual issues by making negative comments in front of others.

C. As treatment has progressed, the abusive partner's negative comments related to sexuality and sexual performance have been discontinued.

9. Critical about Partner's Mental Health (9)

A. The abusive partner often makes critical comments about the other partner's mental health (e.g., "You are crazy," "You need a psychiatrist," "You are paranoid").

B. The psychologically abusive partner often belittles the other partner for seeking mental health treatment.

C. The abusive partner has terminated comments about the other partner's mental health.

10. Threats to Harm (10)

A. The psychologically abusive partner makes vague threats about harming the other partner.

B. The psychologically abusive partner makes specific threats about harming the other partner.

C. As treatment has progressed, threats to do physical harm to the partner have been decreased.

D. The psychologically abusive partner has discontinued the pattern of threatening the other partner with physical harm.

11. Threats to Leave (11)

A. The psychologically abusive partner makes vague threats about leaving the other partner.
B. The psychologically abusive partner makes specific threats about leaving the other partner.
C. As treatment has progressed, the threats to leave the other partner have decreased.
D. The psychologically abusive partner has discontinued the pattern of threatening to leave the other partner.

12. Threats to Have an Affair (12)

A. The psychologically abusive partner makes vague threats about having sex with someone else.
B. The psychologically abusive partner makes specific threats about having another sexual partner.
C. As treatment has progressed, the threats to seek another sexual partner have decreased.
D. The psychologically abusive partner has discontinued the pattern of threatening the other partner with affairs.

13. Blocks Contact with Friends and Family (13)

A. The psychologically abusive partner has forbidden the other partner to have contact with friends and family.
B. The psychologically abusive partner has prevented the other partner from having contact with friends and family.
C. The psychologically abusive partner has punished the other partner for having contact with friends and family.
D. The psychologically abusive partner has now endorsed the need for the other partner to have unrestricted access to friends and family.

14. Prohibits Partner from Leaving Home (14)

A. The psychologically abusive partner has forbidden the other partner to leave the home without supervision.
B. The psychologically abusive partner has prevented the other partner from leaving the home.
C. The psychologically abusive partner has punished the other partner for leaving home against the abusive partner's wishes.
D. The psychologically abusive partner has now endorsed the need for the other partner to have unrestricted freedom to leave the home.

15. Blocks Use of Car (15)

A. The psychologically abusive partner has denied the other partner the use of the couple's motor vehicle.
B. The abusive partner has made it physically impossible for the other partner to use the couple's motor vehicle (e.g., taking the keys away, removing spark plugs or wires).
C. The partners have agreed to unrestricted access to the motor vehicle for both partners.

16. Silent Treatment (16)

A. The psychologically abusive partner often uses the silent treatment when angry.
B. The psychologically abusive partner does not allow the other partner to engage in regular conversation for an extended period of time, due to some perceived slight.

C. As treatment has progressed, the partners have agreed to discuss issues rather than use manipulative tactics, such as the silent treatment.

17. Requires Accounting of Time (17)

A. The psychologically abusive partner makes the other partner account for time.

B. The psychologically abusive partner becomes extremely angry when the other partner does not meet strict expectations about timeliness.

C. When time is not specifically accounted for, the psychologically abusive partner makes accusations about the other partner.

D. As treatment has progressed, the psychologically abusive partner has become more trusting and less demanding of information regarding the other partner's time and whereabouts.

E. Time-accounting demands have ceased.

18. Jealous of Time with Others (18)

A. The psychologically abusive partner reports feelings of jealousy regarding time that the other partner spends with other individuals.

B. The jealous partner becomes especially upset when the other partner spends time with someone of the opposite sex.

C. The abusive partner often expressed feelings of jealousy through intimidation, critical comments, or threats.

D. The jealous partner has become more at ease with the other partner's spending time with other individuals.

19. Discourages Partner's Self-Improvement (19)

A. The psychologically abusive partner often discourages the other partner from opportunities for self-improvement that would increase self-esteem.

B. The psychologically abusive partner has refused the other partner such options as training or education that would create opportunities for career or personal advancement.

C. The psychologically abusive partner is critical of the other partner's opportunities for greater involvement in interests or areas in which that partner might receive greater recognition.

D. As treatment has progressed, the psychologically abusive partner has come to be supportive of the other partner's opportunities for increased self-esteem and advancement.

20. Ordering Around (20)

A. The psychologically abusive partner often orders the other partner around in a dominating, controlling, and belittling manner.

B. The partner being victimized often feels as though there is no other option but to comply with the psychologically abusive partner's pattern of domination, controlling, and belittling.

C. As treatment has progressed, the victimized partner has become less willing to acquiesce to the other partner's domination.

D. The psychologically abusive partner has become less dominating, controlling, and belittling toward the other partner.

INTERVENTIONS IMPLEMENTED

1. Obtain Verbal Commitment (1)

A. The partners were asked to make a verbal commitment not to engage in name-calling or making hostile comments.

B. Positive feedback was provided as both partners agreed to make a commitment to stop hostile comments and name-calling.

2. Advise about Individual Therapy Option (2)

A. The partners were advised about the need for individual therapy if anger cannot be controlled in the conjoint therapy sessions.

B. The partners were advised that individual therapy sessions were necessary, due to the high level of anger within the conjoint sessions.

C. Anger levels have been adequately controlled to allow the use of conjoint therapy sessions to focus on the psychological abuse.

3. Discuss Readiness for Conjoint Therapy (3)

A. Both partners were advised that conjoint therapy will begin only when both partners feel secure and accepting of this approach.

B. Both partners were asked to minimize the probability that any major negative events occur during therapy.

C. The partners were supported for acknowledging that both partners must feel psychologically ready for conjoint sessions.

4. Describe Hurtful Comments (4)

A. Each client was asked to describe comments by the other partner that have been the most hurtful.

B. Support and encouragement were provided to each partner as they reviewed the painful comments that each has made to the other partner.

5. Describe Areas of Vulnerability (5)

A. Each partner was asked to describe their own personal areas of greatest vulnerability.

B. Support was provided as each partner described personal areas of vulnerability.

C. Gentle confrontation was provided to the partners when it was perceived that a partner was denying or minimizing personal vulnerability.

6. Reverse Roles to Increase Empathy (6)

A. The abusive partner was directed to use role-reversal techniques to assume the abused partner's identity, and then describe the emotional impact of the abusive behavior.

B. The abusive partner gained insight and empathy through the use of the role-reversal technique.

C. The abusive partner found it difficult to assume the abused partner's identity and describe the emotional impact of the abusive behavior and was provided with feedback about this area.

7. Confront Abusive Behavior (7)

A. Any displays of abusive behavior were confronted.

B. References to or threats of abusive behavior were confronted as though they were actual abuse behavior.

C. An emphasis was placed on teaching the clients about the consequences of abusive behavior.

8. Obtain Commitment against Coercive Sexual Interaction (8)

A. The partners were asked to commit not to use physical force to coerce sexual interaction.

B. The partners both agreed not to use physical force to coerce sexual interaction and were reinforced for this progress.

9. Educate about Positive Sexual Relationship (9)

A. The partners were taught that a positive sexual relationship dictates that the sexual activity must be acceptable to both partners.

B. The partners were urged to see the sexual relationship as a mirror of the rest of the relationship.

C. The partners were supported for agreeing that sexual activity must be acceptable to both partners for the sexual relationship to be a healthy one and were supported for this expectation.

10. Educate about Effects of Coercive Sexual Activity (10)

A. The clients were taught how the pressure by one partner to engage in sexual activity usually leads to sexual aversions and/or avoidance and dislike by the other partner.

B. The partners were encouraged to provide specific examples of how coercive sexual activity has led to sexual aversions, avoidance, and dislike.

C. The partners were reinforced for displaying understanding of how sexual activity leads to sexual aversions, avoidance, and dislike.

11. Elaborate on Sensitive Nature of Sexual Coercion (11)

A. The partners were taught how sexual behavior is one of the most sensitive of all human behaviors.

B. The partners were taught how aversive control by one partner can quickly lead to disinterest and sexual dysfunction in the other partner.

C. The partners were urged to identify how aversive control has led to sexual dysfunction and disinterest within their relationship.

D. Positive feedback was provided as the partners displayed an understanding of how aversive control leads to dysfunction and disinterest within the sexual relationship.

12. Obtain Commitment against Threats to Have an Affair (12)

A. The partners were asked to commit not to make threats to have sex with someone else.

B. The partners both agreed not to make threats to have sex with someone else and were reinforced for this progress.

13. Obtain Commitment to Maintain Relationship (13)

A. The partners were asked to verbally commit not to threaten to leave the relationship during the term of therapy.

B. The partners were reminded of the length of commitment to therapy developed at the beginning of treatment.

C. The partners were provided with positive reinforcement for giving verbal commitments not to threaten to leave the relationship during the term of therapy.

D. The partners were confronted when making comments about leaving the relationship.

14. Obtain Commitment against Physical Force (14)

A. The partners were asked to make a verbal commitment not to engage in any physical force against the partner for any reason.

B. The partners were informed that when verbal intimidation exists, the risk for physical aggression is also high.

C. The partners made a verbal commitment not to engage in any physical force against each other for any reason; the benefits of the commitment were enumerated.

D. Confrontation of one partner was provided when it was suspected that physical force was being used or threatened.

15. Inquire about Coercion and Violence (15)

A. The partners were asked to describe the extent to which psychological coercion and threats of violence are present in the relationship in general.

B. Each partner was asked individually to identify the extent to which coercion and violence is present in the relationship.

C. The level of coercion and violence in the relationship was reflected to the partners.

D. It was noted that there continues to be physical coercion and threats of violence within the relationship.

E. The partner was reinforced for the fact that no current physical coercion or threats of violence exist within the relationship currently.

16. Inquire about Consequences of Threatened Violence (16)

A. Each partner was asked to identify the perceived or experienced negative consequences of threatened violence.

B. The partners identified negative effects of perceived or threatened violence (e.g., distrust, fear, isolation, and anger) and were positively reinforced for this understanding.

C. The negative effects of threatened violence were reflected to the partners.

17. Refer to Safe Environment (17)

A. The abused partner's fear of violence was estimated to be quite intense, so a referral to a safe environment (e.g. battered women's shelter, abuse hot-line numbers) was provided.

B. The abused partner has followed up on the referral to a safe environment.

C. The abused partner has not followed up on the referral to a safe environment and was reminded about the use of this option.

18. Review Patriarchy (18)

A. The concept of patriarchy in the current society was reviewed.

B. A discussion was coordinated regarding the patriarchal nature of our society.

C. The partners were supported as they described their experience of patriarchy in current society.

19. Review Misuse of Power (19)

A. The partners were directed to discuss how the controlling partner misuses power within the relationship.

B. The abused partner was provided with support and encouragement while reviewing how the controlling partner misuses power within the relationship.

C. The controlling partner was provided with immediate, positive feedback for identification of the misuse of power within the relationship.

D. The abusive partner tended to deny the misuse of power within the relationship and was provided with tentative examples of the misuse of power within their relationship.

20. Educate about Control Leading to Dislike and Avoidance (20)

A. The partners were informed that controlling behaviors by one partner tend to lead to dislike and avoidance by the other partner.

B. The partners were asked to identify how controlling behaviors have led to dislike and avoidance in their own relationship.

C. The partners were provided with support and feedback as they described the pattern of controlling behaviors leading to dislike and avoidance within their relationship.

D. The abusive partner denied any pattern of controlling behaviors leading to dislike and avoidance within their own relationship and was provided with tentative examples in this area.

21. Review Aggression/Low Self-Esteem Connection (21)

A. The clients were provided with evidence regarding the association between psychological aggression and low self-esteem.

B. The partners were provided with evidence regarding the association between psychological aggression and depression.

C. The partners were asked to review how psychological aggression, low self-esteem, and depression are related within their relationship.

D. The partners were asked to identify specific ways to build self-esteem in each other.

E. Positive feedback was provided as the clients have focused on developing positive self-esteem within each other.

22. Educate about Relationship between Social Support and Relationship Satisfaction (22)

A. The partners were taught how external social support (e.g., contact with friends) and relationship satisfaction are positively related.

B. The partners were asked to identify how they have experienced the connection between external social support and relationship satisfaction.

23. Educate about Need for Support (23)

A. The clients were taught the need for each partner to be able to venture out from the relationship with the sense that the other will be supportive.

B. Specific examples of how it is necessary for each partner to venture out from the relationship were provided (i.e., bettering self through education, training, or job enhancement).

C. The partners were asked to identify how support from each other could assist in positive outcomes through venturing out from the relationship.

D. Positive feedback was provided as the partners have supported each other in venturing out from the relationship for self-enhancement.

E. The partners were confronted for continuing a pattern of nonsupport when one partner is attempting to venture out from the relationship for self-enhancement.

24. Identify Underlying Feelings (24)

A. The abusive partner was asked to identify the underlying feelings that motivate the need for controlling behavior.

B. The abusive partner identified the feelings that lead to controlling behavior, including jealousy and fears of inadequacy; strong support was provided for acknowledging these types of emotions.

C. The abusive partner tended to be in denial about the feelings that lead to controlling behavior and was provided with tentative feedback in this area.

25. List Negative Consequences (25)

A. Each partner was asked to list the negative consequences of controlling behavior on the abused partner.

B. The partners were assisted in developing a list of the negative consequences of controlling behavior on the abused partner.

C. Emphasis was placed on the negative consequences that the abused partner has identified (e.g., resentment, avoidance, waning of caring feelings).

D. Emphasis was placed on the negative consequences that the abusive partner was able to identify.

26. Prompt Listening and Paraphrasing (26)

A. Each partner was directed to listen to the other partner about a relationship problem without interrupting and then paraphrase what the other said.

B. Positive feedback was provided as the partners displayed an ability to listen and paraphrase each other's comments.

C. The partners were provided with remedial feedback about the inability to listen without interrupting and the inability to paraphrase.

27. Critique Communication Style (27)

A. Feedback and interpretation were provided to the partners about their communication styles.

B. The partners were provided with feedback about how their communication styles work together.

C. The partners were provided with feedback about how their communication styles may cause conflict with each other.

28. Evaluate Relationship Alternatives (28)

A. In an individual session with the psychologically abused client, the focus was on evaluating the available alternatives to the current relationship.

B. The psychologically abused client has indicated a desire to pursue available alternatives to the current relationship.

C. The psychologically abused partner does not see any alternatives to the current relationship and was provided with feedback about this assessment.

D. The psychologically abused client identified available alternatives to the current relationship, but has elected not to pursue these.

29. Suggest Reading Materials (29)

A. Reading materials were suggested to the abused client .

B. The abused client was encouraged to read *The Verbally Abusive Relationship* (Evans).

C. The abused client has read the assigned materials, and the salient points were reviewed.

D. The abused client has not read the assigned materials and was redirected to do so.

30. Refer to Shelter (30)

A. The psychologically abused partner was referred to a battered women's shelter.

B. The psychologically abused client was referred to an agency that assists women who have been battered.

C. The psychologically abused client has followed up on a referral to a battered women's program, and the benefits of this were reviewed.

D. The psychologically abused client has not followed up on a referral to a battered women's shelter, and her decision was processed.

31. Review Effects on Children (31)

A. Evidence regarding the significant link connecting open hostility between parents and psychopathology in children was reviewed.

B. The increased incidents of conduct problems and anxiety problems in the children were identified as a few of the evidence-based links between open hostility between parents and psychopathology in children.

C. The partners endorsed the connection between open hostility in their relationship, and the potential for psychopathology in their children.

32. Commit to Minimizing Negative Conduct in Front of Children (32)

A. Both partners were asked to minimize negative interactions in the presence of the children.

B. The partners were reinforced for agreeing to minimize the interactions in the presence of the children.

RECREATIONAL ACTIVITIES DISPUTE

CLIENT PRESENTATION

1. Conflict over Leisure Activity Choices (1)*

A. The partners reported frequent conflicts over the leisure activities choices shared.

B. One partner enjoys more physical leisure activities, and the other partner enjoys more sedentary leisure activities.

C. One partner enjoys socially-oriented leisure activities, and the other partner enjoys activities with just the partner.

D. Leisure activities tend to lead to arguments rather than producing relaxation.

E. As communication and compromise have improved, the partners have developed a more mutually satisfying pattern of leisure activities.

2. Conflict over Individual Recreational Time (2)

A. The partners reported a pattern of one or both partners engaging in individual recreational activities without the other partner.

B. The partners often have conflict about the amount of time spent by one partner in individual recreational activities.

C. One partner described feeling left out and unappreciated due to the time spent by the other partner in individual recreational activities.

D. As treatment has progressed, conflicts over time spent by one partner in individual recreational activities have decreased.

3. Feelings of Disconnectedness (3)

A. The partners described a pattern of one or both partners engaging extensively in separate, unshared recreational activities.

B. The partners described feelings of disconnectedness due to the lack of mutual involvement in recreational activities.

C. One partner reports feeling jealous toward the other partner's involvement in separate, unshared recreational activities.

D. The partners have developed a pattern of sharing activities and feeling more connected with each other.

4. Vacation Disagreements (4)

A. The partners reported frequent disagreements over the manner in which vacation time is spent.

B. One partner favors spending most of the vacations at home, while the other partner enjoys traveling.

C. One partner enjoys very active vacations, while the other partner enjoys more relaxing vacations.

*The numbers in parentheses on Client Presentation pages correlate to the number of the Behavioral Definition statement in the companion chapter with the same title in *The Couples Psychotherapy Treatment Planner* (Jongsma, O'Leary, and Heyman) by John Wiley & Sons, 1998. The numbers in parentheses on the Interventions Implemented page correspond to the number of the Therapeutic Intervention statement in the companion chapter in the same book.

D. As communication and compromise have increased, the partners have decreased the frequency of disagreements over the manner in which vacation time is spent.

5. Erosion of Partner-Pleasing Activities (5)

A. The partners described a decrease in the amount of time that each partner spends in partner-pleasing activities.

B. The partners reported a decrease in the quality of time spent in partner-pleasing activities.

C. The partners describe a sense of being intimate strangers.

D. The partners describe an increase in the quality and quantity of time spent in partner-pleasing activities.

INTERVENTIONS IMPLEMENTED

1. Identify Level of Satisfaction with Recreational Activities (1)

A. Each partner was asked about their level of satisfaction with recreational activities that are done individually.

B. Each partner was asked about their level of satisfaction with recreational activities that are done as a couple.

C. The partners' level of satisfaction with recreational activities was reflected to them.

2. Identify Areas for Improvement (2)

A. Each partner was asked to identify elements of recreational activities that are in need of improvement.

B. It was noted that both partners identify a need for a change in the frequency of recreational activities.

C. It was reflected to the partners that both partners see a need to increase the quality of recreational activities available.

D. Both partners were assisted in identifying particular activities that they would like the couple to engage in.

3. Generate a List of Desired Activities (3)

A. The partners were asked to generate a list of desired activities in the following categories: (a) to do alone, (b) to do with partner, (c) to do with partner and other family members, (d) to do with partner and nonfamily members, and (e) to do with nonfamily members.

B. The partners were asked to complete the Inventory of Rewarding Activities (Birchler and Weiss).

C. The partners' lists of desired activities were reviewed in session.

D. The partners have not generated lists of desired activities and were redirected to do so.

4. Discuss List of Desired Activities (4)

A. The partners were directed to discuss the similarities of their lists of desired activities.

B. The partners were directed to discuss the differences between their lists of desired activities.

C. The similarities and differences of the partners' lists were summarized and reflected to them.

D. The partners were noted to have very few similarities, but many differences in desired activities.

E. The partners were noted to have many similarities and few differences in their lists of desired activities.

5. Discuss Important Activities (5)

A. The partners were asked to identify important activities about which they disagree and discuss their points of view by taking turns as speakers.

B. The partners were provided with examples of how to describe their point of view about important recreational activities (i.e., "When I go hunting, I feel alive and part of nature").

C. As the partners reviewed their points of view related to important recreational activities, feedback was provided about how they communicated this information.

6. Direct Paraphrasing of Other Partner's Preferences (6)

A. After one partner has stated preferences for leisure activities, and the reasons for these preferences, the other partner was asked to show respect for the other's point of view by paraphrasing it and refraining from criticism.

B. The original speaker was asked to verify the accuracy of how the other partner reflected the speaker's point of view.

C. Positive feedback was provided as the partners displayed the ability to listen attentively, paraphrase, and refrain from criticism.

D. The listener's ability to paraphrase and refrain from criticism was deficient and additional feedback was provided in this area.

7. Assign Individual Lists of Mutually Satisfying Activities (7)

A. Each client was asked to independently list 5 to 10 activities or behaviors that the other partner would also enjoy.

B. Feedback was provided to the partners as they discussed their lists of activities that the other partner would enjoy.

C. The partners have not completed independent lists of activities that the other partner would enjoy and were redirected to do so.

8. Classify Partner-Enjoyable Activities by Time (8)

A. Each partner was asked to classify the partner-enjoyable activities into those that can be done in 15 to 30 minutes, 1 to 2 hours, 4 to 6 hours, a full day, and a week-end.

B. The partners' lists of time classified partner-enjoyable activities were reviewed.

9. Schedule One Week's Activities (9)

A. The clients were asked to use their list of rewarding activities to schedule one week's activities.

B. The partners were reminded to include work responsibilities, chores, and leisure pursuits while scheduling one week's worth of activities.

C. The partners were reinforced for developing a realistic plan for one week's activities.

D. The partners' schedule of one week's activities seemed to be unrealistic, and they were provided with feedback in this area.

E. The partners have not developed a schedule of one week's activities and were redirected to do so.

10. Assign Arrangement of Partner-Enjoyable Activities (10)

A. The clients were assigned to join in or arrange for their partner at least three activities that are enjoyable for the partner (scaled to fit their time demands) per week.
B. The clients were directed to record the activity and rate the quality of satisfaction for each activity.
C. The partners have joined in or arranged for at least three activities that are enjoyable for the other partner and recorded the satisfaction levels; the results of this involvement were processed.
D. The partners have not joined in or arranged for activities that are enjoyable for the other partner and were redirected to do so.

11. Use "I" Statements to Discuss Pleasurable Activities (11)

A. Each partner was asked to discuss the week's pleasurable activity assignment, using "I" statements.
B. The following example was used to explain the use of "I" statements: "When we went for a walk at the beach this weekend (situation), I felt really peaceful and close to you (emotion). I'd like us to go for a walk at least once a weekend in the future (assertion)."
C. The listener was asked to respond to the speaker using paraphrasing and reflecting skills.
D. The partners were provided with feedback about their communication regarding the pleasurable activity assignment.

12. Review, Troubleshoot, and Reassign Scheduling (12)

A. The clients' use of a one-week's schedule of their activities was reviewed.
B. Problem areas regarding the use of a one-week's schedule were reviewed and problem-solved.
C. The partners were asked to contract to continue to schedule their pleasurable activities on a weekly basis.

13. Brainstorm Involvement in Other's Hobby (13)

A. It was noted that one partner does not share an interest in the other's hobby.
B. The partner that does not share in the other's hobby was asked to brainstorm ways to share in the other's pleasure.
C. The partners were provided with feedback about ways to share the other partner's pleasurable activities.

14. Encourage Displays of Interest (14)

A. Each partner was encouraged to commit to occasionally and sacrificially show an interest or participate in an activity that is pleasurable to the other partner, but not to self.
B. Each partner was reinforced for the occasional and sacrificial display of interest and participation in activities that are pleasurable to the other partner, but not to self.
C. It was noted that the partners experienced enjoyment when showing interest in or participating in activities pleasurable to the other partner.

D. The partners have not shown an interest in or participated in an activity that is pleasurable to the other partner but not to self and were redirected to do so.

15. Contract for Respect of Other's Interests/Hobbies (15)

A. The partners were asked to contract to respect each other's interests and hobbies by not criticizing the other's hobby or other enjoyable activity.

B. The partners reported a decrease in criticism of each other's hobbies or other enjoyable activity, and the positive benefit of this was reviewed.

C. The partners continued to be critical of each other's interests and hobbies and were redirected in this area.

16. Contract against One Hobby Dominating Time (16)

A. The partners were asked to contract to respect each other by not letting any one activity or hobby dominate their own free time.

B. The partners were reinforced for agreeing that one activity or hobby should not dominate one partner's free time.

C. The partners' pattern of not allowing one activity or hobby to dominate each partner's free time was noted and supported.

17. Schedule Both Types of Activities (17)

A. The partners were asked to contract to respect each other's interests and hobbies by scheduling time each week for both mutually enjoyable and individually enjoyable leisure activities.

B. The partners were given positive feedback for scheduling both mutually enjoyable and individually enjoyable leisure activities.

C. The partners' experience of increased respect for each other's interests and hobbies was reviewed and highlighted.

D. The partners have not scheduled both mutually enjoyable and individually enjoyable leisure activities and were redirected to do so.

18. Brainstorm Mutual Enjoyment of Vacation Destinations (18)

A. It was noted that the partners disagreed on vacation sites, and they were helped to brainstorm ways in which they can still enjoy mutual destinations.

B. The partners were provided with examples of mutual enjoyment of the same destination (e.g., since one likes the beach and the other does not, one goes to the beach while the other shops in nearby town).

C. Positive feedback was provided as the partners brainstormed ways to mutually enjoy destinations despite disagreements.

D. The partners failed to brainstorm ways in which they can mutually enjoy vacation destinations and were provided with specific feedback in this area.

19. Include Others in Vacations (19)

A. The partners disagree on vacation sites, so they were assisted in brainstorming ways to include others and thereby increase the attractiveness of the partner's preferred site.

B. The partners developed specific ideas of ways to include others and thereby increase the attractiveness of the partner's preferred site; these were reviewed and feedback was provided.

20. Make Vacation Destination Choices Equitable (20)

A. As the partners disagree on vacation sites, they were assisted in brainstorming ways to make destination choices equitable (e.g., one summer go to the beach, the next to the mountains).
B. The partners have developed plans for making destination choices equitable and positive feedback was provided.
C. The partners were reminded to focus on enjoyment of the present vacation site, despite who made the choice.
D. The partners were urged to keep the reciprocal nature of selecting vacation sites in mind throughout each vacation.

21. Plan a Love Day (21)

A. The partners were directed to plan a Love Day on a periodic basis.
B. The partners were assisted in brainstorming ways in which one partner can provide as many beneficial activities to the other partner as is possible.
C. The partners were provided with the following example of a Love Day: a husband might give his wife a back rub, take care of the children while she exercises, and then prepare a romantic, candlelight dinner.
D. The partners have implemented a Love Day on a periodic basis, and the benefits of this were reviewed.
E. The partners have not implemented a Love Day on a regular basis and were redirected to do so.

22. Alternate Roles in Love Day (22)

A. The partners were asked to alternate who will be the recipient of the Love Day and who will be the giver.
B. The partners were supported for regularly alternating use of a Love Day.
C. The partners have drifted away from the use of the Love Day on a reciprocal basis and were redirected to this technique.

RELIGION/SPIRITUALITY DIFFERENCES

CLIENT PRESENTATION

1. Disagreements about Religious Faith and Practices (1)[*]

A. The partners described frequent, upsetting verbal disagreements over religious faith issues (e.g., core beliefs about life and after-life).

B. The partners reported verbal disagreements about religious practices (e.g., communal worship, prayer).

C. The partners described some progress in resolving disagreements about core issues related to religious faith and practice.

D. As treatment has progressed, the partners report a resolution of disagreements about religious faith and practices.

2. Attempts to Coerce Religious Belief (2)

A. One partner has attempted to coerce the other partner into accepting certain religious and spiritual beliefs, values, and activities.

B. One partner has crossed acceptable boundaries regarding the attempts to evangelize the other partner into specific religious and spiritual beliefs, values, and activities.

C. One partner reports feelings of resentment toward the other partner's attempts to coerce specific religious or spiritual beliefs.

D. As treatment has progressed, the partners report a discontinuation of attempts to coerce acceptance of certain religious and spiritual beliefs.

3. Reduced Intimacy (3)

A. The partners report a pattern of reduced intimacy due to the inability to constructively share deeply held core beliefs and values.

B. One partner reports feeling "unequally yoked" with the other partner due to core differences in deeply held beliefs and values.

C. As treatment has progressed, the partners have developed an increased pattern of intimacy.

4. Conflicts about Children's Religious Training (4)

A. The partners described frequent arguments about their children's religious training and expected attendance at worship services.

B. One partner supports the children's religious training and attendance at worship services, while the other partner does not support such religious involvement.

C. One partner tends to disparage the other partner's involvement of the children in religious training and worship services.

D. As treatment has progressed, the partners have developed a mutually acceptable level of involvement for the children in religious training and worship services.

[*]The numbers in parentheses on Client Presentation pages correlate to the number of the Behavioral Definition statement in the companion chapter with the same title in *The Couples Psychotherapy Treatment Planner* (Jongsma, O'Leary, and Heyman) by John Wiley & Sons, 1998. The numbers in parentheses on the Interventions Implemented page correspond to the number of the Therapeutic Intervention statement in the companion chapter in the same book.

5. Conflicts about Child Discipline Due to Religious Beliefs (5)

A. The partners report frequent arguments about proper child-discipline strategies.

B. The partners identified that they have different child-discipline strategies due in part to differing religious and spiritual beliefs about parenting.

C. The children displayed a pattern of confusion due to the differing child-discipline strategies used by the parents.

D. As treatment has progressed, the partners have developed a more cohesive, unified approach to child-discipline strategies.

INTERVENTIONS IMPLEMENTED

1. Describe Childhood Religious Experiences (1)

A. Each partner was asked to identify the role that religion and spirituality played in childhood home and family experiences.

B. The partners were noted to have had very similar family religious and spirituality practices in their childhood.

C. The partners were noted to have had significantly divergent experiences in their childhood related to spirituality and religion.

2. Trace Changes to Religious Beliefs (2)

A. The partners were asked to trace the changes that have taken place in their religious and spiritual beliefs, values, or activities as they have grown older.

B. The partners described a parallel pattern of changes in religious beliefs, values, and practices, and this was reflected to them.

C. The partners described a pattern of more divergent changes in religious and spiritual beliefs, values, and activities as they have grown older, and this was reflected to them.

3. Review Role of Religion in Early Relationship (3)

A. The partners were asked to discuss the role that religion and spiritual beliefs played in their lives in the early stages of their relationship.

B. The partners' pattern of compatibility regarding religious involvement during the early stages of their relationship was reflected to them.

C. The partners' pattern of incapability regarding religious involvement in the early stages of their relationship was reflected to them.

D. The partners' report of the significant role of religion and spirituality during the early stages of their relationship was reflected to them.

4. Discuss Religious Meaning of Marriage (4)

A. The partners were asked to discuss the meaning of marriage in their respective religious and spiritual belief systems.

B. The partners' very congruent beliefs regarding marriage in their respective religious belief systems were reflected to them.

C. The partners' rather divergent ideas regarding the meaning of marriage in their respective religious and spiritual belief systems were reflected to them.
D. As treatment has progressed, the partners were supported for identifying significant similarities and agreement regarding the role of marriage within their religious and spiritual belief systems.

5. Identify Changes in Religious Beliefs over Time (5)

A. The partners were asked to identify ways that their religious and spiritual beliefs, values, or activities have changed since they met.
B. It was reflected to the partners that the role of religious beliefs and practices has changed in importance and intensity over the course of the relationship.
C. The partners were provided with tentative examples of how their religious and spiritual beliefs, values, or activities have changed since they met.

6. Identify Origins of Spiritual Conflicts (6)

A. The partners were asked to identify when conflict over religious and spiritual beliefs, values, or activities began.
B. Based on the history provided, the partners were assisted in identifying when their conflicts over religious and spiritual beliefs, values, or activities began.
C. The partners' rather recent conflicts over religious and spiritual beliefs, values, and activities were reflected to them.
D. The partners' longstanding conflicts over religious and spiritual beliefs, values, and activities were reflected to them.

7. Describe Context of Disagreements (7)

A. The partners were asked to describe the situations in which they argue or disagree about religious and spiritual beliefs, values, and activities.
B. The partners were asked to describe the manner in which they argue or disagree about religious and spiritual beliefs, values, and activities.
C. The partners were provided with feedback and a summarization of the issues over which they have disagreed about religious and spiritual beliefs, values, and activities.

8. Identify Strengthening Effects (8)

A. Each partner was asked to describe the ways in which personal religious and spiritual beliefs, values, and activities contribute to strengthening the relationship.
B. It was reflected to the clients that their religious and spiritual beliefs, values, and activities lend a great deal of strength to the relationship.
C. It was reflected to the clients that their religious and spiritual beliefs, values, and activities do not seem to strengthen the relationship.

9. Relate Religious Differences to Other Relationship Areas (9)

A. Each client was asked to describe the ways in which religious and spiritual differences accentuate conflict in other areas of the relationship.

B. The partners were able to identify a variety of ways in which religious and spiritual differences accentuate conflict in other areas of the relationship, and these were reviewed and processed.

C. The partners denied any accentuation of conflict by the religious and spiritual differences and were provided with possible examples of such (e.g., role strain, parenting).

10. Contract for Respect of Beliefs (10)

A. The clients were asked to contract to respect each other's religious and spiritual beliefs by not criticizing the other's beliefs, values, and activities.

B. The couple was reinforced for contracting to respect each other's spiritual or religious beliefs.

C. The partners were confronted for failing to respect each other's religious and spiritual beliefs, as they were noted to criticize the other partner's beliefs, values, and activities.

11. Develop Agreement Not to Coerce (11)

A. The clients were asked to contract with each other to respect each other's religious and spiritual beliefs by agreeing not to coerce the other into one's own beliefs, values, or activities.

B. The partners were reinforced for agreeing that an invitation to each other's religious and spiritual activities was acceptable, but attempting to coerce through psychological or physical means was inappropriate.

C. One partner was confronted for attempting to coerce the other into conforming to a specific set of beliefs, values, or religious activities.

12. Discuss Religious Values (12)

A. Each partner was asked to discuss the value placed on commitment in the framework of the other's religious and/or spiritual belief system.

B. Each partner was asked to discuss the value placed on respect in the framework of the other's religious and/or spiritual belief system.

C. Each partner was asked to discuss the value placed on intimacy in the framework of the other's religious and/or spiritual belief system.

D. Each partner was asked to discuss the value placed on forgiveness in the framework of the other's religious and/or spiritual belief system.

E. Each partner's values related to commitment, respect, intimacy, and forgiveness were summarized and reflected back to the partners.

13. Discuss Values as Evidence of Religious Belief (13)

A. Each partner was asked to discuss how the value placed on commitment provides evidence of personal religious and/or spiritual beliefs.

B. Each partner was asked to discuss how the value placed on respect provides evidence of personal religious and/or spiritual beliefs.

C. Each partner was asked to discuss how the value placed on intimacy provides evidence of personal religious and/or spiritual beliefs.

D. Each partner was asked to discuss how the value placed on forgiveness provides evidence of personal religious and/or relationship beliefs.

E. The partners' value placed on commitment, respect, intimacy, and forgiveness as evidence of their religious and/or spiritual beliefs was reviewed and reflected.

14. Identify Religious Conflict's Effect on Sexual Relationship (14)

A. The partners were asked to identify the impact of their differing religious and spiritual beliefs on their sexual relationship.

B. The partners were supported as they identified the effect that their different religious and spiritual beliefs have on their sexual relationship.

C. The idea that the sexual relationship is a mirror of the rest of the relationship, including the religious and spiritual beliefs, was presented.

15. Explain Core Beliefs (15)

A. Each partner was asked to identify his/her core religious beliefs and how that belief system was developed.

B. The partner's core beliefs (e.g., the existence and nature of God, the nature of man, the meaning of human life, the existence and nature of an after-life) were reflected to them.

C. Each partner was supported for identifying the journey that has been taken to come to the current belief system.

D. The partners were assisted in comparing core beliefs and the journeys to these beliefs.

16. Describe How Spiritual Beliefs Have Meaning (16)

A. Each partner was asked to consider and share the ways that religious and spiritual beliefs have added meaning to their lives.

B. The partners were supported as they described the ways in which religious and spiritual beliefs have added meaning to their lives.

C. Similarities and differences regarding the partners' religious and spiritual beliefs and how they have added meaning to their lives were reviewed and processed.

17. Develop How Spiritual Practices Reinforce Core Beliefs (17)

A. Each partner was asked to share the ways that spiritual practices reinforce core beliefs.

B. Each partner was assisted in identifying a variety of ways in which religious and spiritual practices reinforce core beliefs.

C. Similarities and differences in how each partner's religious and spiritual practices reinforce core beliefs were identified and processed.

18. Coordinate Paraphrasing (18)

A. One partner was asked to describe religious and spiritual beliefs that are held.

B. The listening partner was directed to show respect for the speaker's beliefs by paraphrasing the speaker's beliefs, regardless of whether or not there is agreement.

C. As the listening partner paraphrased the speaker's description of religious and spiritual beliefs, this was checked for accuracy with the speaker.

D. The listening partner struggled to accurately paraphrase the speaker's beliefs, often made personal comments about these beliefs, and was redirected in this area.

19. Practice Refraining from Lecturing/Preaching (19)

A. As one partner described important spiritual and religious beliefs, the other partner was reminded to show respect for the speaker's beliefs by not responding with lecturing and preaching.

B. Positive feedback was provided to the listening partner for simply listening to the beliefs, without lecturing or preaching about those areas in which the partners are not in agreement.

C. The listening partner was confronted for responding with lecturing or preaching about those areas in which the speaker and listener do not agree.

20. Guide against Arguing (20)

A. The listening partner was asked to show respect for the speaker's beliefs by not arguing against the speaker's beliefs.

B. The listening partner was reinforced for showing respect for the speaker's beliefs by not arguing about these beliefs.

C. The listening partner was redirected when beginning to argue against the speaker's beliefs.

21. Review Importance of Accepting Beliefs (21)

A. Each client was asked to describe the relative importance of the other partner accepting and adopting the client's religious beliefs.

B. Active listening was used while each partner identified the relative importance of having the other partner adopt the partner's religious beliefs.

C. The partners were asked about how they would constructively cope with a lack of agreement regarding each other's religious beliefs.

22. Identify Acceptable Deviations from Core Beliefs (22)

A. Each partner was asked to identify what deviations from core beliefs can be accommodated or tolerated in the other partner.

B. As each partner described acceptable deviations, positive feedback and encouragement was provided.

C. A summary of both partners' acceptable deviations from core beliefs was presented.

23. Identify Unacceptable Deviations from Core Beliefs (23)

A. Each partner was asked to identify what deviations from core beliefs are not acceptable.

B. Support and encouragement was provided as each partner identified the deviations from core beliefs that are not acceptable, tolerable, or able to be accommodated.

C. A summary of the deviations from core beliefs that cannot be accommodated or tolerated in the other partner was presented.

24. Review Divorce Beliefs (24)

A. Each partner was asked to identify core religious beliefs regarding divorce.

B. Core religious beliefs regarding divorce were discussed and processed within the session.

25. Review Sense of Community (25)

A. Both partners were asked to address the advantages and disadvantages of the sense of community brought to the relationship by each partner's religious and spiritual activities.

B. The partners were supported as they discussed the advantages and disadvantages of the sense of community brought to the relationship by each partner's religious and spiritual activities.

C. Variable patterns of the level of community from each partner's religious and spiritual activities were identified.

26. Develop Needs for Social Support (26)

A. Each partner was asked to identify and verbalize the perceived need for social support from the religious and spiritual community.

B. Each partner was directed to seek agreement as to the other partner's cooperative participation in the spiritual and religious community.

C. The partners have developed a better understanding of each other's needs related to social support from the religious and spiritual community, and this understanding was reviewed with the partners.

27. Ask about Agreements Regarding Religious Training (27)

A. The couple was asked to identify whether an explicit agreement was made regarding the religious training of their children prior to their birth.

B. The partners' denial of any explicit agreements regarding the religious training of their children was reflected to them.

C. The history of agreements regarding the religious training of their children was reviewed.

28. Elicit Current Feelings about Previous Agreements (28)

A. Each partner was queried as to current misgivings about the original agreement regarding their children's religious upbringing.

B. The partners identified current misgivings about the original agreement regarding their children's religious upbringing and were directed to verbalize that position using nonblaming "I" statements.

C. The partners' use of "I" statements to describe the current misgivings about their children's religious upbringing was reviewed and critiqued.

D. The partners were reinforced for identifying no misgivings about their current agreement about their children's religious upbringing.

29. Investigate Current Expectations (29)

A. Each partner was asked to verbalize current expectations for their children's religious instruction or practice.

B. As each partner verbalized current expectations for their children's religious instruction and practice, active listening and supportive feedback were used.

C. It was noted that the partners have very similar expectations regarding their children's religious instruction and practice.

D. It was noted that the partners have verbalized very different expectations regarding their children's religious instruction and practice.

30. Brainstorm Agreements (30)

A. The partners were assisted in brainstorming agreements regarding their children's religious instruction and practice that both partners can abide by.

B. The partners were assisted in developing the details of an agreement regarding the children's religious instruction and practice.

C. The partners were noted to continue to disagree about the children's religious instruction and practice.

31. Identify Religious Effects on Discipline (31)

A. The couple was asked to identify whether either partner's religious or spiritual beliefs guide their approach to discipline.

B. The partners were assisted in identifying specific expectations related to their religious beliefs that affect the way that they parent.

32. Discuss Strengths and Conflicts Regarding Spiritually-Guided Parenting Practices (32)

A. The partners were assisted in a discussion about the strengths and conflicts arising from each partner's religiously influenced parenting practice.

B. It was noted that the partners identified a variety of strengths arising from the religiously based parenting practices.

C. It was noted that the partners have a variety of conflicts arising from the spiritually based parenting practices.

33. Brainstorm Synthesis of Parenting Practices (33)

A. The partners were assisted in brainstorming ways in which strengths can be maintained and conflict reduced in the area of their religiously based parenting practices.

B. The partners developed a variety of ways in which strengths can be maintained and conflict reduced regarding the spiritually based parenting practices, and they were provided with positive feedback in this area.

C. The parents failed to develop mutually acceptable parenting practices and were provided with more specific feedback in this area.

SEPARATION AND DIVORCE

CLIENT PRESENTATION

1. Thoughts of Ending the Relationship (1)*

A. One partner reports having thoughts about ending the relationship.
B. Both partners reported having thoughts about wanting to end the relationship.
C. The partners reported having strong thoughts about ending the relationship, but have not taken any specific steps to do so.
D. As treatment has progressed, thoughts about ending the relationship have ceased.

2. Separation (2)

A. One partner is planning to move out of the home to establish separate living arrangements, due to dissatisfaction with the relationship.
B. One partner has moved out of the home and has established a separate living arrangement, due to dissatisfaction with the relationship.
C. The partners have become less connected with each other since the separation began.
D. The partners expressed feelings of hurt, disappointment, anxiety, and depression related to the separation.
E. The partners have become more motivated to resolve differences since the separation began.
F. The partners have begun living together again.

3. Legal Proceedings (3)

A. One partner has filed a divorce petition.
B. Child custody proceedings have been initiated.
C. The partners expressed feelings of sadness surrounding the legal proceedings related to the divorce.
D. The partners expressed feelings of anger and resentment over the legal proceedings.
E. The partners tend to blame each other for the legal complications related to the divorce.
F. As the partners have resolved conflicts, legal proceedings have been discontinued.

4. Confusion about Children (4)

A. The partners expressed confusion about how to best deal with the feelings that the children are experiencing about the marital crisis.
B. The estranged partners have radically different ideas about how to deal with the children's emotional struggles.
C. The partners often criticize each other for how each deals with the feelings of the children.
D. The partners continue to be on the path of separation and divorce, but feel more competent about how to cope with the children's feelings.

*The numbers in parentheses on Client Presentation pages correlate to the number of the Behavioral Definition statement in the companion chapter with the same title in *The Couples Psychotherapy Treatment Planner* (Jongsma, O'Leary, and Heyman) by John Wiley & Sons, 1998. The numbers in parentheses on the Interventions Implemented page correspond to the number of the Therapeutic Intervention statement in the companion chapter in the same book.

E. The partners have developed a mutually agreeable plan for dealing with the children's feelings and behavior.

5. Emotional Reaction to Loss of Relationship (5)

A. One partner identified feelings of anger, hurt, and fear about the break-up of the partnership.
B. Both partners reported feelings of anger, hurt, and fear due to the break-up of the relationship.
C. The partners have reported having fears of having to face life as a single person.
D. The partners tend to blame each other for the emotions that result from the break-up of the relationship.
E. As the relationship has improved, there is less anger, hurt, and fear expressed.
F. The partners continue on the path of separation and divorce, but have less of an emotional reaction to the loss of the relationship.

6. Spiritual Conflict (6)

A. One partner has identified experiencing spiritual conflict due to the breaking of the marriage vows.
B. Both partners describe spiritual conflict regarding breaking of the marriage vows.
C. The partners have resolved their spiritual conflict by resolving the problems within the marriage.
D. The partner's spiritual conflict has lessened.

7. Grief (7)

A. One partner described feelings of depression as a part of the grief process related to the loss of the relationship.
B. Both partners described feelings of depression as a part of the grief process related to the loss of the relationship.
C. One partner displayed evidence of social withdrawal as a part of the grief process related to loss of the relationship.
D. As the client has worked through the grief related to the loss of the relationship, depression and social withdrawal have decreased.

INTERVENTIONS IMPLEMENTED

1. Assess for Extramarital Problems (1)

A. Each partner's emotional health was assessed.
B. Each partner's physical health was assessed.
C. Each partner's vocational stability was assessed.
D. Each partner's religious conflict over divorce issues was assessed.
E. Extramarital concerns were noted to exist.
F. No extramarital concerns appear to be affecting the current relationship.

2. Postpone Separation until Extramarital Problems Resolved (2)

A. The couple was identified as experiencing significant problems unrelated to the marriage.
B. Each partner was encouraged to postpone any decision about separation until problems unrelated to the marriage have been addressed.

C. The partners were supported for agreeing to postpone any decisions about separation until after problems unrelated to the marriage have been addressed.
D. The partners are pursuing significant changes with the marriage despite needing to resolve extramarital problems and were encouraged to change this focus.

3. Establish Type of Treatment (3)

A. The partners identified that they wanted to work together to try to resolve the marriage problems and were advised to begin conjoint marital therapy.
B. The partners identified individual issues that needed to be treated in order to resolve the marital issues and were referred for individual treatment.
C. The partners indicated no interest in conjoint or individual counseling to improve the marriage and were advised to begin predivorce treatment.
D. The partners were uncertain about the commitment to the relationship, and the type of treatment that might be necessary and this was selected as the focus of current sessions.

4. Assess Steps toward Divorce (4)

A. Each partner was assessed for the steps that have been taken toward divorce.
B. Each partner was administered the Marital Status Inventory (Weiss and Cerreto).
C. Each partner was interviewed about his or her sense of hope and vision of the future for the relationship.

5. Assess Developmental Stage of Marriage (5)

A. The partners were assessed for what developmental stage of marriage they are in.
B. The partners were noted to be in the *early marriage* stage.
C. The partners were noted to be in the *couple with young children* stage.
D. The partners were noted to be in the *long-term marriage* stage.
E. The developmental stage of the marriage was reflected to the couple.

6. Assess History of the Marriage (6)

A. The recent history of the marriage was assessed.
B. As the history of the marriage was assessed, changes in the respective partners' happiness were noted.
C. As the history of the marriage was assessed, the timing of changes regarding the expectations for the marriage were noted.
D. As the history of the marriage was assessed, the timing of thoughts about divorce were noted.
E. The changes occurring during the history of the marriage were reflected to the partners.

7. Assess Current Satisfaction (7)

A. The partners' current satisfaction with the marital relationship was assessed.
B. The partners were administered self-report instruments to assess their current satisfaction with the marital relationship (e.g., Relationship Satisfaction Questionnaire [Burnes]; Marital Adjustment Test [Locke and Wallace]; or Dyadic Adjustment Scale [Spanier]).
C. The partner's current satisfaction with the marital relationship was reflected to the couple.

D. The partners have not completed the self-report instruments regarding marital satisfaction and were redirected to do so.

8. Assess for Affairs (8)

A. Each partner was asked about involvement in an affair.
B. The partners were questioned about their suspicion of extramarital affairs.
C. There is a strong suspicion about extramarital affairs, and this was brought out into the open.
D. It was noted that the partners acknowledged a history of extramarital affairs.
E. It was reflected to the partners that there are not indications of presence or suspicion of extramarital affairs.

9. Assess for Violence/Intimidation (9)

A. In individual sessions, the partners were assessed for the experience of violence or intimidation in the relationship.
B. Violence and intimidation were identified as existing within the relationship, and the partners were advised about the appropriate treatment for these concerns.
C. It was reflected to the partners that there was no evidence of violence or intimidation within the relationship.

10. Review Extended Family History (10)

A. Each partner's extended family history was reviewed with regard to the incidence of divorce.
B. Each partner was asked to verbalize how the extended family history may be effecting the decision to divorce.
C. The review of the extended family history indicated strong prohibitions about divorce, and the effects of this expectation were noted.
D. The review of the extended family history indicated multiple divorces, and little expectation for marriage to last, and this was reflected to the partners.

11. Identify Subcultural Influence (11)

A. Each partner was asked about subcultural identification (e.g., ethnicity, religious affiliation).
B. Discussion was held about the influence of the subcultural identification on attitudes about divorce.
C. A conflict between behavior and beliefs was identified, and the partners were assisted in facilitating a resolution of this conflict.
D. The partners denied any influence of the subculture identification on the attitudes toward divorce and were encouraged to monitor this area.

12. Identify Personal Responsibility (12)

A. Each partner was asked to turn to the other and identify his or her own personal contributions to the downfall of the relationship.
B. Each partner was asked to turn to the other and express personal attempts to make the relationship work.
C. Each partner was reinforced for taking significant responsibility for the relationship.

D. The partners tended to take varying levels of responsibility for the relationship, and this was reflected to them.
E. Both partners take very little responsibility for the relationship, and this was reflected to them.

13. Verbalize Pros and Cons (13)

A. Each partner was asked to verbalize their point of view on the pros and cons of preserving the relationship.
B. Each partner was asked to verbalize their point of view on the pros and cons of separation or divorce.
C. As the pros and cons of preserving the relationship versus divorce were reviewed, the partners' views were noted to be quite congruent.
D. As the pros and cons of preserving the relationship versus divorce were reviewed, the partners' views were noted to be incongruent in their assessment.

14. Review Implications of Divorce (14)

A. Each partner was asked to verbalize the emotional implications of divorce.
B. Each partner was asked to identify the implications of divorce for the rest of the family (including children).
C. Each partner was asked to identify the religious implications of divorce.
D. Each partner was asked to identify the social implications of divorce.
E. As each partner reviewed the implications of divorce, the other partner was asked to paraphrase the first person's statements in each area to increase understanding and empathy between the two partners.
F. Paraphrasing of each partner's identified implications of divorce was verified for accuracy with the partner.

15. Sensitize to Effects on Children (15)

A. The partners were directed to discuss the anticipated effects of separation and divorce on their children.
B. The upheaval that divorce causes for children was highlighted as the partners discussed the anticipated effects on their children.
C. The partners tended to minimize the effects of separation and divorce on the children and were provided with additional feedback in this area.

16. Assign Reading Regarding Children and Divorce (16)

A. The parents were assigned to read information about children and divorce.
B. The following texts were recommended to the parents: *How to Help Your Child Overcome Your Divorce* (Benedek and Brown), *The Parent's Book about Divorce* (Gardener), and *Mom's House, Dad's House* (Ricci).
C. The partners have read the information on children and divorce, and the salient points were reviewed.
D. The partners have not done any reading regarding children and divorce and were redirected to do so.

17. Emphasize Children's Best Interest (17)

A. The partners were asked to verbally contract with each other and the therapist that all decisions in the divorce and separation process will be made with the best interests of the children as the paramount concern.

B. The partners were supported for verbally contracting with each other and the therapist that all decisions in the divorce and separation process will be made with the best interests of the children as the paramount concern.

C. As the separation and divorce process has unfolded, the partners were provided with positive feedback about keeping the best interests of the children as the paramount concern.

D. The partners were confronted when they deviated from the best interests of the children as the paramount concern in the divorce and separation process.

18. Role-Play Informing the Children (18)

A. Role-playing techniques were used to help the partners rehearse telling the children together about the impending divorce.

B. The partners were prompted to include the following elements as they tell the children about the decision to divorce: they both love the children; they plan to divorce; the divorce is not the children's fault; there is nothing that the children can do to get the parents back together; and they will continue to love and see the children.

C. As the partners role-played how to tell the children about the divorce, they were provided with feedback and redirection.

19. Review the Telling of the Children (19)

A. The experience of the partners telling the children about the divorce or separation was reviewed.

B. Probing questions were used to identify the need for further explanation or support for the children.

C. The partners were pressed for an agreement on the further needs that the children have regarding explanation or support.

20. Describe Destructive Anger (20)

A. Each partner was asked to describe times when their own anger was destructive to the other partner.

B. Support and feedback were provided as the partners reviewed destructive anger experiences.

21. Clarify Therapist's Role (21)

A. The therapist's role was clarified to the clients, with an emphasis on aiding the family in making the separation or divorce transition, and helping both partners deal with the turbulent emotions experienced during this process.

B. An emphasis was placed on the therapist's role as serving the best interest of all family members.

C. It was emphasized to the partners that the therapist would not be a mediator or judge.

D. The partners were assessed for their understanding of the therapist's role.

E. As the partners have attempted to place the therapist in the role of mediator or judge, they were redirected.

22. Recognize Gradations of Anger (22)

A. The partners were taught to recognize the gradations of anger.
B. The partners were taught about when they need to take steps to cool down before self-control becomes eroded.
C. The partners were taught cool down techniques (e.g., relaxation and deep breathing exercises, take time-out for 15 minutes, go for a walk).
D. The partners were assessed for their understanding of the gradations of anger and when they need to take steps to cool down.
E. Feedback was provided to the partners regarding their use of cool down techniques when becoming too angry.

23. Identify "Hot Topic" Responses (23)

A. Each partner was asked to identify topics that seem to be "hot" and cause increased emotional responses.
B. After identifying "hot topics," the partners were directed to practice in-session cognitive rehearsal about how to cope with such topics adaptively.
C. Support and feedback were provided as the partners practiced how to deal with "hot topics."
D. As the partners reviewed their adaptive attempts to deal with "hot topics," they were provided with additional feedback and reinforcement.

24. Practice the Time-Out Technique (24)

A. The partners were directed to practice using time-out (agree to pause in the conversation when anger begins to elevate) while discussing an emotional topic in session.
B. Support and feedback were provided to the partners as they practiced using time-out.
C. The partners' ongoing use of time-out during emotional discussions was reviewed and processed.

25. Facilitate Discussion of Separation (25)

A. The partners were advised to obtain legal advice before agreeing to a separation.
B. The discussion regarding a separation was facilitated.
C. The partners were assisted in making a decision about when one partner will move out of the house.
D. Because the partners do not have the financial ability to maintain two homes, the details of an in-house separation were negotiated.

26. Facilitate Agreement about Acceptable Contact (26)

A. The partners were assisted in developing an agreement about what forms of contact are acceptable and prohibited.
B. The partners were supported as they identified typical types of contact that are acceptable during the separation and divorce (e.g., planning around children's activities).
C. The partners were assisted as they identified typical prohibited activities during the separation and divorce (e.g., affection displays, sexual intimacy).

D. The partners were assessed for their adherence to the contract regarding acceptable and prohibited types of contact.

27. Refer for Individual Therapy for Anger and Planning (27)

A. Individual sessions were used on an as-needed basis to allow each partner to express anger, disappointment, and disapproval about what has happened during the separation and divorce.

B. The expressions of hurt were balanced with an elicitation of the partners' goals for coping with short-term and long-term situations with the other partner and children.

C. The partner's were provided with feedback regarding emotional expression and goals for coping.

28. Educate about Marriage Dissolution Choices (28)

A. The partners were informed about the choices available for dissolving the marriage.

B. The partners were taught about litigation, which is an adversarial legal process.

C. The partners were taught about arbitration, involving a third party chosen by both partners, who makes decisions regarding property and custody.

D. The partners were taught about mediation, in which the partners come to their own agreement with the help of a trained mediator.

E. The partners displayed an understanding of the options for dissolution of the marriage and have selected a specific option.

29. Facilitate Co-Parenting Agreement (29)

A. The partners were assisted in developing a co-parenting agreement.

B. The partners' co-parenting agreement was formulated to include a pledge that the children's primary residence will be established in their best interests.

C. The partner's co-parenting agreement was formulated to include a pledge that neither parent will belittle the other parent or that parent's family members in front of the children.

D. The partner's co-parenting agreement was formulated to include promises that the parents will avoid placing the children in loyalty conflicts.

E. The co-parenting agreement that was facilitated included an agreement regarding the terms of financial support for the children.

F. The partners have not come to an agreement on co-parenting and were provided with additional assistance and feedback in this area.

30. Assist in Social Network Development (30)

A. Using individual sessions, each partner was assisted in developing a varied social network.

B. The partners were assisted in developing skills for asking others to socialize; beginning or increasing involvement in club, community, volunteer and/or church activities; and dating.

C. Each partner was reinforced for developing a more varied social network.

D. Remedial assistance was provided for the partner who has struggled to develop a varied social network.

31. Ensure Attendance to Children's Emotional Needs (31)

A. A parent-child session was used to assure that the children's emotional needs are being attended to.

B. The parents were reinforced for giving appropriate attendance to the children's emotional needs.

C. Gaps in attending to the children's emotional needs were identified, and the parents were assisted in attending to these needs.

32. Encourage Support Group (32)

A. The partners were encouraged to attend a local divorce support group.

B. The partners were encouraged to attend a self-help group (e.g., Parents Without Partners).

C. One partner was directed to attend a local divorce support group.

D. One partner was directed to attend a self-help group (e.g., Parents Without Partners).

E. The use of group support options was processed.

33. Assess Affect on Religious/Spiritual Connections (33)

A. The affect of the divorce on either partner's religious and spiritual connections was assessed.

B. As one partner has identified problems with religious or spiritual connection due to the divorce, assistance was provided in problem solving how to re-establish these connections (e.g., switching parishes, investigating congregations that welcome divorced members).

C. The partners were supported for maintaining healthy religious and spiritual connections.

SEXUAL ABUSE

CLIENT PRESENTATION

1. Verbal Demands for Sex (1)*

A. One partner identified that the other partner has made unequivocal verbal demands for sexual interaction.

B. The partner making verbal demands for sexual interaction is inappropriately forceful and persistent.

C. The partner making verbal demands for sexual interaction has acknowledged the inappropriateness of these demands.

D. Inappropriate verbal demands for sexual interaction have been discontinued.

2. Physical Pressure for Sex (2)

A. One partner identified that the other partner often uses physical pressure to get the partner to fulfill sexual demands.

B. One partner acknowledged using physical force to get the other partner to fulfill sexual demands.

C. The partner using physical pressure to fulfill sexual demands has identified the ways in which this damages the relationship.

D. Physical pressure for fulfillment of sexual demands has been discontinued.

3. Threats of Force (3)

A. One partner identified that the other partner has threatened to use force to obtain cooperation with demands for intercourse or other sexual activity.

B. One partner admitted to using threats of force to get the other partner to cooperate with demands for intercourse or other sexual activity.

C. The partner using threats of force for intercourse or other sexual activity has identified the negative ways in which this affects the relationship.

D. Threats of force to get the partner to cooperate with demands for intercourse or other sexual activity have been discontinued.

4. Verbal Demands for Uncomfortable Sexual Activity (4)

A. One partner identified that the other partner has made verbal demands for a type of sexual activity with which the partner is clearly uncomfortable.

B. One partner acknowledged making verbal demands and demeaning comments to the other partner to coerce engagement in sexual activity with which the other partner is clearly uncomfortable.

C. As the partners have developed a better understanding of sexual activity within a committed relationship; verbal demands for uncomfortable sexual activity have been discontinued.

*The numbers in parentheses on Client Presentation pages correlate to the number of the Behavioral Definition statement in the companion chapter with the same title in *The Couples Psychotherapy Treatment Planner* (Jongsma, O'Leary, and Heyman) by John Wiley & Sons, 1998. The numbers in parentheses on the Interventions Implemented page correspond to the number of the Therapeutic Intervention statement in the companion chapter in the same book.

5. **Physical Demands for Uncomfortable Sexual Activity (5)**

A. One partner identified that the other partner has made physical demands for a type of sexual activity with which the partner is clearly uncomfortable.

B. One partner acknowledged making physical demands to the other partner to coerce engagement in sexual activity with which the other partner is clearly uncomfortable.

C. As the partners have developed a better understanding of sexual activity within a committed relationship, physical demands for uncomfortable sexual activity have been discontinued.

6. **Sexual Criticism (6)**

A. One partner has accused the other partner of being "frigid."

B. One partner has accused the other partner of being " impotent."

C. The partners often use criticism of the other partner's sexuality in an effort to coerce sexual activity from that partner.

D. The partners often use criticism of the other partner's sexual performance in nonsexualized situations.

E. As treatment has progressed, criticism of the other partner's sexual performance has ceased.

7. **Threats to Withhold Sex (7)**

A. One partner has made threats to withhold sex from the other partner in the future.

B. Threats to withhold sex have been used for manipulation in nonsexual situations.

C. As treatment has progressed and communication has increased, threats to withhold sex from the other partner have been discontinued.

8. **Threats to Have Sex with Someone Else (8)**

A. One partner has made threats to have sex with someone else.

B. Both partners have made threats to have sex with someone else.

C. Threats to find an alternative sexual partner have been used to manipulate the other partner into sexual involvement.

D. Threats to find an alternative sexual partner have been used to manipulate the other partner in nonsexual situations.

E. As treatment has progressed, threats to find an alternative sexual partner have been discontinued.

9. **Threats to Leave (9)**

A. One partner has made threats to leave the other partner.

B. Both partners have made threats to leave the other partner.

C. Threats to leave the relationship have been used to coerce sexual activity.

D. Threats to leave the relationship have been used in nonsexualized situations.

E. As treatment has progressed and communication has increased, threats to leave the relationship have been discontinued.

10. **Low Sexual Desire Due to Coercion and Fear (10)**

A. One partner identified a very low desire for sexual activity due to resentment or fear related to coercion used by the other partner for sexual activity.

B. The partners have identified how coercion breeds resentment and fear, resulting in decreased desire for sexual interaction.
C. As treatment has progressed and coercion has ceased, desire for sexual activity has increased.

11. Avoidance of Sexual Interaction due to Coercion (11)

A. One partner identified a pattern of avoidance of any sexual interaction due to resentment or fear relating to coercion used by the other partner for sexual activity.
B. The partners have identified how coercion breeds resentment and fear, resulting in avoidance of sexual interaction.
C. The previously avoidant partner has become more sexually interested as forgiveness has occurred relating to coercion formerly used by the other partner for sexual activity.

12. Complaints of Lack of Love and Caring (12)

A. One partner has made complaints about how little love and caring there is within the relationship.
B. Both partners have made complaints about how little love and caring there is within the relationship.
C. The partners have gained insight about how love and caring are decreased due to the problems in the relationship.
D. As the partners have increased communication, the levels of love and caring have also increased.

13. Avoidance of Talking of Sexual Matters (13)

A. The partners identified a pattern of avoidance of communication with each other regarding sexual matters.
B. When one partner brings up sexual matters, the other partner often avoids any type of communication in this area.
C. As the partners have been able to increase communication about sexual matters, their sexual relationship and other portions of their relationship have improved.

INTERVENTIONS IMPLEMENTED

1. Obtain Verbal Commitment against Coercing Sex (1)

A. Each partner was asked to give a verbal commitment not to employ physical force for any sexual interaction.
B. Positive feedback was provided as the partners gave a verbal commitment not to employ physical force for any sexual interaction.
C. The partners have not made a verbal commitment against employing physical force for any sexual interaction, and other treatment was put on hold until this issue could be resolved.

2. Obtain Written Commitment against Coercing Sex (2)

A. Each partner was asked to sign a written commitment not to employ physical force for any sexual interaction.

B. Positive feedback was provided as the partners signed written commitments not to employ physical force for any sexual interaction.

C. The partners have not signed a written commitment against employing physical force for any sexual interaction, and other treatment was put on hold until this issue could be resolved.

3. Educate about Positive Sexual Relationship (3)

A. The clients were taught that a positive sexual relationship is possible only when the sexual activity is acceptable to both partners.

B. The partners were provided with specific examples of how forced sexual activity is detrimental to a positive sexual relationship.

C. The partners were supported for endorsing the desire to have a positive sexual relationship based in sexual activity that is acceptable to both partners.

4. Educate about Effects of Pressure for Sex (4)

A. The partners were taught that pressure to have sexual activity usually leads to sexual aversion.

B. The partners were taught that inappropriate pressure to have sexual activity often leads to avoidance and dislike of the pressuring partner.

C. The partners endorsed an understanding that pressure to have sexual activity usually leads to sexual aversion or avoidance and dislike of the partner.

5. Educate about Aversive Sexual Control (5)

A. The partners were taught that sexual behavior is one of the most susceptible of all human behaviors to aversive control.

B. The partners were taught that aversive control of sexual activity can quickly lead to lack of interest and sexual dysfunction for the partner.

C. The partners were provided with specific examples of how coercive control of sexual activity affects the relationship.

D. The partners were reinforced for their understanding of the susceptibility of sexual behavior to aversive control and the effects of that control.

E. The partners were noted to be providing only a lackluster endorsement of issues related to aversive control.

6. Obtain Verbal Commitment against Sex Out of the Relationship (6)

A. Each partner was asked to give a verbal commitment not to threaten to have sex with someone else.

B. The partners were supported as they gave a verbal commitment not to threaten to have sex outside of the relationship.

C. The partners have not made a verbal commitment against having sex outside of the relationship, and other treatment was put on hold until this issue could be resolved.

7. Obtain Commitment to Fidelity (7)

A. An individual session was used with each partner to obtain a commitment from each partner not to have sex with someone else during the course of therapy.

B. The sexually abusive partner was supported for making an individual commitment not to be sexually involved with anyone else during the course of therapy.
C. The partner who has been sexually abused was provided with positive feedback for making commitment not to be sexual with anyone else during the course of therapy.
D. The clear ground rules related to threats or to having sexual activity with anyone outside of the relationship were emphasized to both partners.

8. Obtain Commitment to Remain in the Relationship during Therapy (8)

A. A verbal commitment was requested from each partner not to threaten to leave the relationship during therapy.
B. A particular span of time for therapy was emphasized as the duration of the commitment not to leave the relationship.
C. The partners were supported for making a commitment not to threaten to leave the relationship during the course of therapy.
D. The clear ground rules that there will be no threats to leave the other partner during the therapy process were emphasized to both partners.

9. Obtain Verbal Commitment against Physical Force (9)

A. Each partner was asked to give a verbal commitment not to employ physical force for any reason.
B. The partners were reinforced for giving a verbal commitment not to employ physical force for any reason.
C. The partners have not made a verbal commitment against employing physical force for any reason, and other treatment was put on hold until this issue could be resolved.

10. Obtain Written Commitment against Coercing Sex (10)

A. Each partner was asked to give a written commitment not to coerce sex for any reason.
B. The partners were reinforced for giving a written commitment not to coerce sex for any reason.
C. The partners have not made a written commitment against coercing sex for any reason, and other treatment was put on hold until this issue could be resolved.

11. Review Psychological Coercion (11)

A. Both partners were asked to describe the extent to which psychological coercion is used in the relationship.
B. It was reflected to the partners that there was a significant level of psychological coercion used within the relationship.
C. It was reflected to the partners that very little psychological coercion is used within the relationship.

12. Review Physical Aggression (12)

A. Both partners were asked to describe the extent to which physical aggression is used in the relationship.
B. It was reflected to the partners that there was a significant level of physical aggression used within the relationship.

C. It was reflected to the partners that very little physical aggression is used within the relationship.

13. Discuss Fears in Relationship (13)

A. Both partners were asked to describe any fears that they have of the other partner.
B. As the partners described fears of the other partner, support and encouragement was provided.
C. The partners were asked to identify how fear of the other partner affects the intimate aspects of the relationship.
D. Support was provided as the partners identified the effects of fear on the intimate aspects of the relationship.
E. The partners denied any pattern of fear within the relationship, and this was accepted.
F. The partners denied any effects of fear on the intimate aspects of the relationship and were provided with additional information in this area.

14. Review Patriarchy (14)

A. The concept of patriarchy in the current society was reviewed.
B. A discussion was coordinated regarding the patriarchal nature of our society.
C. The partners were supported as they described their experience of patriarchy in current society.

15. Review Misuse of Power (15)

A. The partners were directed to discuss how the controlling partner misuses power within the relationship.
B. The abused partner was provided with support and encouragement while reviewing how the controlling partner misuses power within the relationship.
C. The controlling partner was provided with immediate positive feedback for identification of the misuse of power within the relationship.
D. The abusive partner tended to deny the misuse of power within the relationship and was provided with tentative examples of the misuse of power within their relationship.

16. Educate about Control Leading to Dislike and Avoidance (16)

A. The partners were informed that controlling behaviors by one partner tend to lead to dislike and avoidance by the other partner.
B. The partners were asked to identify how controlling behaviors have led to dislike and avoidance in their own relationship.
C. The partners were provided with support and feedback as they described the pattern of controlling behaviors leading to dislike and avoidance within their relationship.
D. The abusive partner denied any pattern of controlling behaviors leading to dislike and avoidance within own relationship and was provided with tentative examples in this area.

17. Identify Initial Expectations (17)

A. The partners were asked to describe their initial expectations about their sexual life.
B. The partners' initial expectations about their sexual life were explored and paraphrased back to them to assure accuracy.

C. The partners described very similar initial expectations about their sexual life, and this was reflected to them.

D. It was noted that the partners had very divergent views regarding the initial expectations about their sexual life.

18. Identify Changes in Expectations (18)

A. The partners were asked to describe how their expectations about their sexual life changed with the beginning of conflict over intimacy.

B. The partners were provided with support and encouragement as they described changing expectations about their sexual life since the beginning of conflict over intimacy.

C. The changes that have occurred in the partners' expectations about their sexual life since the beginning of conflict over intimacy were underscored.

19. Interpret Sexual Encounters versus Age Norms (19)

A. The clients were asked to identify the frequency, nature, and satisfaction of their sexual encounters.

B. The partners were provided with factual information regarding the frequency, nature, and satisfaction of sexual encounters for others of their age in our culture.

C. The partners were assisted in comparing the frequency, nature, and satisfaction of their sexual encounters to others of their age in our culture.

D. The partners were noted to have a level of frequency, nature, and satisfaction regarding sexual encounters that corresponds to others of their age in our culture.

E. The frequency, nature, and satisfaction of the partners' sexual encounters do not correspond to that of others of their age in our culture, and this was reflected to them.

20. Emphasize Positive, Nonsexual Aspects of Relationship (20)

A. The partners were asked to describe the positive, nonsexual aspects of their current relationship.

B. Support and encouragement were provided as the partners reviewed the positive, nonsexual aspects of their current relationship.

C. The partners were noted to have many positive, nonsexual aspects in their current relationship.

D. The partners were noted to have very limited positive, nonsexual aspects in their current relationship.

21. Emphasize Positive Sexual Aspects of Relationship (21)

A. The partners were asked to describe the positive sexual aspects of their current relationship.

B. Support and encouragement were provided as the partners reviewed the positive sexual aspects of their current relationship.

C. The partners were noted to have many positive, sexual aspects in their current relationship.

D. The partners were noted to have limited positive, sexual aspects in their current relationship.

22. Practice Communication on Nonsexual Matters (22)

A. The partners were directed to practice communication with each other about nonsexual matters.

B. The listening partner was directed to listen without interrupting while the other partner spoke about a nonsexual matter, and then validate what the other had said (without interruption from the other partner).
C. The partners were provided with feedback regarding their communication about nonsexual matters.
D. The partners were redirected when their communication pattern was interrupted.

23. Practice Communication on Sexual Matters (23)

A. The partners were directed to practice communication with each other about sexual matters.
B. The listening partner was directed to listen without interrupting while the other partner spoke about a sexual matter, and then validate what the other had said (without interruption from the other partner).
C. The partners were provided with feedback regarding their communication about sexual matters.
D. The partners were redirected when their communication pattern was interrupted.

24. Critique Communication Styles (24)

A. Feedback and interpretation were provided to the partners about their communication styles.
B. The partners were noted to have fairly healthy communication styles.
C. The partners were provided with a variety of ways to improve their communication styles.

25. Inquire about Causes for Sexual Decline (25)

A. The partners were asked to describe the perceived causes for decline in frequency and enjoyment of sexual activity.
B. The partners identified causes for a decline in frequency and enjoyment of sexual activity, and these were processed.
C. The partners could not identify significant causes for the decline in frequency and enjoyment of sexual activity and were provided with tentative examples of reasons why this may occur.

26. Explore Abusive Partner's History of Abuse (26)

A. The abusive or critical partner was asked about a possible history of physical abuse of self or others in the childhood family experience.
B. Support was provided as the abusive partner discussed the history of physical abuse in the childhood family experience.
C. The abusive partner indicated no history of physical abuse of self or others in the childhood family experience, and this was accepted.

27. Explore Abused Partner's History of Abuse (27)

A. The abused partner was asked about a possible history of physical abuse of self or others in the childhood family experience.
B. Support was provided as the abused partner discussed the history of physical abuse in the childhood family experience.
C. The abused partner indicated no history of physical abuse of self or others in the childhood family experience, and this was accepted.

28. Explore Anger toward the Opposite Sex (28)

A. The concept of anger toward the opposite sex that is rooted in unresolved childhood experiences was presented to the abusive partner.

B. The abusive partner was asked about the possible presence of anger toward the opposite sex that has roots in unresolved childhood experiences.

C. The abusive partner endorsed a history of anger toward the opposite sex that is routed in unresolved childhood experiences, and support and encouragement were provided for this insight.

D. The abusive partner immediately minimized any ideas related to unresolved childhood experiences prompting anger toward the opposite sex; the abusive partner was encouraged to reconsider this dynamic.

E. After careful consideration, the abusive partner denied any connection between unresolved childhood experiences and anger toward the opposite sex, and this was accepted.

29. Question Expectation of Noncoercive Sexual Activity (29)

A. The abusive partner was asked about the level of trust that the other partner would freely and happily engage in sexual activity if coercion was not present.

B. The abusive partner's ability to trust others and feel loveable was questioned and discussed.

C. Emphasis was placed on the abusive partner's ability to feel loved and trust others, rather than the victimized partner's responsibility.

D. The abusive partner was reinforced for stating a positive expectation that sexual activity would be freely and happily engaged in if coercion was not present.

E. Support was provided as the abusive partner admitted to feeling unlovable and having difficulty trusting others.

30. Confront Domination (30)

A. The use of sexual coercion or belittling criticism was identified as a means of domination that degrades the other partner from a lover to that of a victim.

B. The sexually coercive or belittling partner was confronted about degrading the other partner through domination.

31. Identify Traumatic Sexual Experiences (31)

A. The partners were asked to identify traumatic sexual experiences.

B. Support and encouragement were provided to the abusive partner as sexually traumatic experiences were reviewed.

C. Support and encouragement were provided to the victimized partner as sexually traumatic experiences were reviewed.

D. The partners were reinforced for providing support to each other as they reviewed traumatic sexual experiences.

E. The partners denied any history of traumatic sexual experiences, and this was accepted.

32. Discontinue Traumatizing Sexual Activity (32)

A. The partners were advised to cease any sexual activity that triggers memory of traumatic events.

B. The partners have identified sexual activity that triggers memories of traumatic events, and this type of sexual activity has been terminated; the emotions related to these changes were processed.
C. The partners were confronted for failing to cease sexual activity that triggers memories of traumatic events.

33. Teach Sensate Focus (33)

A. The couple was taught about the use of sensate focus techniques so each partner can provide pleasure to the other.
B. The partners were quizzed about their understanding of the sensate focus technique.

34. Obtain Feedback about Sensate Focus Exercises (34)

A. The partners were asked about their use of the sensate focus exercises.
B. Support and encouragement were provided as the partners described their experiences with the sensate focus exercises.
C. The partners were assisted in minimizing any behaviors that affect either partner negatively.
D. The partners were reinforced for their healthy use of the sensate focus techniques.
E. The partners were provided with remedial information about the sensate focus techniques.

35. Focus on Alternatives to Current Relationship (35)

A. In an individual session, a discussion was held with the sexually abused client regarding the alternatives to remaining in the current relationship.
B. The abused partner was assisted in listing the options available regarding the relationship (maintenance, separation, divorce).
C. The session focused on the abused partner's emotional response to separating or terminating the relationship.

36. Assess Alternatives to Current Relationship (36)

A. In an individual session, a discussion was held with the sexually abused client regarding the alternatives to remaining in the current relationship.
B. The abused partner identified the pros and cons of alternatives of remaining in the current relationship.
C. Support and encouragement was provided to the abused partner as decisions were made about alternatives to the current relationship.

37. Refer to Domestic Violence Shelter (37)

A. The abused partner has been referred to a domestic violence shelter.
B. The abused partner was assisted in getting in touch with a domestic violence shelter.
C. The abused partner declined a referral to a domestic violence shelter and was encouraged to maintain this as an option.

SEXUAL DYSFUNCTION

CLIENT PRESENTATION

1. Lack of Sexual Desire (1)*

A. One member of the couple describes a consistently very low desire for or pleasurable anticipation of sexual activity.

B. The interest in sexual contact is gradually increasing.

C. The couple verbalized an increased desire for sexual contact, which is a return to previously established levels.

2. Avoidance of Sexual Contact (2)

A. The couple reported a strong avoidance of and repulsion for any and all sexual contact, in spite of a relationship of mutual caring and respect.

B. The partner's repulsion for sexual contact has begun to diminish.

C. There is no longer a strong avoidance of sexual contact.

D. The partners have expressed pleasure about their sexual contact.

3. Lack of Physiological Sex Response (3)

A. The sexually dysfunctional client has experienced a recurrent lack of the usual physiological response of sexual excitement and arousal.

B. Instead of an arousal response to sexual contact, the sexually dysfunctional client's physiological response to excitement is not present.

C. The sexually dysfunctional client is gradually regaining the usual physiological response of sexual excitement and arousal.

D. The couple reported that sexual contact resulted in a satisfactory level of physiological response of sexual excitement.

4. Lack of Subjective Enjoyment (4)

A. The sexually dysfunctional client reported a consistent lack of a subjective sense of enjoyment and pleasure during sexual activity.

B. The sexually dysfunctional client reported an increased sense of pleasure and enjoyment during recent sexual contact.

C. The couple reported a satisfactory level of enjoyment and pleasure during recent sexual activity.

5. Delay In/Absence of Reaching Orgasm (5)

A. The couple reported a persistent delay in or absence of reaching orgasm after achieving arousal and in spite of sensitive sexual pleasuring by a caring partner.

B. The couple reported an improvement in the ability to reach orgasm during sexual contact.

C. The couple reported a satisfactory response time to reaching orgasm during sexual contact.

*The numbers in parentheses on Client Presentation pages correlate to the number of the Behavioral Definition statement in the companion chapter with the same title in *The Couples Psychotherapy Treatment Planner* (Jongsma, O'Leary, and Heyman) by John Wiley & Sons, 1998. The numbers in parentheses on the Interventions Implemented page correspond to the number of the Therapeutic Intervention statement in the companion chapter in the same book.

6. Genital Pain (6)

A. The sexually dysfunctional client reported persistent genital pain before, during, or after sexual intercourse.

B. The sexually dysfunctional client's genital pain associated with sexual intercourse has diminished.

C. The sexually dysfunctional client reported no experience of genital pain before, during, or after sexual intercourse.

7. Vaginismus (7)

A. The sexually dysfunctional client reported a consistent or recurring involuntary spasm of the vagina that prohibits penetration for sexual intercourse.

B. The couple reported experiencing minimal vaginal penetration during sexual contact without the experience of pain.

C. The couple reported normal vaginal penetration during sexual intercourse without any experience of involuntary contraction or pain.

8. General Relationship Dissatisfaction (8)

A. One partner has made comments about a general sense of dissatisfaction with the relationship.

B. Both partners have made comments about a general sense of dissatisfaction with the relationship.

C. As treatment has progressed, the partners have displayed increased satisfaction with the relationship.

9. Complaints of Lack of Love and Caring (9)

A. One partner has made complaints about how little love and caring there is within the relationship.

B. Both partners have made complaints about how little love and caring there is within the relationship.

C. The partners have gained insight about how love and caring are decreased due to the problems in the relationship.

D. As the partners have increased communication, the levels of love and caring have also increased.

10. Avoidance of Talking of Sexual Matters (10)

A. The partners identified a pattern of avoidance of communication with each other regarding sexual matters.

B. When one partner brings up sexual matters, the other partner often avoids any type of communication in this area.

C. As the partners have been able to increase communication about sexual matters, their sexual relationship and other portions of their relationship have improved.

11. Criticism about Lack of Sexual Responsiveness (11)

A. One partner often makes negative comments about the other partner's lack of sexual responsiveness.

B. One partner calls the sexually dysfunctional partner "frigid."

C. One partner calls the sexually dysfunctional partner "impotent."

D. As the couple has progressed in treatment, the partners have displayed a pattern of mutual support regarding the sexual dysfunction problems, discontinuing negative or pejorative comments about the other partner.

12. Low Self-Esteem (12)

A. The partner with the sexual dysfunction often makes statements reflective of low self-esteem.

B. The partner with the sexual dysfunction sees the problem as a personal deficiency.

C. As treatment has progressed, the sexual dysfunction has been ameliorated, and the self-esteem of that partner has increased.

13. Low Self-Esteem for Partner (13)

A. The partner without the specific sexual dysfunction perceives the sexual problem to be due to own personal deficiencies.

B. The partner without the sexual dysfunction makes self-blame statements (e.g., "It's my fault").

C. As treatment has progressed, the sexual dysfunction has been ameliorated, and the other partner feels less guilty.

D. The partner without the sexual dysfunction has learned not to take personal responsibility for the other partner's sexual dysfunction, but to seek ways to assist in conquering the problem.

14. Depressed Mood (14)

A. The partner with the sexual dysfunction displayed a depressed mood.

B. The partner without the sexual dysfunction displayed a depressed mood.

C. Both partners displayed a depressed mood.

D. As treatment has progressed, mood and affect have improved.

INTERVENTIONS IMPLEMENTED

1. Assess Frequency of Sexual Interactions (1)

A. The partners were questioned regarding the current frequency of sexual interactions.

B. The partners were asked about the frequency of sexual interactions across the history of the relationship.

2. Assess Enjoyment of Sexual Interactions (2)

A. The partners were questioned regarding the current enjoyment of sexual interactions.

B. The partners were asked about the enjoyment of sexual interactions across the history of the relationship.

3. Ask about Perceived Causes of Decline (3)

A. The partners were asked to each provide the perceived causes of decline in the frequency of their sexual activity.

B. The partners were supported as they emphasized situational factors that have led to the decline in the frequency of their sexual activity.
C. The partners were supported as they focused on problems within the relationship that have led to the decline in the frequency and of their sexual activity.
D. The partners were uncertain about possible causes in decline in sexual activity and were provided with tentative examples in this area.

4. Review Positive Aspects at Start of Relationship (4)

A. The partners were asked to describe the positive, nonsexual aspects of the beginning of their relationship.
B. As the partners identified a variety of positive, nonsexual aspects that were important to the beginning of their relationship, these were reinforced and processed.

5. Identify Positive Aspects in Current Relationship (5)

A. The partners were asked to describe the positive, nonsexual aspects of their current relationship.
B. As the partners identified a variety of positive, nonsexual aspects that are important to the current relationship, these were reinforced and processed.
C. The partners failed to identify positive, nonsexual aspects of their current relationship and were provided with tentative examples in this area.

6. Review Positive Sexual Aspects at Start of Relationship (6)

A. The partners were asked to describe the positive, sexual aspects of the beginning of their relationship.
B. As the partners identified a variety of positive, sexual aspects that were important to the beginning of their relationship, these were reinforced and processed.

7. Identify Positive Sexual Aspects in Current Relationship (7)

A. The partners were asked to describe the positive sexual aspects of their current relationship.
B. As the partners identified a variety of positive sexual aspects that were important to the current relationship, these were reinforced and processed.
C. The partners failed to identify positive sexual aspects of their current relationship and were provided with tentative examples in this area.

8. Practice Paraphrasing about Nonsexual Matter (8)

A. While one partner was serving as the speaker, the other partner was directed to paraphrase, by rephrasing the speaker's major point, with a focus on a nonsexual matter.
B. The speaking partner was asked to acknowledge whether the paraphrasing partner had accurately described the intended message.
C. The partners were provided with positive feedback as they displayed several examples of appropriately paraphrasing each other's comments.

9. Practice Paraphrasing about Sexual Matter (9)

A. While one partner was serving as the speaker, the other partner was directed to paraphrase, by rephrasing the speaker's major point, with a focus on a sexual matter.

B. The speaking partner was asked to acknowledge whether the paraphrasing partner had accurately described the intended message.
C. The partners were provided with positive feedback as they displayed several examples of appropriately paraphrasing each other's comments.

10. Provide Feedback about Communication (10)

A. Feedback was provided to the partners about their communication styles.
B. The differences in the partners' communication styles were highlighted to them.
C. The partners' understanding of the differences and similarities in their communication styles was checked for accuracy.

11. Identify Early Sexual Expectations (11)

A. Each client was asked to describe initial expectations about their sexual lives.
B. The partners were supported as they described very similar expectations about their sexual lives early in the relationship.
C. It was noted that the partners described very divergent expectations related to their sexual life.

12. Identify Expectations That Have Changed (12)

A. The partners were asked to describe how expectations about their sexual life have changed.
B. The partners identified ways in which their sexual life has changed; these were summarized and clarified.
C. The partners were unable to identify specific ways in which their sexual life has changed and were provided with tentative examples.

13. Compare Sexual Activity with Age Norms (13)

A. The partners were asked how they compare their sexual encounter frequency and satisfaction with those of others in their age range.
B. The partners were provided with factual information regarding the frequency and satisfaction of sexual encounters for others in their age range.
C. The partners' sexual dysfunction was interpreted as being a factor of higher expectation regarding sexual encounter frequency and satisfaction than is accurate for their age range.
D. It was reflected to the partners that their reported frequency and satisfaction with sexual encounters is commensurate with the norms of their age range.
E. It was reflected to the partners that the frequency and satisfaction with sexual encounters is less than should be expected for their age range.

14. Discuss Traumatic Sexual Experiences (14)

A. The partners were assessed for a history of sexual abuse.
B. One partner identified a history of sexual abuse as a child, and acknowledged how this abuse has had a negative impact on current sexual feelings and thoughts.
C. Both partners identified a history of sexual abuse as a child and acknowledged how this abuse has had a negative impact on sexual feelings and thoughts.
D. No history of sexual abuse was identified.

15. Probe for Negative Triggers (15)

A. The partner identifying a history of sexual trauma was assessed regarding whether these traumas create negative emotions during sexual overtures or activities.

B. The partners denied any negative emotions during sexual activity, and this was accepted.

C. The focus of treatment was shifted to resolving the past traumas that impact the couple's current sexual pleasure.

16. Examine Religious Beliefs (16)

A. The partners' religious beliefs and training were examined to identify whether such beliefs interfere with engaging in sexual activity desired by either partner.

B. The partners were supported as they denied any interfering effects of religious beliefs and training on the sexual activity desired.

C. The partners were assisted in neutralizing the impact of religious beliefs and training on desired sexual activity.

D. The partners were assisted in defining acceptable sexual practice, considering religious beliefs and training.

17. Recommend Cessation of Trauma-Triggering Activity (17)

A. Since specific sexual activity seems to trigger memories of traumatic events, the partners were recommended to cease such sexual activity until traumatic memories are properly resolved.

B. The partners were praised for their agreement to care for each other by ceasing trauma-triggering sexual activity.

C. The partners have not ceased the trauma-triggering sexual activity and were redirected to do so.

18. Explore Family of Origin Sexual Attitudes (18)

A. The partners were asked to describe their perceptions of sexual attitudes that were learned from their respective families of origin.

B. The partners outlined the sexual attitudes that are perceived as causing sexual inhibition, feelings of guilt, fear or repulsion associated with sexual activity; these attitudes were summarized and clarified.

C. The partners denied any family of origin sexual attitudes that affect their current sexual functioning and were provided with tentative examples in this area.

19. Explore and Detach from Early Family Emotions (19)

A. The partners were assessed for feelings related to early family experiences that have a negative impact on the current sexual experience.

B. The partners endorsed the presence of emotions related to early family experiences and were encouraged to differentiate between the past and the here-and-now.

C. Support and feedback were provided as the partners were able to identify the differences between early family experiences and current experiences.

D. The partners had a difficult time differentiating early family experiences and current experiences and were provided with remedial feedback and assistance in this area.

20. Assess Biochemical Causes for Dysfunction (20)

A. The role that substance abuse, diabetes, hypertension, or thyroid disease may have on the sexual functioning was explained and assessed.

B. The sexually dysfunctional client identified a pattern of substance abuse that could have a very negative affect on sexual functioning; a recommendation for chemical dependence treatment was provided.

C. The sexually dysfunctional client identified a medical condition that may have an impact on sexual functioning, and a referral to a physician for further evaluation was made.

21. Review Medications (21)

A. The sexually dysfunctional client's use of medication was reviewed as to the medication's possible negative side effects on sexual functioning.

B. The sexually dysfunctional client was referred to the primary physician for a more comprehensive review of the medications taken and their impact on sexual functioning.

C. The sexually dysfunctional client acknowledged that medication side effects might be a powerful contributing factor to the sexual problems and this was processed.

22. Explore Feelings about Body Image (22)

A. Each partner's feelings regarding body image were explored with a focus on identifying causes for a decrease in frequency and range of sexual activity.

B. One partner was identified as experiencing body image concerns (e.g., increased body weight, lack of muscle tone, or residual affects of surgery).

C. The partner with body image concerns was confronted for being too self-critical and expecting perfection.

D. The partner with body image concerns was encouraged to be more self-accepting of a body with normal flaws.

E. The partners were reinforced for verbalizing a more positive body image and for increasing the range and frequency of sexual activity.

23. Encourage Positive Body Image (23)

A. The partners were asked to list the assets of their bodies about which each feels positive.

B. The partners were encouraged to be less critical about their body image.

C. As the partners have become less critical regarding body image, they have developed greater freedom of sexual expression.

24. Assign Body Image Enhancers (24)

A. The partner with a negative body image was encouraged to begin a program of exercise, in conjunction with that partner's physician.

B. The partner with a negative body image was encouraged to begin a program of dieting, in conjunction with that partner's physician.

C. The partner with the negative body image was encouraged to change patterns of dress.

D. The partner was supported for implementing changes to improve body image and increase feelings of sexual attraction.

25. Assess Self-Esteem (25)

A. The role of self-esteem in sexual functioning was assessed for each of the partners.
B. Factors within the relationship were probed to determine their impact on each partner's self-esteem.
C. The couple identified factors within the relationship which have led to low self-esteem and decreased sexual function.
D. As the partners have worked on increasing each other's self-esteem, sexual functioning has increased as well; the benefits of this were reviewed.

26. Probe about Extramarital Affairs (26)

A. In individual sessions, the partners were asked about secret sexual affairs that have contributed to sexual dysfunction with the partner.
B. The partners were probed for feelings of suspicion related to a secret sexual affair.
C. One partner acknowledged the presence of a secret sexual affair.
D. Both partners acknowledge the presence of a secret sexual affair.
E. The partners were advised about the need to immediately terminate any affairs in order to work on the sexual relationship with the partner.
F. No evidence of secret sexual affairs was identified.

27. Assess Homosexual Thoughts/Activities (27)

A. In individual sessions, each partner was assessed for the presence of homosexual thoughts or activities.
B. One of the partners identified homosexual urges that have predominated any heterosexual interests.
C. The partner was supported for acknowledging that the homosexual attraction is a major factor in the sexual dysfunction with the partner.
D. The partner with a homosexual interest has agreed to share this information with the partner and was encouraged to discuss the future of the relationship.
E. No homosexual thoughts or activities were identified as interfering with the heterosexual functioning of the relationship.

28. Explore/Identify Sexual Orientation Implications for the Relationship (28)

A. As one partner has identified homosexual activities or fantasies that interfere with the couple's relationship, this issue was more completely explored.
B. The implications of the homosexual activities and fantasies for the future of the heterosexual relationship were a primary focus of the discussions regarding sexual orientation.
C. The partners were supported as they have decided to try to continue the relationship despite the homosexual orientation of one partner.
D. The partners were supported as they have decided to dissolve the relationship due to one partner identifying a homosexual orientation.

29. Encourage Sexual Fantasies (29)

A. The couple was encouraged to indulge in normal sexual fantasies that could mediate and enhance sexual desire.

B. The couple reported success at becoming aware of and indulging in sexual fantasies that have increased sexual desire.

C. The couple reported resistance to indulging sexual fantasies due to feelings of guilt, embarrassment, and shame.

30. Assign Written Material on Sexual Fantasies (30)

A. The partners were directed to read material on sexual fantasies.

B. The partners were referred to read *My Secret Garden* (Friday), *Women on Top* (Friday), or *Becoming Orgasmic: A Sexual Growth Program for Women* (Heiman and LoPiccilo).

C. The partners have read the material on sexual fantasies, and the important points from this material were processed.

D. The partners have not read the assigned written material regarding sexual fantasizing and were redirected to do so.

31. Assign Educational Videos (31)

A. The partners were assessed for whether their religious and moral views permit the purchase of educational videos of sexual activities.

B. The partners were directed to purchase educational videos of sexual activities to teach enhancement of fantasy, masturbation, and a variety of heterosexual sexual behaviors.

C. The partners were directed to purchase videos (e.g., *Self-Loving* [Dodson], *Better Sex Videos: Vols. I–3* [Sinclair Institute]).

D. The partners have purchased educational videos to teach enhancement of fantasy, masturbation, and a variety of sexual behaviors, and the benefits of these were reviewed.

E. The partners have not purchased or viewed educational videos on sexual activities and were redirected to do so.

32. Suggest Books on Sexual Behavior/Functioning (32)

A. The partners were directed to read books on sexual behaviors and sexual functioning.

B. The partners were referred to books such as *Sex for Dummies* (Westheimer), *The New Male Sexuality* (Zilbergeld), *The New Joy of Sex* (Comfort), *The Gift of Sex* (Penner and Penner), or *When a Woman's Body Says No to Sex* (Valins).

C. The partners have read information on sexual behavior and sexual functioning, and the salient points of this information were reviewed.

D. The partners have not read information on sexual behavior and sexual functioning and were redirected to do so.

33. Instruct about Sensate Focus (33)

A. The partners were instructed about the use of sensate focus exercises to learn how to touch each other for sexual pleasure.

B. The partners were reinforced for displaying an adequate understanding of the sensate focus techniques.

C. The partners reported on the use of sensate focus and their use was processed.

D. The partners have not used the sensate focus techniques and were redirected to do so.

34. Obtain Feedback about Sensate Focus Exercises (34)

A. The partners were asked about their use of the sensate focus exercises.
B. Sensate focus behaviors that affect either partner negatively were identified.
C. Sensate focus behaviors that affect either partner negatively were focused on to help minimize these affects and maximize sexual pleasure.

WORK/HOME ROLE STRAIN

CLIENT PRESENTATION

1. Perception of Misplaced Emphasis (1)*

A. One partner reported a perception that the relationship or family is not placed as a high enough priority in the other partner's life because of too great an emphasis on employment interests.

B. The partners often have arguments due to one partner's emphasis on employment interests that take priority away from the other partner or family relationships.

C. As treatment has progressed, the emphasis on the marital relationship, family, and employment has been shifted to more equitable levels.

D. As treatment has progressed, the partners have become satisfied with the level of priority given to the relationship, family, and employment interests.

2. Perceived Failure to Meet Responsibilities (2)

A. One partner contends that the other partner is not meeting that partner's fair share of responsibilities in the relationship, the family, home maintenance, or work duties.

B. Both partners complain that the other partner is not meeting the fair share of responsibilities in the relationship, the family, home maintenance, or work duties.

C. As communication has increased, the partners have developed a more equitable and attainable division of responsibilities in the relationship, the family, home maintenance, or work duties.

D. The partners describe satisfaction that each is meeting responsibilities within the home and family.

3. Conflict over Allocation of Time (3)

A. The partners have conflict over the allocation of time made by one partner to work duties.

B. The partners disagree about how much time should be spent doing home and other chore roles.

C. The partners have developed a better appreciation of the responsibilities that each partner has regarding work, home, and chore roles, and this has reduced conflict between the partners.

D. The partners no longer disagree about the amount of time allocated to work.

4. Arguments over Role Imbalances (4)

A. The partners often argue about differing expectations regarding roles.

B. Discussions about role needs often develop into more involved arguments regarding core issues of role imbalances.

C. As treatment has progressed, the partners have developed skills to openly discuss their roles and expectations.

*The numbers in parentheses on Client Presentation pages correlate to the number of the Behavioral Definition statement in the companion chapter with the same title in *The Couples Psychotherapy Treatment Planner* (Jongsma, O'Leary, and Heyman) by John Wiley & Sons, 1998. The numbers in parentheses on the Interventions Implemented page correspond to the number of the Therapeutic Intervention statement in the companion chapter in the same book.

5. Perceived Difficulty in Meeting Role Expectations (5)

A. One partner reported difficulties in meeting role expectations.

B. Both partners reported difficulties in meeting role expectations.

C. Although there is a perception by one partner that role expectations are not being met, the other partner reports satisfaction with how well roles are fulfilled.

D. As treatment has progressed, discussion about meeting role expectations has been more open and has resulted in mutual satisfaction.

6. List Organizational Inefficiencies (6)

A. There is a perception of disorganization by one partner in the attempt to meet key role responsibilities.

B. There is a perception of time inefficiencies by one partner in an attempt to meet key role responsibilities.

C. As partners have been informed about the perception of disorganization or time inefficiencies, these area's have improved.

D. Perceived disorganization or time inefficiencies were identified as actually being the most effective ways to meet key role responsibilities.

E. There no longer are complaints regarding disorganization or time inefficiencies.

INTERVENTIONS IMPLEMENTED

1. Assess Satisfaction (1)

A. Each partner's satisfaction with work roles was assessed.

B. Each partner's satisfaction with family roles was assessed.

C. The partners' level of satisfaction with work and family roles was summarized, compared, and contrasted.

D. It was reflected to the partners that they are fairly satisfied with work and family roles.

E. It was reflected to the partners that there is significant dissatisfaction with work and family roles.

2. Probe Stress Levels (2)

A. Each partner's stress level was assessed in regard to work/home role strain.

B. It was reflected to the partners that there is relatively little stress due to work/home role strains.

C. The partners indicated a great deal of stress due to work/home role strain, and this was verified with each partner.

D. It was reflected that the partners experience uneven levels of stress due to work/home role strain.

3. Query about Work Schedules (3)

A. The partners were asked about their work schedules.

B. The partners were asked about hours worked, what shift is worked, and whether they bring work home.

C. The partners' work schedules were summarized and reflected back to them for accuracy.
D. The partners' work schedules were indicative of a low degree of role strain, and this was reflected to them.
E. The partners' work schedules were indicative of a high degree of role strain, and this was reflected to them.

4. Describe Typical Days (4)

A. The couple was asked to describe a typical workday and a typical weekend day.
B. A summarization was provided as the partners described typical days, including when they get up, their morning routine, their workday, the evening routine, and any variability within each day.
C. It was noted that the partners have strong boundaries between work and home roles.
D. It was noted that the work and home roles have not been significantly separated.

5. Develop Etiology of Current Role Arrangement (5)

A. The partners were asked to describe how the current role arrangement came about.
B. It was reflected to the partners that they have taken adequate time to discuss their current family/work time allocations.
C. Supportive listening techniques were used as the partners described how their current arrangement evolved.

6. Assess Chore Division (6)

A. The partners were asked about how the chores at home are divided between family members.
B. The partners were asked about whether there is an explicit plan to divide chores between family members.
C. The partners were supported for having specific plans for how to divide family chores.
D. It was noted that the family does not have an explicit plan for how to divide chores.

7. Assess Satisfaction with Partners' Parenting (7)

A. An assessment was completed regarding each partner's satisfaction with the other's involvement in caring for the children.
B. The partners agree that each partner is appropriately involved in caring for the children; this was reflected to them.
C. Both partners were noted to be dissatisfied with the other's involvement and caring for the children.
D. It was reflected to the partners that they have varying levels of satisfaction with how involved each is with the children.

8. Identify Family Interference with Employment (8)

A. The couple was asked to describe the ways that family demands interfere with the employment role.
B. The couple was asked to provide specific examples of situations in which family demands have interfered with the employment role.

C. Supportive listening was provided as the couple described the ways in which the demands of family or relationships interfere with work responsibilities.

9. Identify Employment Interference with Family (9)

A. The couple was asked to describe the ways that employment demands interfere with the family roles.
B. The couple was asked to provide specific examples of situations in which employment demands have interfered with the family roles.
C. Supportive listening was provided as the couple described the ways in which the demands of work responsibilities interfere with family and relationship expectations.

10. Connect Stress to Relationship Conflicts (10)

A. The partners were asked to describe the ways in which work/home roles have precipitated relationship conflicts.
B. The partners were supported as they described specific examples of how work stress precipitated relationship conflicts.
C. The couple tended to minimize any connection between work stress and relationship conflicts and was provided with specific examples of how this occurs.

11. Contrast Expectations (11)

A. Each partner was asked to write down, in two columns, the behaviors that are expected of them at work and at home.
B. The partners were asked to read their behavioral expectations at work and at home, and discuss any incompatible expectations.
C. The partners were supported as they described incompatible expectations between work and home (e.g., having to travel during a child's important athletic event, working when the children are being put to bed).
D. The partners denied any incompatible expectations between work and home roles, and more specific questions were asked in this area.

12. Assign Reading on Values (12)

A. The partners were assigned to read information that focuses on personal guidelines or values that are expected to influence important life-role enactment.
B. The couple was directed to read *Seven Habits of Highly Effective Families* (Covey).
C. The partners have read the assigned material, and the salient points of this information were reviewed.
D. The partners have not read the assigned material and were redirected to do so.

13. Write Personal Mission Statement (13)

A. For a homework assignment, the partners were asked to write their personal mission statement that reflects their personally held values and to bring this to the session.
B. The partners have completed their mission statement, and these were reviewed in session.
C. The partners have not completed the mission statement and were redirected to do so.

14. Question Mission Statement Validity (14)

A. The partners were asked to read their mission statement within the session.

B. The partners were asked about whether they are carrying out their mission statements (e.g., Does the time allocation/quality reflect the priorities of the mission statement?).

C. It was reflected to the partners that they are being consistent between the identified mission statement and the allocation/quality of their resources.

D. Inconsistencies between the identified mission statements and actual prioritization between home and work allocations were reflected to the partners.

15. Identify Influences on Expectations (15)

A. Each partner was asked to describe what expectation they perceive that friends, subcultural groups, and society have for them in their work and home roles.

B. The partners describe the expectations that they perceive others have for them in their work and home roles; it was reflected to the partners that these expectations were consistent with general cultural norms.

C. It was reflected that the partners had rather divergent understanding about what expectations others have for the partners' work and home roles.

16. Define Dilemmas (16)

A. Each partner was asked to define the other partner's dilemmas that are faced in trying to meet varied and sometimes competing role demands.

B. Each partner's description of the other partner's dilemmas was checked with the other partner for accuracy.

C. It was reflected to the partners that they both have a clear understanding of the other partner's dilemmas in trying to meet varied and sometimes competing role demands.

D. It was reflected to the partners that they have struggles in understanding each other's varied and competing role demands.

17. Teach Paraphrasing (17)

A. While one partner was serving as the speaker, the other partner was directed to paraphrase, by rephrasing the speaker's major point and empathizing with the speaker's dilemma regarding work and home role conflicts.

B. The speaking partner was asked to acknowledge whether the paraphrasing partner had accurately described the intended message.

C. The partners were provided with positive feedback as they displayed several examples of appropriately paraphrasing each other's comments.

18. Identify Emotional Effects of Role Arrangement (18)

A. Each partner was asked to describe how both the positive and negative aspects of the current role arrangement affect that partner emotionally.

B. Active listening skills were used as the partners described how the positive and negative aspects of the current role arrangements have created emotional effects.

19. Direct Validation and Empathizing (19)

A. While one partner serves as the speaker, the other partner was directed to validate and empathize with the partner's perspective regarding the gains and losses of the current role arrangement.

B. The partners' ability to identify, validate, and empathize about gains and losses was reviewed and summarized to the partners.

C. The listening partner was encouraged for the use of validation and empathy without substitution of own perspective.

D. When the listening partner began substituting a personal perspective for validation and empathy of the partner's perspective, redirection was applied.

20. Assign Self-Talk Homework (20)

A. The partners were directed to write out the thoughts or self-talk conclusions associated with negative feelings over the current role arrangement.

B. The partners have completed the self-talk homework regarding conclusions and negative feelings over the current role arrangements, and this was reviewed and processed in the session.

C. The partners have not completed the homework regarding self-talk and negative feelings over the current role arrangement and were redirected to complete this.

D. The partners were provided with examples of self-talk conclusions that might lead to negative feelings over the current role arrangement.

21. Direct Reading of Thought-Tracking Homework (21)

A. Each partner was asked to read the thought-tracking homework within the session.

B. The partners were assisted in developing the thought-tracking and self-talk conclusions associated with the negative feelings over the current role arrangement.

22. Assess Self-Talk (22)

A. Each self-talk thought or conclusion was assessed for helpfulness, specificity, and accuracy.

B. Each self-talk thought or conclusion was assessed for whether it would be helpful in getting the desired outcome if it was verbalized.

C. Each self-talk thought or conclusion was assessed for whether it is directly related to the specific situation described (i.e., is situationally specific, not global).

D. Each self-talk thought or conclusion was assessed for accuracy (i.e., actual evidence can be cited to support the conclusion).

E. It was noted that the partner's self-talk thought or conclusions were helpful, specific, and accurate.

F. It was reflected to the partner that some self-talk thoughts or conclusions were not helpful, specific, or accurate.

23. Rework Nonuseful Self-Talk (23)

A. Some of the partners' thoughts or conclusions were noted to fail to meet all three criteria (e.g., helpful, specific, and accurate).

B. The nonuseful self-talk thoughts or conclusions were reworked to make certain that they were helpful, specific, and accurate.
C. The partner was noted to be able to rework self-talk thoughts or conclusions so that they are helpful, specific, and accurate.
D. The partner failed to grasp how to rework self-talk thoughts or conclusions and was provided with the following example: "He doesn't care about his children" can become "he seems to be having a hard time finding time for both work and home lately. After the kids are in bed, I'll ask him if he feels up to discussing the strain."

24. Identify Needed Behavior from Partner (24)

A. For each self-talk conclusion identified, the client was asked to state the preferred behavior from the other partner, rather that stating what the other partner is doing negatively.
B. The partner was supported and encouraged as requests for proactive behavior from the other partner were made.
C. When the partner experiencing the negative self-talk reverted to complaints about the other partner's behavior, redirection was used.

25. Identify Action Steps to Increase Partner's Desired Behavior (25)

A. Each partner was asked to identify action steps that could be taken to increase the probability of attaining desired behavior from the other partner.
B. The partner was supported for identifying behaviors that will increase the probability of attaining desired behavior from the other partner.
C. The partner was confronted when responses became merely complaining about the other partner's behavioral faults.
D. The partner struggled to identify ways to increase the probability of attaining desired behavior from the other partner and was provided with the following example: "She doesn't spend enough time at home," can become "I want to be supportive so that our home is one she would want to come home to."

26. List Current Home and Work Activities (26)

A. Each partner was asked to identify and list the current activities that must be performed at home and work.
B. Each partner's list of activities to be performed at home and work was reviewed, and areas of omission were added.
C. Each partner's current activities that must be performed at home and work were summarized and reflected to the partners.

27. Identify Goals and Allocate Time (27)

A. Each partner was asked to prioritize the key short-term and long-term goals in their work, family, and chore roles.
B. The partners were asked to allocate weekly work, family, and chore time based on the identified priorities.
C. The partners were reinforced for reprioritizing their time for work, family, and chores based on their short-term and long-term goals.

D. It was noted that the partners' short-term and long-term goals are not consistent with their allocated time to work, family, and chores.

28. Direct Pinpointing and Paraphrasing to Discuss Allocation of Time (28)

A. One partner was upset about the proposed allocation of time, and was directed to use pinpointing skills to identify the problem.
B. One partner was directed to use paraphrasing and/or reflection to indicate understanding of the reasons why the other partner is upset with the proposed allocation of time.
C. The partners were reinforced as they discussed issues in a specific, direct manner, which decreased emotional overreaction.
D. The partners were confronted when they slipped out of pinpointing and paraphrasing skills.

29. Brainstorm Assistance for Role Demands (29)

A. The partners were asked to brainstorm possible sources of assistance to ease home and work demands.
B. The partners were supported as they developed a variety of possibilities for assistance to ease home and work demands.
C. The partners failed to identify any ways to ease home and work role demands and were provided with examples (e.g., family members, child care, household help, project delegation).

30. Brainstorm Allocation of Time (30)

A. The partners were asked to brainstorm ways of reallocating their time to provide mutual support and benefits.
B. The partners were supported as they developed creative solutions to reallocate their time to provide mutual support and benefits.
C. The partners struggled to develop any ideas for reallocation of their time to provide mutual support and benefits and were redirected in this area.

31. Choose Preferred Solution (31)

A. The partners were assisted in evaluating the pros and cons of the brainstormed time allocation solutions.
B. The partners were assisted in choosing a mutually preferred time allocation solution to help ease home and work role demands.
C. The partners were supported for their wisdom in choosing time allocation solutions to help ease home and work role demands.
D. The partners failed to choose a specific time allocation solution to help ease home and work role demands and were redirected in this area.

32. Discuss Enacting Solution (32)

A. The partners were assisted in discussing and agreeing on exactly how the brainstormed solution for allocating time should be carried out.
B. The partners were directed to contract with each other to enact the time allocation solution.
C. The partners were asked to write down their perceptions of the results (for discussion in a future session) of the time reallocation implementation.

D. The partners were supported for their discussion on enacting the brainstormed time allocation solution.
E. The partners did not come to an agreement about how the time allocation solution should be carried out and were provided with redirection in this area.

33. Discuss Results of Brainstormed Solution (33)

A. The partners were asked to discuss the results of implementation of their brainstormed solution to reallocate their time.
B. The partners were asked to identify ways in which their brainstormed solution could be improved.
C. The partners were assisted in developing additional ways to solve time allocation problems.

34. Write and Sign Contract for Work/Home Responsibilities (34)

A. The partners were directed to write and sign a work/home contract that details explicit expectations, requirements and rewards for each partner in carrying out specific responsibilities.
B. The partners have developed a contract for work and home; this was reviewed and critiqued within the session.
C. The partners were supported for committing to explicit expectations, requirements, and rewards for carrying out assigned expectations.
D. The partners have not developed a work/home contract and were redirected to do so.

35. Develop Written Contract for Daily Work/Home Strains (35)

A. The partners were directed to discuss specific areas of daily work/home strain.
B. The partners were directed to develop a written plan for dealing with difficult work/home strains.
C. The partners were reinforced for developing an agreement regarding specific work/home daily strains.
D. The partners have not developed solutions for daily work/home strains and were directed to develop more specific techniques in this area.

36. Modify Standards to Meet Resources (36)

A. It was reflected to the partners that their time and energy resources are insufficient to meet current standards (i.e., there is not enough time at the end of the day to fully clean the home every day).
B. The partners were directed to identify situations in which standards can be explicitly modified to meet time and energy resources (e.g., partners will clean for company and to maintain adequate hygiene levels, but otherwise will fully clean the home only once per month).
C. The partners were provided with positive feedback for their adjustment of standards to meet time and energy resources.
D. The partners have not adjusted standards to meet time and energy resources, and were provided with additional direction in this area.

37. Establish Routines to Maintain Family Contact (37)

A. It was reflected to the partners that work schedules make family time difficult to schedule.
B. The partners were directed to establish brief routines that maintain some family contact and closeness (e.g., a short evening phone ritual during the working partner's break).
C. The partners were supported and reinforced for their use of brief routines to maintain family contact and closeness.
D. The partners have not used brief routines to maintain family contact and closeness and were reminded about the importance of this technique.